NEFESH SHIMSHON

Shabbos Kodesh

Rav Shimshon Dovid Pincus

Nefesh Shimshon

Shabbos Kodesh

Making the most of Shabbos:
Inspiring insights into the meaning
and purpose of Shabbos

FELDHEIM PUBLISHERS
JERUSALEM NEW YORK

For cassettes and CDs of the Rav's talks: +972 (527) 625-966

ISBN 978-1-59826-283-4

FELDHEIM PUBLISHERS
POB 43163 / Jerusalem, Israel

208 Airport Executive Park
Nanuet, NY 10954

www.feldheim.com

10 9 8 7 6 5 4 3 2 1

Printed in Israel

Contents

Inspirational Essays

Shabbos with Rav Pincus

Introduction to the English Edition

It is with feelings of great joy and gratitude to *Hashem Yisbarach* that we proudly present this English translation of *Nefesh Shimshon* on the topic of Shabbos, by our father, *zt"l.*

After the passing of our father, *zt"l,* we were blessed by Heaven with the opportunity to publish a series of books adapted from his taped lectures. These *sefarim* touch on a wide variety of subjects including Yomim Tovim and Shabbos. The Hebrew books enjoyed wide circulation and were well received by circles of *bnei Torah* as well as by the Jewish public in general. Many people's lives were illuminated by these *sefarim.*

Repeated requests have been coming in over the years for us to translate these books into English for the benefit of the greater public. Although various factors delayed this, we now, *baruch Hashem,* are presenting the first English book in this series containing lectures given by our father, *zt"l,* about *Shabbos Kodesh.* It is our hope that this book will enlighten the public regarding this important topic.

In the Hebrew edition we offered a brief description of the *sefer*:

> The book *Shabbos Malkesa,* written entirely by Rav Pincus himself, earned its place in Torah circles as a definitive work

on the deeper aspects of Shabbos, containing inspiration as well as practical application. Despite the breadth and depth of that important book, we've seen fit to publish this "companion volume" based on Rav Pincus's lectures. The spirit and feeling of a live talk, which we have strived to preserve, adds immeasurably to one's appreciation and understanding of this important topic.

Furthermore, as Rav Pincus was constantly adding and developing insights into the topics about which he spoke, this book contains additional significant material not found in *Shabbos Malkesa*. Rav Pincus's articles from the weekly publication *HaMa'ayan* are also included in this *sefer* in the second section.

However, we wish to emphasize that the main themes of Shabbos are elucidated in *Shabbos Malkesa* in the Rav's own meticulous wording. Thus, readers seeking a deeper and more precise understanding of this subject are directed there.

The publication of this book is a moving moment for us. We remember well how our father, *zt"l*, conducted himself regarding Shabbos. We witnessed how he made Shabbos an event, as he was wont to encourage others to do. People naturally treat the coming of a Yom Tov as something significant and prepare excitedly for the special day. Yet Shabbos is greater than all the Yomim Tovim! Regarding Shabbos it is said, "You blessed it above all days and sanctified it above all times." Treating Shabbos as a key event in one's life was one of the special messages Rav Pincus conveyed to others, not only through his many well-known lectures on the subject, but through his own conduct as well. The way he prepared for and observed Shabbos was unparalleled.

Chazal say, "Beautiful are the words spoken by those who practice them" (*Bereishis Rabbah* 34:14). For this reason, and due to popular demand, we have included an appendix detailing our father's unique Shabbos practices. We hope that this section will inspire us all, each on his own level, to enhance and uplift our observance of this holy day.

As this edition goes to print, we wish to express our gratitude to our friends R' Yehonasan Posen and R' Yaakov Posen, who after the passing of our father, *zt"l,* took upon themselves the task of publishing his lectures, working day and night to this end. Thanks to them, we have merited to see the lectures of our illustrious father published in more than ten impressive volumes. This is an eternal *zechus* for them; may they be blessed by the Source of all blessings in this world and the next.

In the same vein we wish to thank R' Aharon Schwartz, who has been of invaluable assistance in everything connected with publishing the books, and who has devoted himself to disseminating the teachings of our father, *zt"l,* by means of audio cassettes as well. Now he has undertaken the task of preparing the books for publication in English. He worked without rest to complete the fine volume that we see before us today.

We also wish to mention and thank R' Tzvi Yosef Shechter who masterfully adapted and prepared the lectures for the Hebrew edition. We also thank R' Ilan Greenwald for his work in editing and preparing the Hebrew edition for publication. We also thank R' Meir Lombarsky for his help in preparing the appendix at the end of this book, which details the unique Shabbos practices of our father, *zt"l.*

With the appearance of the English edition, we wish to express our deep gratitude to the translator, R' Shmuel Globus. His abundant understanding graced this English edition with the tasteful and thoughtful form that we see before us today. We are grateful to R' David Schallheim for his fine editing. We also wish to mention Feldheim Publishers' talented staff for putting the finishing touches on this edition. And we thank all the others who assisted with the publication of this book in any way.

May all of them be blessed by Hashem. May Hashem reward them with much *nachas* and happiness, blessing and joy, all the days of their lives in this world and the next.

We wish to mention the *Shalheves* organization in the framework of which our illustrious father, *zt"l,* delivered many of his lectures. May they merit to disseminate Torah and *yiras Shamayim,* and bring many people back to Hashem's Torah.

We hereby offer our apologies in the name of all the people who took part in this work. The process of adapting the lectures and translating them was done with great emphasis on precision and on translating according to the original text. However, translation is known to be a very difficult task and it is possible that there are deviations from what was originally said. And it is surely possible that we have failed to comprehend the full depth of the subjects discussed, due to their great profundity. Therefore, any mistake that is found in this book should certainly be attributed to us.

In conclusion, we extend our hands in prayer to the Master of all: Just as Your mercy has helped us until now, so may You never abandon us. May it be His will that this *sefer* be an *ilui neshamah* for our father HaRav HaGaon Shimshon Dovid ben Rav Chaim Avraham, *zt"l,* and our righteous mother Chayah Mindel bas Rav Mordechai Leib, *a"h,* and our beloved sister Miriam bas Rav Shimshon Dovid, *a"h,* who were suddenly taken to Heaven on 12 Nisan 5761. May their souls be bound in the bond of eternal life.

The Pincus Family
Tammuz, *shemittah* year 5768

NEFESH SHIMSHON

Shabbos Kodesh

קבלת שבת – קבלת פני שכינה

1

Welcoming Shabbos Is Akin to Greeting the Shechinah

Not Just a Mitzvah

One of the most beautiful aspects of Shabbos is greeting and receiving Shabbos when it begins, and escorting it out when it ends.

No Yom Tov or any other special time receives a welcome like this. It is only on the holy day of Shabbos that we have this special mitzvah of *Kabbalas Shabbos,* where we greet the Shabbos Queen. We address her as if she were a person, and say: *Bo'i Kallah, Bo'i Kallah, Shabbos Malkesa!*

And when Shabbos ends, we escort her out with a special meal called the *Melaveh Malkah,* "the escorting of the Queen." Perhaps there's a mitzvah to eat a meal after Yom Tov too, but that meal isn't called a *Melaveh Malkah.* Only Shabbos do we escort and address as "Queen."

Chazal frequently refer to Shabbos as a definite being. For instance:

> Shabbos said to HaKadosh Baruch Hu: *"Ribbono shel Olam,* to all of them You gave a mate. [Each of the weekdays, of which there are an even number, pairs off with another, forming a couple.] But I have no mate."

HaKadosh Baruch Hu said to her: "*Knesses Yisrael* is your mate."[1]

We see that Shabbos conducts itself as a person. She comes and leaves. She speaks up and makes claims. We honor her and take care not to insult her. And according to *Sefer Yerei'im* there is a special mitzvah of fearing Shabbos: We are to be in fear and awe of her greatness.[2]

But what is the meaning of all this? Why is Shabbos in particular treated as an actual individual? We refer to Shabbos as a guest in our home. None of the Yomim Tovim or other mitzvos are depicted as personalities, besides Shabbos. Tefillin is a mitzvah, mezuzah is a mitzvah, and Pesach and Shavuos are also mitzvos.

Shabbos is a personality.

If so, let us understand who Shabbos is. Whom are we welcoming when the sun sets on Friday? We are not asking, "What is Shabbos?" Rather, we are asking, "*Who* is Shabbos?"

Three Halachos of Receiving the Shechinah

The Brisker Rav, *zt"l,* wrote something astounding about *Kabbalas Shabbos*.[3] This "reception ceremony" is actually learned from what took place when the Jewish people stood at Har Sinai. There, the Jewish people greeted and received the *Shechinah* in the same manner that a king is greeted and received.

He explains that there are three halachos of *Kabbalas Shabbos,* resembling the three instructions given to the Jews when they received the *Shechinah* at Har Sinai.[4]

1. *Bereishis Rabbah* 11:8.
2. *Siman* 410.
3. See *Gry"z al HaTorah, parashas Yisro.*
4. *Shemos* 19:9-7.

1. *"They shall wash their garments."* When one comes to greet the King, HaKadosh Baruch Hu, one must don nice clothing in His honor.

2. *"And they shall be ready for the third day."* When Hashem arrives, one must be ready as if a great king were expected to arrive. One should be sitting and waiting for Hashem, lest He arrive while one is busy with other matters.

3. *"Moshe brought the people out to greet God."* There is a special halachah to go out and greet the *Shechinah.*

These three halachos, says the Brisker Rav, apply to *Kabbalas Shabbos* as well.

The first is to don nice clothing. Men observe this halachah pretty well, because they are usually dressed in their Shabbos clothes when Shabbos arrives. But it is important for women to know about this halachah as well. Often a woman is still dressed in a simple weekday robe when she lights Shabbos candles. But really by the time Shabbos begins, we should *already* be wearing our finest clothing; we shouldn't put them on just for the meal, because at the time of candle-lighting, the *Shechinah* is already arriving.

The second halachah is not to be busy when Shabbos arrives. This is something men should know. Many men utilize the moments before candle-lighting to take care of last-minute details. They are busy putting *muktzeh* items away and completing various small tasks. But this is not the proper way; one should be sitting and waiting for *Shabbos Kodesh* to arrive. The Rambam also speaks about this:

> And one should be sitting respectfully and looking forward to greeting Shabbos as one would go to greet the king.[5]

5. *Mishneh Torah, Hilchos Shabbos* 30:2.

The third halachah is to go out to greet Shabbos—*bo'u v'neitzei likras kallah*. The Rambam says about this:

> The earlier Sages would gather their *talmidim* on *erev Shabbos* and don their cloaks and say: "Come, let us go out to greet Shabbos, the King!"[6]

Our generation is not accustomed to doing this. If we were to go out into our streets as they are today, it is not Shabbos we would find there...Nevertheless, we can and should find Shabbos within our homes.

Focusing on Greeting Hashem

Why is it that we have this special halachah of *Kabbalas Shabbos*, greeting Shabbos?

There are two kinds of mitzvos. The majority of mitzvos, such as eating matzah or putting on tefillin, fall into the first category. When we fulfill these mitzvos, the main focus is that we are doing as Hashem commanded.

But there is another kind of mitzvah. For example, *"Three times a year, all your males shall appear before Hashem, your God, in the place He will choose."*[7] This is the mitzvah of coming to the Beis HaMikdash for the *Shalosh Regalim* in order to "see" Hashem's presence and be "seen" by Him. Here, fulfilling the mitzvah is more than just doing as Hashem commanded. It is actually greeting and receiving Hashem's presence. It is a personal relationship with Hashem.

So it is with *Shabbos Kodesh*. It is the main mitzvah in which we develop a personal relationship with Hashem.

When we greet Shabbos, we are actually greeting the *Shechinah*. Some commentaries explain that when we say the words *bo'i kallah* in the *piyut* of *Lecha Dodi*, the word *kallah* refers

6. Ibid.

7. *Devarim* 16:16.

to Shabbos itself. Others say that *kallah* refers to the *Shechinah*. But in truth it's the same thing. Greeting Shabbos *is* greeting the *Shechinah*.

Let us imagine a very, very busy man who has no time even to buy matzos for Pesach. Comes Seder night and everyone has matzos except him. He goes to the neighbor's house, knocks on the door, and asks for a few matzos. "I forgot to buy," he explains. "I was too busy." What an embarrassing moment!

For him it may be embarrassing, but at least he didn't hurt anyone's feelings through his negligence. The matzos weren't "insulted" by the fact that he forgot to buy them.

Now let us imagine that this busy man's dear parents inform him that they are planning to come for Shabbos. "We will arrive on Thursday with the six o'clock train." And indeed, after a long journey, they arrive, very weary from their trip. They step off the train only to discover that there is no one waiting for them at the station. They call up their son, and he says with a sigh, "Oh, I forgot!"

So they catch a cab and arrive at their son's home. They remove their bags from the cab and call out, "Hello, is anyone home?" A reply emanates from somewhere: "Everyone is very busy right now; just come in, sit down, and make yourselves comfortable. We are looking forward to seeing you Friday evening at the Shabbos table."

We wouldn't do this to our dear parents. When our mother and father come for a visit, we drop everything and welcome them. The first thing we do is say a nice hello, give them a kiss, and bring them into the house. Anything less would hurt their feelings.

If someone's parents arrive only to find no one waiting for them, they'll be insulted. They'll feel snubbed and might even consider spending Shabbos elsewhere! We can imagine them saying, "After all, why do we have to spend Shabbos here? It doesn't seem that we're wanted... Do they think they're the only address in town? We have plenty of friends here who will be happy to see us."

Shabbos Kodesh is coming to our home—but we are too busy. Hashem Himself is knocking at our door—but we don't open it. "Just wait another few minutes," we say. We're not ready when Shabbos arrives, and we aren't awaiting her. If we fail to welcome the precious Shabbos and show we care about her, she might decide she has somewhere else to go, so to speak, leaving our home devoid of Shabbos's wonderful *kedushah* and *berachah*.

Some people recite *Shir HaShirim* when Shabbos begins. What's the idea behind this custom? The main theme of *Shir HaShirim* is, "*May He kiss me with the kisses of His mouth.*" As we mentioned above, when our mother or father come for a visit, we give them a kiss. When Shabbos arrives in our home Hashem comes with her, and we want to express how happy we are that He came.

The *kedushah* of Shabbos completely transforms us and our home. We become like *Kohanim* in the Beis HaMikdash. (This concept will be explained in further chapters.) The moment that creates this tremendous transformation is at the moment we welcome Shabbos and usher her in.

Greeting Shabbos is a glorious moment, a moment of "*May He kiss me with the kisses of His mouth,*" in which every Jew receives a kiss from Hashem. But, just at this special moment, the children are wandering around with nothing to do. Have them sit next to their father in shul, or next to their mother at home listening to stories of Shabbos in the homes of tzaddikim. These are special moments!

Indescribable Closeness to Hashem

Song plays a special role in *Kabbalas Shabbos*. We begin *Kabbalas Shabbos* with the words "*Lechu neranenah laShem.*" The word *neranenah* comes from the root of *rinah*, song. Next we say "*Shiru laShem shir chadash,*" again emphasizing *shirah*, song.

We continue with the joyous song of *"Lecha Dodi."* Then comes *"Mizmor shir l'yom haShabbos,"* again highlighting song with the double expression *"mizmor shir."*

When Shabbos enters, our entire *avodah* is through song. Why?

Some things simply cannot be expressed in words. For example, let us imagine a person in pain; something is hurting him. He meets a friend who has never experienced pain in his life. (Of course, there is no such person. But let us pretend for a moment that there is.) Now, there is no way in the world that the person in pain will succeed in explaining to his friend the meaning of, "It hurts me." Only someone who has felt pain himself can relate to "It hurts me." He recalls the pain he once felt and understands what the person is telling him.

Another thing that cannot be expressed in words is the taste of food. We can say a certain food is bitter or sweet, but no one in the world can explain what "bitter" or "sweet" is. We can say only, "Do you remember when you ate that sweet thing? What you tasted then, I taste now."

The only language for communicating things too deep for words is song. If our ear is attuned, we hear the moving message borne by the melody. But a coarse and insensitive person will miss it.

When Shabbos begins, we attain such closeness to Hashem that it cannot be expressed in words. So, at this exalted moment, we don't talk; we sing. Nothing less will do. Whoever has an attuned ear understands that there is no other way to express the *neshamah*'s joy over the coming of *Shabbos Kodesh*. If someone doesn't understand, there is no way to explain it.

Shabbos touches the deepest feelings in the heart of the Jewish people. At this time we meet *HaKadosh Baruch Hu,* and an indescribable love is aroused. All we can say is: *"Mizmor shir l'yom haShabbos, tov l'hodos laShem!"*

This is what Shabbos is all about. It strikes a chord hidden deep within the Jewish heart. It is the point of connection between us and Hashem.

We asked before: "Who is Shabbos? Who is this personality?" Now we can answer: This "personality" is actually Hashem. For *Chazal* tell us that "Shabbos" is one of Hashem's Names.[8]

Love of Shabbos flows from a love for Hashem. And desecrating Shabbos is the opposite of this love.

Today, we live with the unfortunate reality that so many of our brethren desecrate Shabbos. They drive their cars, go to the movies Friday night, etc. It is very painful for us to see them trampling on something that is so beloved to us. But who is it that we love so? Whom are the cars running over? Who is being trampled underfoot by all those entering the movie theaters?

Chazal say that when Titus entered the Beis HaMikdash, he took a sword and pierced the curtain hanging at the entrance to the *Kodesh HaKodashim*.[9] Miraculously, blood oozed out. When Titus saw the blood, he thought he had "killed" Hashem.

Had Titus lost his mind? How could he think he had killed the Supreme Being? In truth, this teaching of *Chazal* contains a profound message. Death signifies departure, while blood is the *nefesh*, the life force. When Titus saw the blood on the ground, he concluded that Hashem had departed. He thought God had ascended to Heaven, no longer to be involved in earthly affairs.

What was Titus' mistake? Blood indeed spilled out of the *Kodesh HaKodashim*, but it wasn't at all as Titus thought. God didn't ascend to the heavens above. He didn't leave us, and His involvement with this world didn't cease.

That blood on the ground symbolized Hashem on the ground, still with us, but in Galus, and treated with contempt.

8. Zohar, *Yisro* 88b.

9. *Gittin* 56b.

And when people drive their cars on Shabbos, it's the same thing. HaKadosh Baruch Hu is sprawled on the ground, so to speak, under the wheels of those cars.

Shabbos is Hashem's name. These days, when the *Shechinah* is sprawled on the ground for all to trample on, Hashem is seeking a home in which He may find refuge. And this is *Kabbalas Shabbos*. We greet Hashem and say to Him: "Hashem, in my home You can find rest and refuge. The house is clean, both physically and spiritually. I have rid my home of all the 'idolatry' that so sullies the world today. There are no foreign influences here. It is a wholly Jewish home. Please come in."

Fortunate is he who can say this on *Shabbos Kodesh*. And even more fortunate is he who can say all week long, "In my home there is only Torah. Not Torah plus other things. Only Torah. Only *Yiddishkeit*. If we want to tell a child a story, we tell him only stories of tzaddikim. Here we are involved only with the holy *Shechinah*."

As soon as Hashem finds a place to rest, He will no longer be rolling under the wheels of the cars outside.

My dear fellow Jews, we are responsible for the fact that Hashem is sprawled on the ground, homeless. If our homes were pure and holy, like the Beis HaMikdash, everything would be different.

"Home" means a clean place where we may be alone with Hashem, without the presence of strangers. Only holiness and purity. This is especially true of those special moments of *Kabbalas Shabbos*. We should be ready early and sit down and say: "Hashem, we're waiting for You. Here, You can find peace."

Shabbos Preparations Are Personal

What does it mean to prepare for Shabbos? Let us consider, for instance, the mitzvah to clean the house of chametz before Pesach. If we failed to search our homes and remove the chametz, it would be a sin, even a grave sin. But it wouldn't be an insult. However, if someone neglects to fulfill the mitzvah of shining his shoes for Shabbos, it is not only a sin. It is also an insult to Shabbos, to Hashem.

It's like going to a wedding wearing filthy shoes or an old, beat-up jacket with a big stain right in the middle. Such a person has slighted the *chasan*.

When Shabbos comes, a "*chasan*" is here: Hashem. This is the essence of Shabbos; it is Hashem's day. When we polish our shoes on Friday afternoon, it is in His honor. It's "personal." When we prepare a Shabbos meal or set the table, we remember in Whose honor we'll be serving the food. We think of Who will be present in our home for the meal.

One reason we don't feel the presence of Shabbos is because we don't know how to greet her. We don't give her the welcome she deserves. If we work on this, we will feel the holiness of Shabbos much more, and this feeling will open up the great fountain of *berachah* that Shabbos is, showering goodness and blessing upon us all week long.

"והיה ביום הששי והכינו את אשר יביאו"

2

What Shabbos Preparations Do for Us

The Role of Preparations

THE MIDRASH TELLS US about the great importance of Shabbos:

> Said R' Elazar bar Avina: We find it written in the Torah, the *Nevi'im,* and the *Kesuvim* that Shabbos is equal to all the mitzvos...
>
> HaKadosh Baruch Hu said to the people of Israel: If you are worthy and keep Shabbos, I consider it as though you kept all the mitzvos in the Torah. And if you desecrate it, I consider it as though you desecrated all the mitzvos.[1]

We see that Shabbos is so important—it equals everything else put together! So let us devote some time to discussing how we can merit the greatness of Shabbos.

We know that every Yom Tov has its special mitzvah. Pesach has matzah, Sukkos has sukkah and lulav, and Rosh Hashanah has shofar. But what is the special mitzvah of Shabbos? What can we do to bring about this unique *kedushah* of Shabbos?

There is one mitzvah: *"And on the sixth day they prepared what they brought."*[2]

1. *Shemos Rabbah* 25:12.
2. *Shemos* 16:5.

This *pasuk* describes how *b'nei Yisrael* in the *midbar* prepared the manna that fell on Friday, making it ready for Shabbos use. But *Chazal* tell us that this *pasuk* is more than that. It is a mitzvah for every Jew in every place and time to prepare for Shabbos. According to the halachah, this is considered a Torah-ordained mitzvah.[3]

And this is the special mitzvah of Shabbos! We tap into Shabbos's great *kedushah* by preparing tasty food for the day: fish, kugel, cake, etc.

But, this sounds a little strange. On Rosh Hashanah we need to blow a shofar, which is a powerful spiritual act with many deep meanings. Similarly, eating matzah on Pesach has tremendous spiritual power and significance. The same goes for the sukkah and lulav on Sukkos. But what do we do when it comes to Shabbos, which is equal to all the mitzvos? On Friday we prepare some fish or shine our shoes. Is this all we need to do in order to reach the holiness of this sacred day?

In truth, preparing fish will not enable us to attain this greatness and holiness of *Shabbos*. Neither will anything else. This is because *Shabbos Kodesh* is a special gift from Hashem. And there is only one way to get it: to want it!

We do not have to "generate" the *kedushah* of Shabbos by doing special mitzvos such as shofar and matzah. This is because the *kedushah* of Shabbos comes as a gift from Heaven. It is given to anyone who desires it and truly yearns for it. And someone who makes an effort to prepare special food to honor the Shabbos is showing that he eagerly anticipates its arrival. He is looking forward to it. Shabbos is on his mind, and that is why he is making a big deal preparing for it. That is how he attains the wonderful gift of Shabbos.

3. See *Bei'ur Halachah* 243, s.v. *vehu mi-kevod*.

Longing for Shabbos

This is true as well for other spiritual gifts so great that we cannot successfully attain them on our own.

How did *b'nei Yisrael* get out of the Egyptian exile? The Torah tells us: *"And they cried out."*[4] They really wanted to leave Mitzrayim.

Rashi[5] tells us that four-fifths of the Jewish People died in the *makkah* of *choshech* and never went out of Mitzrayim. What did they do wrong? They were guilty of only one sin: They didn't want to go. They liked living in Egypt and felt no need to leave. They wanted their burdens lightened, to be sure, but they didn't really want to leave Mitzrayim altogether. And there they stayed.

The same is true with our current exile. We will merit *geulah* only by wanting it. When we really want to leave *galus,* Hashem will take us out of it.

The Chofetz Chaim illustrates this point with a story about how the great R' Yosef Dov Soloveitchik, known as the Beis Halevi, came to be the rabbi of a city. The people of the city repeatedly urged him to accept the position, but the Beis Halevi refused again and again. Only when someone told him that an entire community of 30,000 Jews was eagerly awaiting for him to come, he could not refuse.

The Chofetz Chaim says the same is true about the coming of *Mashiach.* If the entire *Klal Yisrael* would eagerly await *Mashiach*'s arrival, he would surely come! If we would truly cry out to Hashem, He would save us immediately.

This is how it works when it comes to Shabbos. We attain the *kedushah* of Shabbos as a gift from Hashem by yearning for It and desiring it.

4. *Shemos* 2:23.
5. *Shemos* 13:18.

Making a Big Deal Out of Shabbos

An effective way to strengthen our yearning for Shabbos is to make a big deal out of it. This means remembering Shabbos and thinking about it well before it arrives. There is even a special halachah to remember Shabbos on all six preceding days. No other mitzvah has such a halachah. It is not written that we must remember Pesach all year, or any other holiday, for that matter. Only with Shabbos do we have such a mitzvah. Every day in Shacharis we recite the *shir shel yom* and say: *"Ha-yom yom rishon b'Shabbos," "Ha-yom yom sheini b'Shabbos...."* All week long we remember Shabbos.

It is a very good practice that beginning on Wednesday, which is the fourth day of the week, we think to ourselves, "In two days it will be Shabbos." When we pass a store, we can think to ourselves, "I will buy such and such food in honor of Shabbos, because in two days Hashem Himself will visit me. I will be in the *Kodesh HaKodashim,* in the Beis HaMikdash. I want to buy a treat in order to honor *Shabbos Kodesh*!"

Starting Friday morning, we should think about Shabbos constantly. When we see our mother preparing the fish, we can ask her to let us add a little salt, in honor of Shabbos. We are excited that Shabbos is coming!

Even greater is following in the footsteps of the great Torah sages who started preparing for Shabbos already at the beginning of the week. It is said about Shammai:

> When he found a choice animal, he would say: "This one is for Shabbos." When he found a better one, he would designate the second one and eat the first one.[6]

The *Mishnah Berurah* states that although we generally follow the dictum of Beis Hillel, with regard to this we follow the

6. *Beitzah* 16a.

practice of Beis Shammai.[7]

I better appreciated the value of early preparations when my son was getting married. We were expecting approximately one hundred guests to arrive for the *aufruf*. Of course we didn't wait until Thursday to begin preparing. We began baking cakes two weeks in advance, and on the Sunday before we did the shopping.

This is how we should prepare for Shabbos. We should start getting ready on Sunday, because on Shabbos we will have a guest—Hashem. On Monday, we should be occupied with thoughts of Shabbos. We should be thinking about Shabbos as much as possible. On Thursday, we should hurry to prepare the fish. On Friday, we should think to ourselves, "Shabbos is almost here!"

And when Shabbos finally arrives, there is nothing special we have to do anymore. All we need to do is remember that today is Shabbos. The table is a Shabbos table, the *shtender* is a Shabbos *shtender*, the sky is a Shabbos sky, the stars are Shabbos stars... On this day, everything is different, for today we are living in the home of HaKadosh Baruch Hu Himself.

Singing about Shabbos Itself

There is an amazing thing that occurs only on Shabbos, not on the other holidays: We sing about the day itself. We sing, "*Shabbos, Shabbos ha-yom laShem*" or "*Yom zeh m'chubad mikol yomim....*"

On the other holidays we sing songs connected to the theme of the day, to its special event and message. But did we ever hear someone sing, "Pesach, Pesach" or "Shavuos, Shavuos"? Yet on Shabbos that is what we do. We sing about Shabbos herself, remembering her and delighting in her. We are saying, so to speak, that everything else has ceased to exist. There is only

7. *Mishnah Berurah* 250:2.

Shabbos, only Hashem.

Especially, on Shabbos itself, we should think about Shabbos all the time, remembering that "Shabbos" is a Name of Hashem. Anyone who does this will suddenly discover wondrous worlds. This is not because he has suddenly climbed to higher *madreigos*; rather, it is because he is meeting Hashem in His own home, so to speak. On Shabbos, Hashem accepts every Jew with love and a kiss, regardless of his spiritual level.

All six days of the week are blessed by Shabbos. Therefore, it is appropriate for a person to acquire the habit that the whole week be "*Shabbosdik*" for him.

Don't Let Go

Someone who brings Hashem into his life in this way will experience a world full of light. This world is not the dark, dreary place that people sometimes think it to be. Not when you have the wondrous *siyata di'Shemaya* that Shabbos bestows.

Chazal recount how Yosef HaTzaddik would constantly pray and mention Hashem as he went about his mundane affairs. He was with Hashem all the time and, indeed, he received tremendous *siyata di'Shemaya*. It is most unfortunate to go through life without being with Hashem. For without Him, it is indeed a dark world.

We are all concerned about what tomorrow will bring. No one knows what will be. An awesome verse from *Eichah* sheds light on this point. "*To their mothers they will say, 'Where is grain and wine?'*"[8] Here we are talking about children under severe siege conditions, whose tongues stick to their palates due to extreme thirst. But they don't ask for water. They ask for wine! Why are they thinking about delicacies? The answer is clear: If this is what a child asks for, this must be what he was used to

8. *Eichah* 2:12.

drinking. Until a week or two ago, the house was full of everything good. The destruction came upon them swiftly, seemingly out of nowhere.

I cannot forget the experience I had during the Six-Day War. The war was about to break out and fear gripped Eretz Yisrael. Everyone was worried about what might happen. It was about two months after I'd gotten married, and I was not afraid. "I'm an American citizen," I told myself. "I can board a plane and get out of here any time I want!" All I needed was a passport for my wife, too.

So, I went to the office of the Interior Ministry in Jerusalem to get her a passport. The clerk looked at me and told me that if I could, I should get out of here as fast as possible. Who knew what would happen here in Israel? He promised to do whatever he could to rush-order a passport for my wife, although a first-time passport usually took two weeks. Then, he examined the papers and remarked disappointedly, "Mister, your files are in Tel Aviv. I can't help you."

What now? My father in New York contacted his senator to do something about the situation, diplomats sent urgent telegrams to Israel, and *baruch Hashem*, the next day, I was holding my wife's passport with a visa to the U.S. But that day war broke out, and Israel's airport was closed ...

I cannot describe to you the feeling I had at that moment. I had thought I was safe. An American citizen. Now everything looked completely different, as I realized I was stuck here with everyone else!

"To their mothers they will say, 'Where is grain and wine?'" Only yesterday they were drinking wine, and today they didn't even have bread and water.

The wisest of all, Shlomo HaMelech, declares, *"What has been is what will be."*[9]

9. *Koheles* 1:9.

People are concerned about the dangers that lie in wait, since history repeats itself. But there is something we can do—grab hold of Hashem, and don't let go! You'll see what a happy life you'll have.

"I found the One my soul loves; I took hold of Him, and I won't let go of Him."[10] If you are holding onto Hashem, you have nothing to worry about. We all meet Hashem three times a day. Don't just go through the "routine" of davening—seize the opportunity and speak to Him! Shout and cry to Him! Then you'll see how far-reaching is His kindness.

The ultimate thing is to meet Hashem on *Shabbos Kodesh,* for then He is smiling and especially benevolent. He greets us with a kiss. On an ordinary day, a person needs a sin-offering to atone for his sins before he is worthy of Hashem's listening to him. But on Shabbos it is different; there is no sin-offering. Why? Because there is no sin! Shabbos has the only *musaf*-offering without a sin-offering. On Shabbos, it doesn't matter who you are. Hashem treats everyone as if he were a great tzaddik without sin.

Getting Ready

There is a practical way to merit the *kedushah* of Shabbos. All we need to do is welcome Shabbos when it arrives, and give it a proper greeting. Our problem is that when Shabbos arrives, we're usually not ready. We are still rushing about, doing last-minute things. As much as we try to be ready on time, it doesn't work. Why is it so hard to be ready to greet Shabbos when it comes?

This is not just a matter of time mismanagement—there is a spiritual reason for it. A person can begin early in the morning and still barely make it at the last minute. Something strange is going on here.

10. *Shir HaShirim* 3:4.

It is written in Torah sources that all the forces of evil that plague us all week, disappear on Shabbos. The *yetzer ha-ra* knows it is about to be put out of commission—it will be banished for twenty-four hours—so it works hard and makes an extra effort beforehand. This effort generates many obstacles and delays on our path as we are trying to properly prepare for Shabbos.

But this is our chance to tap into the tremendous potential of Shabbos. However we begin Shabbos, is how it continues. So when Shabbos arrives, let us grab hold of HaKadosh Baruch Hu with all our strength. How do we do this? All we have to do is believe that it is Shabbos and that Shabbos is a special day. It is Hashem's day! Just don't take your mind off Shabbos. You see that flower? It's *lichvod Shabbos*. You have a glass of soda? It's *lichvod Shabbos*. When you sit down for the meal, you are at the table of HaKadosh Baruch Hu. It is His meal; He paid for it. You are His guest, enjoy His company!

Think about Shabbos all the time; don't take your mind off it even for a moment. *"I found the One my soul loves; I took hold of Him, and I won't let go of Him!"*[11]

11. Ibid.

"זכור את יום השבת לקדשו"

3

Shabbos Is the Day We Can Find Hashem

Joy on Motza'ei Shabbos

SHABBOS IS SURROUNDED by joy on all sides.

Said R' Chanina: A person should always set his table for a meal on *motza'ei Shabbos*.[1]

Commenting on this statement, Rashi explains why a meal is served when Shabbos ends. He says that to honor Shabbos, one should respectfully escort it out, just as he escorts the king out of the city.

We greet Shabbos joyfully, and when she departs we escort her out joyfully and even hold a meal in her honor, just as we would escort a king upon his departure. But why the *joy* as we escort the Shabbos Queen? Shouldn't we mourn her departure?

There is a story about one of the rebbes of Slonim, who every *motza'ei Shabbos* would give his wife money for the coming week's expenses. One week he had no money to give her, and when his wife saw this, she burst into tears. The rebbe, who was totally immersed in holy matters, assumed she was crying simply because Shabbos had left. It didn't occur to him that she would cry over a lack of money. So he turned to her and said,

1. *Shabbos* 119b.

"Don't feel bad, next week Shabbos will come again."

It would seem that crying when Shabbos leaves is a proper response. Yet *Chazal* tell us the opposite. They instruct us to joyfully escort the Shabbos Queen as she leaves, and that is the halachah.[2] What is this joy all about?

Let's imagine a certain Jew who owns a grocery store. The Pesach season arrives and his store is extremely busy. As fast as he fills up the shelves, people empty them. After Pesach, he's not sad at all because his pockets are bulging from all the holiday purchases. Pesach came and went, leaving behind abundant blessing.

So it is with every Jew, even those who don't own grocery stores. Pesach leaves behind its blessing for each and every one of us. The matzah we eat during Pesach blesses us with the power of *emunah* and heals our souls.

Now let's say the king comes to us for a visit. It is the way of royalty to leave behind a token of His Majesty's appreciation for the hospitality he has received. Thus, when the king leaves, although we so enjoyed his presence, we surely have something to be happy about—the generous gifts he brought to give us, which have made us rich!

The same is true with Shabbos. When it arrives, we happily welcome it. And when it leaves, we joyfully escort it out because of all the wonderful blessings we have received. Shabbos was with us for twenty-four hours, and now we're in a different state than we were on *erev Shabbos*. We are enriched! The joy of *motza'ei Shabbos* may even surpass that of *erev Shabbos*.

The Special Blessing That Shabbos Brings

We might ask: What exactly do we expect Shabbos to give us? What kind of gifts does it leave behind?

2. *Shulchan Aruch, Orach Chayim* 300.

The gifts of the other holidays are clear. Thanks to Rosh Hashanah, we grow in our *yir'as Shamayim*. Thanks to Sukkos, we grow in our *simchah*. But what is the special blessing that Shabbos leaves behind?

Really what we are asking is: What is Shabbos? The answer is, that Shabbos is the day of Hashem.

The word "Shabbos," coming from the root of *shevisah*, denotes cessation. On Shabbos, everything in the world stops. It all ceases, and then what remains? *"V'nisgav Hashem levado bayom ha-hu."*[3] We remain alone with Hashem.

Foundations

There are three foundations of *Yiddishkeit*: faith, love, and fear. These Torah-ordained mitzvos of *emunas Hashem, ahavas Hashem*, and *yiras Hashem* correspond to our forefathers, Avraham, Yitzchak, and Yaakov. People think these are very difficult mitzvos to fulfill. But in truth, there is nothing so hard about them.

Faith in Hashem — how is it possible not to believe in Hashem? Let us imagine, a man noticing a fluorescent lamp attached to the ceiling, asks, "Where did this come from?" His friend answers, "It didn't come from anywhere. It just emerged by itself from the ceiling ... " Obviously, that is pure silliness.

We go outside and see the sun, moon, stars. We look at ourselves and recognize that we have eyes, fingers, a brain, etc. All the computers in the world cannot do what the average human brain does. Who made all this?

David HaMelech exclaims, *"If I go up to Heaven, You are there. And if I lie to rest in the netherworld, You are there."*[4] Hashem is found everywhere. His kindness surrounds us at every moment.

3. *Yeshayahu* 2:11.
4. *Tehillim* 139:8.

Indeed, it is extremely difficult *not* to believe in Hashem.

Love of Hashem—how is it possible not to love Hashem? Imagine someone who has a very wealthy father. When he needs to marry off his children, his father says to him, "Don't worry, I'll pay for the apartment." When his father finds out that his son needs a car, he buys him the latest model. His father is also a world-class physician, and when his grandson falls ill and the hospital diagnoses the baby with severe heart disease, he heals him. In short, the father solves any problem that can possibly arise, providing for all needs immediately. This type of father is loved dearly! We would only want to give him a kiss and a hug and tell him how wonderful he is.

Now, we all believe our lives come from Hashem. Our livelihood comes from Hashem. Our children come from Hashem. To take an extreme example, imagine that a speaker ascends to the podium, and suddenly his ears fall off. Who keeps a person's ears in place? Hashem. Who makes sure a person's nose doesn't fall off? Hashem. Who keeps us alive? Hashem. How is it possible not to love Him?

Fear of Hashem—how is it possible not to fear Hashem? Let us imagine a man leaning on the counter of a snack bar, buying himself a drink. Across the street is a mental institution. A patient breaks out, and it is written all over his face that he is totally mad. Eyes bulging and mouth drooling, he runs forward and shrieks, "Don't drink, it's poison!" At that moment, men in white coats catch him and carry him back inside.

Does the man at the snack bar have any reason to think that his drink is poison? No. But for some reason he suddenly doesn't feel like drinking. If a person has any doubt—even one in a million—that the drink has been poisoned, he won't drink it.

Yet when it comes to the existence of Gehinnom's punishments, there isn't any doubt. We all believe in the World to Come. There is Gan Eden and there is Gehinnom; we all know it. If so, how is it possible not to fear Heaven?

Where Lack of Faith Comes From

Now, we come to something truly amazing. As we all know, we don't always manage to do the things that we know are important. But it's not because we fail to realize their importance. Even if we put a "Don't speak *lashon ha-ra*" sticker on the phone, how many of us manage to refrain from *lashon ha-ra* completely? We know we shouldn't get angry, we shouldn't insult those who insult us, and yet…

Why aren't we afraid of Hashem?

Furthermore, many people don't even believe in Hashem or don't love Him. This is really astounding. How do they manage to evade such obvious truths?

The answer is that it's a miracle. In fact, this could be the greatest miracle of our times. This miracle of being able not to believe in Hashem is described by *Chazal* as follows:

> *"You placed darkness—and it was night"* (*Tehillim* 104:20). This refers to this world, which resembles nighttime.[5]

Hashem covered our world with darkness, like a person would cover something with a blanket. In this way, Hashem miraculously enabled man not to believe in Him. Imagine someone traveling into New York City at night. He gets to Fifth Avenue in midtown Manhattan and asks somebody, "Where is the Empire State Building?" Why doesn't he see it himself? The answer is that if it's dark enough, you don't see even what's right in front of your nose. You can be surrounded by Hashem's kindness and awesomeness, yet be totally unaware of it.

5. *Bava Metzia* 83b.

Shabbos Is When Hashem Can Be Found

It is written, *"And God completed on the seventh day ...."*[6] When was the completion of Creation? It didn't actually take place on Shabbos day. Everything was completed at the onset of night, at the last moment of *erev Shabbos*. If so, it should be written, "And God completed on the seventh *night*." This would be more accurate, but the Torah didn't write it, because it's not such an appropriate expression. For Shabbos has no night. It is all day! Nowhere in the Torah do we find the phrase "the night of Shabbos," only "Shabbos day."

Regarding Yom Tov, there is night and day. We take a *lulav* on Sukkos day but not on Sukkos night. We blow the shofar on Rosh Hashanah day but not at night. Yet when it comes to Shabbos, there is no distinction between daytime and nighttime. This is because "night," the blanket of darkness that hides Hashem from us, is not present on Shabbos. This is a twenty-four hour period when it is all day—all light—and Hashem may be found everywhere.

What does this mean, practically speaking? Let's say a person is looking to attain Torah—Shavuos is the special time for this. If he's looking to attain joy, Sukkos is the special time. And to attain freedom, we have Pesach. What if we're looking for Hashem? The time to find Him is on Shabbos, when HaKadosh Baruch Hu is not shrouded in darkness.

But what does it mean to look for Hashem? Sometimes people seek Hashem desperately. They're in trouble, and they really need Hashem's help. What do they do? They try to pray with *kavanah,* begging Hashem to save them. Let's say a family member is sick. His relatives pray fervently and tearfully for his recovery. Or someone urgently needs ten thousand dollars. He prays, "Please help me, *Ribbono shel Olam*. I need the money so badly!"

6. *Bereishis* 2:2.

But can we really call this davening with true *kavanah*? Having *kavanah* doesn't mean telling Hashem how badly we want something. Rather, increasing *kavanah* in our prayers means that we are increasing our awareness of Who Hashem is. We recognize His great powers and appreciate what He and only He can do. We say, for instance, "Hashem, I know that only You can help me!"

Let's say someone approaches a wealthy man for a very large loan and says, "You don't know how important this is to me! I really need the money." In such a case, the wealthy man will likely respond, "I understand you need the money, but I can't right now; try someone else." To which the prospective borrower might reply, "I looked around and there really is no one else who can help me — only you. I know you have a heart of gold, and besides, you are my dear friend, and I know you care for me a lot." What is the prospective borrower doing? He is showing that he appreciates whom he's talking to and acknowledging that this wealthy man can do what no one else can.

This serves as a parable for how to increase *kavanah* in our prayers. If we speak to Hashem and just express with great emotion how much we're suffering, this is not *kavanah*. If a person goes out to the street, looks around, and says to Hashem, "There are so many nice cars on the street. Why do I have to drive around in this beat-up old clunker?" This is not *kavanah*. But if he says, "Hashem, You are so good and kind. You give people such nice cars. Don't You have a nice car for me too?" — this is *kavanah*. If we would speak to Hashem like a person speaks to his friend, as a real live personality, life would be absolutely marvelous — there would always be Someone to talk to.

The key is to recognize with Whom we are speaking. Shabbos is the time when the cover of darkness is removed, and this becomes clear. This doesn't mean that Shabbos is the time to request our needs. But it does mean that Shabbos is the time to increase our awareness of Hashem — this is the time to build up our relationship with Him.

The Beis HaMikdash of Our Times Is Shabbos

In the olden times, there was a place to find Hashem — in the Beis HaMikdash. A Menorah burned there continually, and the loaves of bread on the Shulchan were always as fresh as when they came out of the oven. These mitzvos demonstrated how real Hashem's presence was in the Beis HaMikdash. If you would go into a house and find the rooms empty and dark, you would understand that no one lives there. But if you would see that the light is on, and there's fresh bread on the table, you would know someone is living there.

In Temple times, a Jew would just walk into the Beis HaMikdash and feel Hashem's presence, and love Him. He would know that He's our Father in Heaven, that He's involved in our lives, and that He loves us and cares about what happens to us. He understood that Hashem is a "living God," not an abstract concept. The source of this awareness was the Beis HaMikdash.

Today, the only Beis HaMikdash we have is *Shabbos Kodesh*. On Shabbos we can find Hashem more than on any other day, and that's why we were given Shabbos. On Shabbos there is no mention of sin. Hashem relates to us as if to Yishai, the father of David. Yishai was one of four great tzaddikim who never sinned and who died only because of the sin of Adam HaRishon.[7] Perhaps, during Shabbos, we don't *feel* we're in the Beis HaMikdash, and perhaps we've spent hundreds of *Shabbosos* not feeling Hashem's presence. But that's because the darkness of this world is very pervasive. It penetrates the

7. *Shabbos* 55b.

world's very essence, making it hard to find Hashem.

As explained, this is the great miracle of man's inability to see Hashem, fear Him, and love Him. But there is a way to "rid ourselves" of this miracle and find Hashem. On Shabbos the thick blanket of darkness thins out. We still must make an effort to peel it off, or we won't find Hashem on Shabbos either. But if we are truly looking for Him, it is very easy to find Him on Shabbos.

There is no question about it. If you seek Hashem and want to bring Him into your life, on Shabbos you will surely find Him.

Remembering Shabbos Is the Avodas HaYom

Now the question is: What should we do on Shabbos?

The Torah tells us what to do: "*Remember the Shabbos day.*"[8] To grasp what this means, let's start with something we already understand. We're all familiar with the main message of Rosh Hashanah. Rosh Hashanah is a day of judgment, of Kingship, and of *yiras Hashem*. What do we do on Rosh Hashanah? The first thing to do is to know that today is Rosh Hashanah. One must be aware that this day is unique.

The following scene could take place on an ordinary weekday. A Jew is driving between two towns and realizes it will soon be sunset. So, he stops by the roadside and davens Minchah. He doesn't have the greatest concentration because cars are whizzing by and there's a child whining in the back seat. When he finishes davening, he thinks to himself, "Well, that wasn't the greatest Minchah I've ever davened in my life, but tomorrow, *b'ezras Hashem*, I'll have another opportunity to daven, and I will try to do better then."

8. *Shemos* 20:7.

Now imagine that it's Yom Kippur, and it's time for Minchah. This same person has been in shul all day. He is tired and weak from the fast. He says to himself, "Well, if I don't manage to daven Minchah so well today, I can try again tomorrow. Maybe I'll have better *kavanah*." Does this second scenario make sense? Not really. Today he has the opportunity to recite *Al Cheit* and atone for the year's sins, whereas tomorrow he'll be busy building his sukkah! He won't be able to "try again tomorrow," because tomorrow won't be Yom Kippur anymore.

So it is with *Shabbos Kodesh*. This is an opportunity we don't want to miss; it's a very special day. What we can do today, we cannot accomplish tomorrow. That is why we must constantly be aware that today is Shabbos.

Let us describe more specifically what this awareness entails. When the *Shulchan Aruch* describes Shabbos, *bitachon* in Hashem is emphasized: "It is a mitzvah for a person not to think about [his business and work] at all, and it should be in his eyes as if all his work were done."[9] On *Shabbos Kodesh*, a person puts all his work behind him and doesn't worry at all about where his *parnasah* will come from.

On Shabbos, we also don't read secular books. Why? The answer is simple: Imagine that someone's parents came from afar to visit him and his family. What does he do? Does he ignore them and pick up the newspaper?

It is forbidden to cook or bake on Shabbos. Why did the Torah forbid cooking on Shabbos *for* Shabbos, whereas on Yom Tov it is permitted to cook for the day's needs? We can explain with the above example of the parents' visit. Imagine that the father comes in, greets his son-in-law, and asks, "Where's Rachel?" The son-in-law replies, "She's in the kitchen baking a cake." The father replies, "I didn't come here to eat cake. I

9. *Orach Chayim* 306:8.

have plenty of cake at home! I came to spend time with my family. Tell her to come sit down, and let's enjoy each other's company."

That is what Hashem wants of us on Shabbos. That's what "remembering Shabbos" is all about. If you prepared delicacies before Shabbos, great. Let us partake of them now together. But if something went wrong on Friday, and you weren't able to prepare, now is not the time to do so. Hashem has plenty of kugel and cake—everything in the world is His. Now is the time to sit down together, speak words of Torah, and enjoy each other's company.

On Shabbos we're in Hashem's company. As *Chazal* say, "They [the Sages] barely permitted people to greet each other on Shabbos."[10] Why was greeting a friend barely permitted? It's simple: When you're in the company of a powerful king, an emperor, you don't greet others. When your friend walks in, you don't turn away from the king and say, "Oh, hi! How are you doing?"

How do we create this lofty sense of being in Hashem's presence? We don't have to "create" it. It already exists. All we have to do is remember that today is Shabbos. Just don't spoil it; don't forget. The table should be a Shabbos table. We must know Who is sitting at this table. In the *zemiros* we say, "*Askinu se'udasa ... da hi se'udasa d'Atika Kaddisha.*" This means, "We have prepared a meal ... this is the meal of the Holy Ancient One." We are sitting at Hashem's table, with Him!

This is the precious gift we look forward to receiving from Shabbos. This is the wealth that *Shabbos Kodesh* bestows upon us: that we can truly sense and understand the wonderful fact that Hashem exists. He's a living reality in our lives. We can spend time with Him and sit at His table, partaking of His food.

10. *Talmud Yerushalmi, Shabbos* 15:3.

Shabbos showers us with all the precious gifts that during the rest of the week seem so hard to attain: *emunah, bitachon, ahavas Hashem, yiras Hashem*. All the facets of relating to Hashem are within our grasp on Shabbos. All we have to do is take advantage of this time. That's why Shabbos is *ma'ayan ha-berachos*, the fountain of all blessing.[11]

On Shabbos There Are No Requests—Just Relationship

Among the special halachos of Shabbos is the prohibition of praying for the recovery of a sick person. We don't pray for *refuah* on Shabbos unless the situation is serious, in which case we are permitted to say Tehillim for the ill person. *Chazal* said, "Shabbos is not a day for crying out, and the healing will arrive quickly.... She [Shabbos] is capable of showing compassion."[12] This means that Shabbos itself can save us from trouble and sickness. Let us understand why we don't pray for material needs on Shabbos.

There is a story about a very successful *meshulach*, a *tzedakah* collector. Before approaching a wealthy potential donor, he would ask around about the man's family, history, and so on. Then he would sit down and converse with the fellow about his town, grandfather, uncle, etc. Eventually, the wealthy man would ask, "Did you come for something specific?" The *meshulach* would answer, "No, not really. But it sure was nice talking to you. I'll come visit again." And so it went. He would come repeatedly, and over time he developed a warm relationship with his potential patron. After all was said and done, instead of a donation of $18 he would walk out with $1,800.

A similar story is told about the Brisker Rav, *zt"l*. He once approached a wealthy potential benefactor and requested only

11. See Ramban, *Bereishis* 2:3.

12. *Shabbos* 12a.

fifteen minutes of his time. During those fifteen minutes, he just chatted and began to develop a relationship with him, without mentioning a word about the purpose of his visit.

This is actually what we do on Shabbos. We speak with Hashem at length, but we don't ask for anything—not for *refuah* and not for *parnasah*. We only want to be friends, so to speak—to develop a relationship. We take out a *Chumash* or a Tehillim or a Gemara. And after Shabbos we say to Hashem, "We're friends, aren't we? So please heal so-and-so. It's very important to me." Through developing our relationship over Shabbos, we gain the opportunity to ask for everything all week long—since Hashem remains closely in touch with us, so to speak.

But if we make requests on Shabbos, we spoil everything. This is not the time; today we have to put all such business aside. For this is a happy day. We dress nicely and serve special food, all in a festive spirit.

And it's a lot easier than we think! All we have to do is remember that today is Shabbos, and Hashem will shower us with all His blessings. And the greatest blessing of all is to develop a true relationship with Him. And all this comes through doing the special *avodah* of *Shabbos Kodesh*.

קדושת השבת - כקדושת בית המקדש

4

The Sanctity of Shabbos and the Beis HaMikdash

1. THE "MYSTERY" OF SHABBOS

People Don't Understand Shabbos

OF ALL OUR HOLY days, only about Shabbos do we say, *"U'veirachto mi-kol ha-yamim v'kidashto mi-kol ha-zemanim."* This means that Shabbos is blessed and sanctified more than any other day or time.

There is no other mitzvah that we live and experience like Shabbos. Shabbos takes up more than a seventh of our life! Every seventh day is Shabbos, and it spills over into Friday afternoon and Saturday night. Thus, Shabbos is the mitzvah we experience more than any other.

Shabbos is essential to the life of a Jew. It is the fount and source of all blessing. Yet it seems to be the time least utilized, and it is the least understood among all the holy days. Not that we're ignorant of its halachos, *chas v'shalom*; we are all familiar with the basic halachos of Shabbos. But how many of us are successful in drawing from this miraculous wellspring? How many of us walk away from Shabbos with depth, understanding, and growth in our *avodas Hashem*?

Most people gain something from the other Yomim Tovim. We walk out of Rosh Hashanah enriched with *yiras Hashem*. We walk out of Shavuos enriched with Torah. But when Shabbos arrives, although we look forward to it, we don't really know what we are supposed to be doing. For instance, in the summertime many people find Shabbos too long. The afternoon seems to stretch on forever, and they don't know how to keep themselves busy. We all keep Shabbos, but for some reason it doesn't excite us as it should. We don't know how to appreciate Shabbos, and we don't understand its purpose.

Let us focus on two points:

1. What is the definition of Shabbos? When it comes to Yom Tov, the prayers we say clearly define Pesach as *zeman cheiruseinu,* Shavuos as *zeman matan Toraseinu,* and Rosh Hashanah as *yom ha-zikaron*. But what is Shabbos? If there were a similar phrase in the Shabbos prayers, what would it be? *Zeman* of gefilte fish and cholent?

2. What is the special *avodah* we should be doing on Shabbos? When Pesach arrives, we have a Seder, eat matzah, and are careful all seven days not to consume even the tiniest particle of chametz. On Rosh Hashanah and Yom Kippur we know exactly what to do. These are days of growing in our *yir'as Shamayim* and *teshuvah*. On Shavuos, we stay up all night learning. Sukkos has plenty of special mitzvos too. But what do we do on Shabbos? Sometimes people just pass the time by strolling around, visiting friends, and engaging in light conversation. Unfortunately, the tremendous potential of this special day goes virtually unnoticed, and this is mainly because we don't know what Shabbos is really all about.

Shabbos Conceals a Special Secret

Chazal tell us that Shabbos contains a secret.

Hashem said to Moshe Rabbeinu, *"See that Hashem gave you the Shabbos."*[1] This is

1. *Shemos* 16:29.

strange. Why did Hashem have to inform us that He is giving us this gift? Isn't it obvious that it comes from Him?

Chazal say:

> Said Rava bar Machseya...in the name of Rav: Someone who gives his friend a gift must inform him. For it is written [regarding Shabbos] (*Shemos* 31:13), "*To know that I, Hashem, am sanctifying you.*" Hashem said to Moshe: "I have a good gift in My treasury, and it's called 'Shabbos.' I wish to give it to the people of Israel. Go and inform them."[2]

We learn a halachah from the above Gemara. If someone gives someone else a gift, he should include a card bearing his name so the person will know who it came from. But if the recipient will recognize who gave him the gift, the Gemara says there is no need to inform him.

Won't the people of Israel know Who gave them Shabbos? Why does Hashem have to specifically tell them?

In answer to this question, *Chazal* say there is an aspect of Shabbos that is hidden—its reward.[3] Shabbos offers a special reward that we don't receive by any other mitzvah. Of course we cannot fully fathom the depth or reward of any of the mitzvos, but in Shabbos there is something deeper and more exceptional. The fact that Shabbos goes by so unutilized is itself proof that this day conceals a great secret. Therefore, Hashem instructed Moshe to go and explicitly tell *b'nei Yisrael* about the gift of Shabbos, otherwise we never would have discovered its true depth.

This secret is described as a delightful gift that is found in Hashem's "treasury." Shabbos is like a diamond, a precious jewel guarded from public view. Hashem didn't show it to everybody; He only showed the beauty of *Shabbos Kodesh* to the

2. *Shabbos* 10b.
3. Ibid.

people of Israel. He said to them, "Look, this is My wonderful Shabbos!"

Shabbos and the Exodus, Shabbos and Creation

There are other aspects of Shabbos that seem to make no sense. In the *Aseres HaDibros,* as written in *Sefer Shemos,* Shabbos is described as *zeicher l'ma'aseh bereishis,* "A remembrance of the creation of the world." But in *Sefer Devarim,* Shabbos is called *zeicher litzias Mitzrayim,* "A remembrance of the exodus from Egypt."

The connection between Shabbos and *Yetzias Mitzrayim* is not so obvious. Shabbos, having come into being on the seventh day of Creation, existed in a certain form even before the Exodus.

Furthermore, the connection between Shabbos and Creation is not as obvious as it sounds. Imagine a man works long and hard to construct a great building. When the structure is finally complete, he retires to an easy chair, stretches out his legs, and takes a good rest. If we wanted to imitate something he did during the construction in order to commemorate his work, would we specifically choose his resting? Would this be the appropriate symbol to remind us of all his hard work? Wouldn't bricks and girders and power tools be better representations of his act of construction?

Likewise, let's say we wanted to commemorate the creation of the world. The most appropriate way would be to work hard, to perform various forms of creative work on Shabbos. We should engage in all thirty-nine forms of *melachah,* reciting a special *berachah* saying that our labors are in remembrance of the work done by Hashem when creating the world.

But the Torah commands us not to work on Shabbos, but rather to rest. What is the meaning of rest? In Minchah of Shabbos we say, "A rest of love and generosity, a rest of truth and faith, a rest of peace and tranquility and quiet and security."

What are all these kinds of rest?

On Shabbos, "Work" Is Not Forbidden

Let us consider for a moment the mystery of *hilchos Shabbos*. The acts forbidden on Shabbos are the thirty-nine forms of *melachah* that were done for the Mishkan, and whatever is similar to these *melachos*. We all know that *melachah* doesn't mean "work." For instance, carrying heavy burdens on Shabbos is permitted by Torah law. Although the Rabbis forbade it, it is not considered a *melachah*.

The Torah-forbidden forms of work are what is called *meleches machsheves,* creative work. Any *melachah* that needed to be done in building the Mishkan is forbidden on Shabbos. And since the Mishkan is called "a miniature world," any act of creation of the world is forbidden on Shabbos. This is what is called *meleches machsheves*.

Now why should we want to forbid acts of creation? The greatness of the human being lies in his ability to create. If creating is forbidden, it's as if the Torah is telling us: On Shabbos, do not be a human being!

Had the Torah forbidden hard labor, such as carrying burdens, etc., we would have understood the message. The Torah is instructing us not to act like animals; we shouldn't carry around loads as a beast of burden does. But this is not the Torah's message. Work is permitted; creating is not. Writing two letters, kindling a flame—any activity that involves creating is forbidden. In other words, that which makes the human being special is forbidden on Shabbos. This is quite surprising.

The Confining Shabbos

Let's look at this from a different angle. Imagine for a moment what Shabbos looks like to a person ignorant of Torah. What would happen if we suddenly placed him in an environment in which he had to keep Shabbos?

Every person has different hobbies. One person likes to travel, another enjoys music, and someone else finds fulfillment in drawing. Now it's Shabbos, and this is their only day off. We say to them, "You cannot travel, you cannot play music, and don't draw even a single line!" They are taken aback: Why not? How do such innocent activities desecrate Shabbos? As a non-observant Jew once remarked, "I can't even call my poor mother and wish her a good Shabbos?"

Try explaining to someone ignorant of Torah what's so terrible about using a bar of soap. About making a cup of tea. About closing the fridge if you forgot to disconnect the light bulb. Almost everything he wants to do, we jump up and say, "No, that's forbidden!"

Torah-observant Jews fully accept that these activities are forbidden by halachah. They have no problem following the Torah's instructions. But we have to admit there is some kind of a mystery here. Why does the Torah limit us so severely on Shabbos? Why does it forbid almost every activity, to the point where it looks to an outsider as if we were being held in prison?

And not only physically are we not allowed to function as on a weekday. Also intellectually we have to behave differently. We don't have any way to find out what's going on in the world. The radio is off, there is no newspaper, nothing. People love to know what's happening in the world, since curiosity is a powerful human trait. Yet all this is forbidden on Shabbos.

The whole format of Shabbos is limiting. Sometimes it seems the only things we can do on Shabbos are eat, sleep, and go to shul...

Why does the Torah want it to be this way?

The Severe Punishment for Shabbos Desecration

Another puzzling aspect of Shabbos is the tremendous stringency connected to its desecration. If a person transgresses even the slightest *melachah* on Shabbos, by Torah law he is liable for *sekilah,* stoning, the most severe form of punishment that exists. This punishment is even more severe than the one for murder.

Indeed, Shabbos is the weightiest of all the mitzvos. Its desecration is equal to idolatry. Shabbos is as important as everything put together, as *Chazal* say, "Desecrating Shabbos is like denying the truth of the entire Torah."[4]

Still, this doesn't really explain why halachah treats Shabbos desecration so severely. Let's say that, *chas v'shalom,* someone deliberately burns a *sefer Torah.* He maliciously intends to reduce every single word in the Torah to ashes. What is his punishment? He is flogged for each erasure of Hashem's holy Name, but he doesn't incur the death penalty. Yet someone who flips on a light switch on Shabbos does. Why?

Usually the Torah metes out the death penalty to someone who has committed a major sin: A person sacrificed to an idol; he engaged in an incestuous relationship; he kidnapped and sold a Jew. But when it comes to Shabbos, even a little thing like skimming all the cream off the milk or striking a match is punishable by death. What's behind this?

Of course, we fully accept all the dictates of halachah. We observe the Torah's laws whether or not we understand them. But by raising questions and answering them, perhaps we can increase our understanding of the meaning of Shabbos. This will bring us more pleasure and satisfaction from this holy day.

In this chapter we won't be able to answer *all* the questions we've raised, but we will set down general foundations.

4. *Bemidbar Rabbah* 15:34.

Subsequent chapters will discuss the various issues of Shabbos in more detail, drawing on the basic principles elucidated here in this key chapter.

2. SHABBOS AND THE BEIS HAMIKDASH — THE HEART OF THE WORLD

"And the Stranger Who Draws Close..."

There is one other place in the Torah where the slightest deviation from halachah carries the death penalty. It is the Beis HaMikdash.

Let's say a Jew who is not a *Kohen* goes into the Beis HaMikdash and offers a *korban* to Hashem. He is liable for the death penalty, delivered by Heaven. Why? Because it is written, *"And the stranger who draws close shall die."*[5] All he did was offer a *korban* to Hashem with the best intentions. He didn't kill anybody or commit some shocking act. But in the Beis HaMikdash, deviation from the halachah is punishable by death.

If a *Kohen* goes into the *Beis HaMikdash* to offer a *korban* without washing his hands and feet, he too incurs the death penalty. And if the *Kohen* is not wearing all the required *bigdei Kehunah,* or if his garment is too long or too short, he receives *misah bidei Shamayim* as well. And if his garment is stained, the *Minchas Chinuch* writes that he too is executed by Heaven.[6]

All this pertains to the service performed in the *Kodesh* of the Beis HaMikdash, i.e., the *Azarah.* But when we're talking about entering the *Kodesh HaKodashim, Chazal* tell us that even an improper thought invalidates the service. If the *Kohen Gadol*'s thoughts weren't holy when he went into the *Kodesh HaKodashim* on Yom Kippur, he paid with his life. Because of this, a rope was tied around his waist, in case they would have to pull out his corpse.

5. *Bemidbar* 3:10.

6. Mitzvah 99.

Why such severity in the Beis HaMikdash?

Vital Organs

We can explain with the following allegory.

A man has a small growth on his leg. His doctor determines that an operation is needed to remove the growth. It goes without saying that a good surgeon should be used; an operation is a serious thing. But even if the surgeon was a little careless, and his hand slipped an inch to the right or the left, this wouldn't endanger the patient's life. It could cause some damage, but it wouldn't be fatal.

If the surgeon is operating on the heart or brain, however, he must be extremely precise. A deviation of even a fraction of an inch can make all the difference. Brain surgery requires such tremendous accuracy that it is performed under a microscope. In these cases, the surgeon is entering the person's "*Kodesh HaKodashim*," touching upon his source of vitality and the dwelling place of his soul. Extreme caution must be exercised with such vital organs.

This analogy explains the great stringency the Torah applies to the laws of Shabbos and the Beis HaMikdash.

Chazal tell us that Shlomo HaMelech planted every kind of fruit tree that exists, even pepper trees, in Yerushalayim.[7] But we all know that each kind of tree needs its own climate. Some fruits grow only in Africa; others only in India. There is no one place where they all flourish. How did Shlomo HaMelech get all those trees to grow and bear fruit?

The Midrash answers our question: Shlomo in his great wisdom knew the invisible lines that extend out from Yerushalayim — the heart of the world — to every place on earth. Thus, he planted the pepper tree on the line leading to the land of Kush, so it bore fruit right away.

7. *Midrash Tanchuma, Kedoshim* 10.

The whole world depends upon its heart. Underground "arteries" reach from Yerushalayim to Africa, India, and every country on earth. Shlomo knew which artery goes where, so he planted the appropriate fruit tree on top of each.

Yerushalayim, and especially the Temple Mount and the Beis HaMikdash, is the very heart of the world. That's why even the slightest sin carried out during the service of the Beis HaMikdash is punishable by death. If something is wrong with the heart, it affects everything else.

The same goes for Shabbos. *Shabbos Kodesh* is the spiritual heart which contains all the *kedushah* of the world. Shabbos pumps life into the world just as a heart pumps life-giving blood into the body. The six days of the week derive all their vitality from Shabbos. That's why Shabbos is so stringent. It is the heart, just like the Beis HaMikdash.

In addition, Shabbos desecration mars the very depths of a Jew's heart. It affects his intrinsic *kedushah* as a Jew, his *emunah,* for he who publicly desecrates Shabbos is considered, regarding certain halachos, as a non-Jew.

If Tishah B'Av Falls on Shabbos, It Is Still Shabbos

Let us consider the message of this familiar *Chazal*:

> On Tishah B'Av that falls on Shabbos, one may eat and drink whatever one wishes and have a table as laden even as that of Shlomo HaMelech in his prime.[8]

What are *Chazal* telling us? Tishah B'Av is a day on which we realize that we have no real life without Hashem being in our midst. Unless the *Shechinah* dwells among us in the Beis HaMikdash, we might as well just sit on the ground and cry,

8. *Ta'anis* 29b.

for we have nothing. The Beis HaMikdash was a place where any Jew who sought Hashem could find Him!

But amazingly enough, if this day falls on Shabbos, we eat meat and drink wine as if nothing happened. What is the meaning of this? Where did the *churban Beis HaMikdash* disappear to?

The answer is: We have Shabbos! But this doesn't mean that the *kedushah* of Shabbos diverts our minds from the *churban Beis HaMikdash*. On the contrary, the *kedushah* of Shabbos fills the vacuum left by that destruction. In a sense, on Shabbos we have the Beis HaMikdash! For in its simple sense, the Beis HaMikdash is the "House of Hashem." And Shabbos is the *day* of Hashem.

The Beis HaMikdash Is the House of Hashem

What do we mean by the "House of Hashem"?

If I want to visit my neighbor, I just go to his house and knock on the door. If I want to visit a friend who lives in a different town, I travel there and knock at his door. I meet him there, where he lives. So it is with the "House of Hashem." Simply speaking, this is HaKadosh Baruch Hu's house. This was where we could meet Him. Three times a year, Jews would go visit Hashem in His great house, because this was where the *Shechinah* dwelt. Anyone, whatever his level, could go to the Beis HaMikdash to pray and Hashem would hear his request. *"For My House is a house of prayer for all the peoples."*[9]

And so too it is with Shabbos. When Shabbos arrives, we say: *"Ufros aleinu sukkas shelomecha*—And spread over us Your shelter of peace." On Friday toward evening, a shelter of *kedushah* is spread over us. We are entering the Beis HaMikdash,

9. *Yeshayahu* 56:7.

so to speak — the House of Hashem. Torah sources write that Shabbos and the Beis HaMikdash are essentially the same.

When Shlomo HaMelech built the Beis HaMikdash, he placed two *keruvim* in the *Kodesh HaKodashim*.[10] These *keruvim* resembled a boy and a girl, representing the relationship between Hashem and the Jewish people. But Shlomo did not place them facing each other in an embrace; rather, they turned a bit to the side.[11] In this physical world, we cannot live in a perfect embrace with HaKadosh Baruch Hu all the time. Yes, we pray three times a day, but afterward we have to go to work and take care of various material needs, so we don't experience Hashem to the utmost degree.

But during the *Shalosh Regalim*, when all Jews came to the Beis HaMikdash, what would the *Kohanim* do? They would roll back the *paroches* and show the people the *keruvim* in an embrace and say to them, "See how beloved you are to Hashem — like the love between a man and a woman."[12]

This was the Beis HaMikdash at the most sacred moments: face to face with Hashem, a moment of embrace between each Jew and his Maker.

Likewise, Shabbos is when we are face to face with Hashem. It is, so to speak, a twenty-four-hour embrace and kiss with HaKadosh Baruch Hu!

Beis HaMikdash — Connecting Heaven and Earth

As we all know, Heaven is very different from earth. Heaven is described as a place where, "*Glory and splendor are before Him*."[13] The angels stand and sing praises before Hashem. On earth, things are quite different.

10. *I Melachim* 6:23-28.
11. *Bava Basra* 99a.
12. *Yoma* 54a.
13. *Tehillim* 96:6.

Most people are busy attending to their mundane business, unaware of Hashem.

And this world is very different from what will be when *Mashiach* arrives, because then everything will change. Even according to the Rambam's ruling that the only difference between nowadays and the days of *Mashiach* is that then the Jewish people will no longer be subjugated to the nations, still, the Jewish people will be on the level of prophecy. This is a whole different reality, a whole different world.

As Jews, we believe that our mundane world of today is directly connected with the *kedushah* that fills the heavens and the World to Come. For example, let us consider the events surrounding the coming of *Mashiach*. *Chazal* tell us that the period just before he comes is called *ikvesa d'Meshicha*, "the heels of *Mashiach*." This term seems strange. Wouldn't it be more appropriate to call it "the heels of the *galus*," since the heels are located at the end of the body? Or maybe we should call it "the head of *Mashiach*," since the head is located at the beginning of the body? "The heels of *Mashiach*" sounds like a real misnomer!

However, this phrase expresses a profound truth. For whenever two things are joined, they need a link. Imagine the links of a chain. One part of each link connects with the preceding link and enters its realm, while the other part connects with the following link, entering its realm. So too, *ikvesa d'Meshicha* is the period that links the "heel" days of *galus* to the "head" days of *Mashiach*. Consequently, the last days of *galus* contain some of the wonderful qualities of the days of *Mashiach*, since the light of *Mashiach* enters them. This is because *ikvesa d'Meshicha* is the link that enters both realms.

Today we see miracles and wonders identifiable only with the days of *Mashiach*. One of these tremendous events is the *teshuvah* movement of our day. This is an absolute miracle the likes of which have never been seen. Tens of thousands of people who had sunk to the lowest levels of *tum'ah* suddenly wake up and make a 180-degree turn. People who lived lives of atheism and *chillul Shabbos* become accomplished Torah scholars! This is surely a miracle of the days of *Mashiach*.

But it works in the opposite direction, too. We like to think that the moment *Mashiach* comes, everything will be perfect. But this is not so:

> Why do peoples gather and nations speak for nothing? The kings of the earth stand themselves up, and leaders consult together, against Hashem and against His *Mashiach*.[14]

When *Mashiach* comes, all the nations will join together to fight him, for the influence of *galus* will enter the days of *Mashiach*. In the beginning, there will still be some aspects of *galus*. (Of course, the efforts of the nations will be in vain, as it says in the very next verse, "*He Who sits in Heaven will laugh*.") All this is because *ikvesa d'Meshicha* is the link that enters both worlds.

Now let us apply this idea to the Beis HaMikdash. Our world is earthly and material, whereas Heaven is a world of *kedushah — serafim, ofanim,* the *kisei hakavod;* it is a place of tremendous *avodas Hashem*.

Yaakov Avinu slept at the future site of the Beis HaMikdash and dreamt of a ladder. "*Behold, a ladder is standing on the ground, and its head reaches to Heaven*."[15] This ladder was the Beis HaMikdash. Part of it was in Heaven, and part on earth. It linked the two worlds. That is what the Beis HaMikdash does. It is the place where Heaven enters our earthly world, and vice versa.

It is written regarding the *Kohen Gadol* when he entered

14. *Tehillim* 1:1–2.

15. *Bereishis* 28:12.

the *Kodesh HaKodashim*: "*And no man shall be in the Ohel Moed when he enters to atone in the holy place, until he exits.*"[16] This verse teaches that no human being was permitted to be anywhere in the vicinity when the *Kohen Gadol* entered the *Kodesh HaKodashim*. For at that moment, when the *Kohen Gadol* went behind the *paroches,* the glory of Heaven would be revealed. No human being was capable of being there. Even the *Kohen Gadol* himself was transformed into an angel with a face of fire.

Shabbos Is the Link

Shabbos Kodesh, as well, links our ordinary, physical world with the world of *kedushah* in Heaven. It is our lifeline, our connection to Hashem. And through it comes all blessing. Anyone severed from Shabbos is in effect severed from Hashem, because Shabbos is the link between us and Hashem.

Regarding the creation of the earth, it is written: "*And the earth was astonishingly void, and darkness was upon the face of the deep* [waters]."[17] This description tells us about the nature of our world. On its own, it is a place of darkness, an infinite abyss in which a person can constantly fall. But certain things connect our world with Heaven, namely, the Beis HaMikdash and *Shabbos Kodesh.*

This is why someone who publicly desecrates Shabbos is equivalent to a non-Jew regarding certain halachos, for he has only this mundane world. He has lost the link. And this explains why Shabbos is treated so stringently, as mentioned. Shabbos is our connection to life. It is the main "artery." As long as a person keeps Shabbos intact, he remains alive.

All the mitzvos we do — tzitzis, tefillin, etc. — are done in *Olam HaZeh,* in this world. Shabbos, however, has an aspect of

16. *Vayikra* 16:17.
17. *Bereishis* 1:2.

Olam HaBa. By way of comparison, when a person entered the Beis HaMikdash, he was enveloped in *kedushah*. When he ate, he was eating from the table of Hashem; all his actions were a form of *avodah*. And so it is on Shabbos. It is more than other mitzvos, for which we will get reward in *Olam HaBa* — it's a whole different life, one connected directly to *Olam HaBa* itself.

3. FINDING THE BEIS HAMIKDASH IN YOUR SHABBOS

When we examine the details of Shabbos and the Beis HaMikdash, we see amazing similarities. We find that all the beauty and all the expressions of *kedushah* that were in the Beis HaMikdash can be found in Shabbos too.

Forgiveness of Sin

The most beautiful aspect of the Beis HaMikdash was its atonement for sin. It cleansed and purified us. *Chazal* say:

> Said R' Yehudah son of R' Shimon: There never was a person in Yerushalayim with sin. How so? The *tamid* of the morning would atone for the sins of the [previous] night, and the *tamid* of the evening would atone for the sins committed in the day. Thus, in any case, a person would not go to sleep in Yerushalayim with sin. As it is written (*Yeshayahu* 1:21), "*Righteousness shall sleep in it.*"[18]

When we sing *Dayeinu* in the Pesach Haggadah, we recount a series of great gifts that Hashem gave us: "He took us out of Egypt, He gave us Shabbos, He gave us the Torah ... ." And what is the pinnacle of it all? "And He built for us the Temple to atone for all our sins." That is the goal of everything — to be completely free of sin.

But why is that the ultimate goal? "*For your sins have*

18. *Bemidbar Rabbah* 21:21.

separated between you and your God."[19] There is a partition created by our sins that separates us from Hashem, and we would like to remove it. We all have sins of various kinds, involving our thoughts, speech and actions.

Everyone has misfortunes of various kinds—illness, family problems, financial difficulties, etc. Why do these things happen to us? We all know and believe that calamities befall us because of sin. If so, what could be better for us than getting rid of our sins?

This is the beauty of the Beis HaMikdash. It is the place where the sins of Yisrael are expiated through the offering of *korbanos*. Anyone who went into the Beis HaMikdash walked out purified of sin.

And so it is with *Shabbos Kodesh*:

> Said R' Chisda, in the name of Mar Ukba: [Regarding] anyone who prays on Shabbos evening and says *Va'yechulu*, the two ministering angels who escort a person will place their hands on his head and say to him, *"Your iniquity has departed, and your sin is purged"* (*Yeshayahu* 6:7).[20]

When a Jew comes home on Shabbos evening, he raises a Kiddush cup and says, *"Va'yechulu ha-shamayim v'ha'aretz v'chol tzva'am...."* He is declaring Hashem as the Creator of everything, and thus he merits atonement for his sins as if he had offered *korbanos* in the Beis HaMikdash. Thus, one of the first things that happen to a Jew on Shabbos is that his sins are erased.

On Shabbos, Hashem considers us perfect tzaddikim who've never sinned. Therefore, on Shabbos, the *korban musaf* contains only two sheep; there is no goat for a sin-offering. There's no need for one, because on Shabbos, there's no sin.

19. *Yeshayahu* 59:2.
20. *Shabbos* 119b.

How can this be?

Sins are committed only when a person feels the world belongs to him and he can do what he pleases. But when a person stands up and declares over a cup of wine that the world has a Creator and Ruler, he understands that it is out of the question to act contrary to God's will.

Why do we recite *Va'yechulu* over wine? If a person stands up and says Hashem created the heavens and the earth, perhaps he is just a philosopher who expresses lofty ideas but doesn't live by them. But if he declares his belief together with drinking a cup of wine, he solidifies his declaration. He is declaring that just as the wine he is drinking is real, so too is the declaration that goes along with it. The fact that Hashem created the world is just as much of a reality to him as the wine he drinks.

The moment we realize we're in Hashem's hands, there's no more sin. We're in Hashem's house, in His embrace. Everything is different now.

When I was a young *yeshivah bachur,* I once heard a certain speaker who gave a talk on Shabbos on the subject of *teshuvah.* I said to him, "But we're not supposed to do *teshuvah* on Shabbos!" (I meant to say that we don't recite *viddui* on Shabbos.) He chuckled and said, "Shabbos is not a day of *teshuvah*? On the contrary, Shabbos is all about returning to Hashem! Of course, we don't say *viddui* on Shabbos, but that's because Shabbos itself brings us close to Hashem."

Chazal say that just as *Aseres Yemei Teshuvah* is a special time of "*Seek Hashem when He may be found,*"[21] and prayers offered during those ten days don't go unanswered, so it is regarding Shabbos.[22] Praying on Shabbos is like praying on Yom Kippur;

21. *Yeshayahu* 55:6.

22. *Tikkunei Zohar, Tikun* 21.

it has a special power.

On Shabbos there isn't even a hint of sin, because it is written, *"Evil cannot dwell with You."*[23] In other words, there is no sin where Hashem is. All darkness just evaporates in the presence of such light. Once a week we live in Hashem's house, so to speak, where no iniquity can dwell.

The Priestly Garments

As we know, there is a special halachah of wearing Shabbos clothes:

> *"And you shall bathe and anoint yourself and put on your garments"* (*Rus* 3:3). Said R' Elazar: These are the garments of Shabbos.[24]

The idea of changing into Shabbos clothes is learned from the *bigdei kehunah*:

> What is the source in the Torah for changing one's garments? It is written (*Vayikra* 6:4), *"And he [the Kohen] shall remove his garments and wear different garments."*[25]

From here we see that Shabbos clothes are like the *bigdei kehunah*. Just as the *Kohanim* in the Beis HaMikdash had special garments, on Shabbos we have special garments.

A person's clothing expresses who he is. The *bigdei kehunah* are actually the garments of the angels. The angel Gavriel is called, *"The man clothed in linen,"*[26] and the garments of the *Kohanim* are made primarily of linen. When the *Kohanim* enter the Beis HaMikdash, they are as devoted to serving Hashem as are the angels in Heaven. Thus they wear the garments of angels.

23. *Tehillim* 5:5.
24. *Shabbos*113b.
25. *Shabbos* 114a.
26. *Daniyel* 12:7.

As a child in Williamsburg, Brooklyn, we had a neighbor who had a very menial job. I would see him walking around all week in his soiled work clothes. But when Shabbos came, he donned a splendid *shtreimel* and a *bekisheh* with a lovely floral design; with his long beard, you could think he was a Rebbe. I didn't even recognize him!

On Shabbos, we all wear special and different clothing because then we are different, more elevated people. We are as dedicated to holiness and purity as the *Kohanim* in the Beis HaMikdash.

The Menorah

In the Beis HaMikdash there was a Menorah. There were three mitzvos involving this Menorah. Two are well known: *hadlakas ha-neiros* and *hatavas ha-neiros*.

Hadlakas ha-neiros means lighting the Menorah. *Hatavas ha-neiros* means preparing the Menorah to be lit. (According to the Rambam, the *Kohen* would remove the old oil and wicks, and then set up the new ones.) This is a Torah mitzvah, and only a *Kohen* may carry it out.

Shabbos also has these two mitzvos. There is the mitzvah of lighting Shabbos candles, which is incumbent upon the woman (because she is the "*Kohen*" of the home). And there is an additional mitzvah of preparing the candlesticks (polishing them, inserting the oil and wicks, or candles, etc.). And the *Mishnah Berurah* deems it proper for the husband to do this preparation.[27] *Hatavas ha-neiros* is the man's mitzvah.

I learned this halachah when I was engaged and buying candlesticks for my *kallah*. I saw some fancy, decorated candlesticks on display that looked really nice. The storeowner told me, "Actually, it's quite hard to clean these candlesticks. But

27. 263:12.

you'll do it—it's *your* mitzvah to clean the candlesticks *lichvod Shabbos!*"

The husband prepares, and the wife lights. In this way the *hadlakas ha-neiros,* which resembles the lighting of the golden Menorah in the Beis HaMikdash, creates a perfect unity and harmony between husband and wife.

There is a third mitzvah regarding the Menorah. This mitzvah is simply that there should be a Menorah in the Beis HaMikdash. This mitzvah also has a parallel in Shabbos—we find that the Shabbos candlesticks are compared to the Menorah. Rabbeinu Yitzchak ben HaRa'avad is quoted in the *Rishonim* as saying that if the utensil holding the oil of the Shabbos lights is not a proper *keli*—for instance, it is too wobbly and cannot stand on its own without support—it is invalid for the Shabbos lights. Just as the lights in the Beis HaMikdash were placed inside the Menorah, so, too, the Shabbos lights need to be placed inside a proper *keli*. (Of course, it remains to be clarified whether the halachah follows this opinion.)

On this basis, we can explain the common custom of buying silver candlesticks. The candlesticks are similar to the Menorah,[28] and they are an intrinsic part of the mitzvah of kindling Shabbos lights.

Bathing

When the *Kohen* entered the Beis HaMikdash, before he started his *avodah,* he had to wash his hands and feet at the *kiyor*. If he didn't, his service was invalid.

However, there were two levels: the basic requirement of washing his hands and feet, and an additional requirement

28. Although the Menorah that was in the Beis HaMikdash was preferably made of gold, silver was also considered a worthy material. See *Rosh Hashanah* 24b.

instituted by *Chazal* that the *Kohen* should immerse himself in a *mikveh*.[29]

There is a similar mitzvah regarding Shabbos. The halachah states that it is a mitzvah to bathe one's whole body, and if one cannot do so, to wash one's face, hands, and feet in hot water on *erev Shabbos*.[30] As we know, many people also have the custom to immerse in a *mikveh* before Shabbos.

The Table

In the Beis HaMikdash, the *lechem ha-panim* rested upon a golden Shulchan. Similarly, we have the Shabbos table. Torah sources describe special specifications for the Shabbos table, how it should be positioned and where it should be located, etc. This is because our Shabbos table resembles the Shulchan of the Beis HaMikdash.

And what do we do while sitting around the Shabbos table? It is a universal Jewish custom to sing *zemiros*. These are not just nice songs; the singing is a special form of *avodas Hashem*. It is like the singing of the *Leviyim* in the Beis HaMikdash.

It's customary to place roses (*shoshanim*) on the Shabbos table, perhaps for their pleasant fragrance. "Just as the rose is prepared for Shabbos and Yom Tov, so is Yisrael...."[31]

Sometimes I buy a few roses for Shabbos. Once, I went to a store and saw some beautiful roses. When I asked the storekeeper to wrap some up for me, he asked me a very difficult question: "How many?" I was stumped. I know that a bridegroom buys twelve roses for the bride, but how many roses does one buy in honor of Shabbos, the day of Hashem? Should one buy twenty-four, or perhaps the entire store?

In the end, I took three roses, because it's impossible to buy

29. *Yoma* 30a.
30. *Shulchan Aruch, Orach Chayim* 260:1.
31. *Shir HaShirim Rabbah* 2:6.

enough. No matter how many you buy, it will never fully honor Hashem and His *Shechinah,* so you need some kind of practical framework within which to work. I chose the number three, which corresponds to the three *Avos*. But the main thing is that you should know for Whom you're buying the roses! We have to remember—this is Hashem's *se'udah,* Hashem's house; it is His Shabbos table.

Eating from the Korbanos

When people ate in the Beis HaMikdash, it wasn't an ordinary eating. Someone who offered a *korban* in the Beis HaMikdash would receive a portion of the meat, depending on what type of *korban* it was. (Some *korbanos* had no edible portions, others had portions only for the *Kohen,* and with others, most of the meat was given to the person who brought the *korban.*) Now that the person received his portion of meat, we may ask a halachic question: Did this meat belong to him?

Let's say a man wants to perform *kiddushin,* to betroth a woman. Nowadays, the groom gives the bride a gold ring while standing under the *chuppah*. But halachically speaking, he may perform *kiddushin* anywhere by giving her any object worth at least a *perutah*. What if he wants to betroth a woman by giving her his portion of meat from a *korban*? Is the *kiddushin* valid? It says in the Gemara[32] that it is not valid because the meat is not defined as his property. It is not his, and in order to perform a proper *kiddushin,* he must give her something that is his own.

I was once at a wedding, and during the *chuppah,* the officiating rabbi asked the *chasan* to take out the ring. The *chasan* started looking for it. He searched through all his pockets, but couldn't find it. His mother tried to solve the problem: "Take my ring and give it to the *kallah*." The rabbi, upon hearing this,

32. *Kiddushin* 52b.

exclaimed, "No, no! He cannot perform *kiddushin* with a ring that doesn't belong to him." The mother responded, "In that case, I am giving him the ring as a gift." Only when the ring became his property was the *chasan* able to perform *kiddushin*.

The Gemara explains why one cannot perform *kiddushin* with a portion of meat from a *korban*. This is because the man received this portion *mi-shulchan Gavo'ah,* "from the table of the Most High." What does that mean?

When a person eats lunch at his friend's house, the halachic authorities debate whether the food he eats is considered his or belongs to his host. That is, may the guest take the food home with him, either to eat it, or to do with it as he wishes? But in the Beis HaMikdash, there is no such question. According to all opinions, he is eating "from the table of the Most High." The food definitely belongs to Hashem, Who "invites" this Jew to partake at His table. Thus the meat is not his property, and he cannot perform *kiddushin* with it.

So it is with the Shabbos table. We are not saying that, halachically speaking, if a man performs *kiddushin* with Shabbos food, she is not betrothed to him. What we are saying is that the idea is the same. On Shabbos we sit at Hashem's table and eat His food. In the *zemiros* of Shabbos we say. *"Da hi seudasa d'Atika Kaddisha*—This is the meal of the Holy Ancient One." I once asked someone what he thinks this means. He answered, "It means that we are inviting Hashem to our table." I replied, "No, it is exactly the opposite. It means that Hashem is inviting us to *His* table. He is the host and we are guests."

Shabbos Kodesh resembles the *Beis HaMikdash*. We sit at Hashem's table and partake of His food!

"Borrow on My Account"

What we just explained about the Shabbos table sheds light on the following statement of *Chazal*:

> HaKadosh Baruch Hu said to Yisrael, "My children, borrow on My account and sanctify the day of Shabbos

> [through reciting Kiddush over wine]. Have faith in Me, and I will pay."[33]

It is also stated:

> All of a person's sustenance is allotted to him between Rosh Hashanah and Yom Kippur, except for expenses related to Shabbos, to Yom Tov, and to teaching his sons Torah. For if he spent less, he is given less, and if he spent more, he is given more.[34]

Rashi explains that all the money a person is destined to earn during the year is allocated at this time, so he should be careful not to overspend. If he does, extra income will not be granted to him, and he will lack what he needs. But this is not so with regard to Shabbos expenses. For such outlays, a person is supplied by Heaven according to what he is accustomed.

Let's say a person goes into debt to buy a new car he doesn't need. He's not living within the budget Hashem allotted him. What will happen? He'll be lacking in his sustenance. But this doesn't apply to expenses for Shabbos and Yom Tov (and Rosh Chodesh, according to Tosafos). There is no limit on what we can spend for them! Hashem says to us, "Borrow on My account, and I will pay."

The same goes for the expenses of teaching Torah to one's sons. If your child is having trouble in school, hire a private tutor. (And surely if he is an excellent student, treat him to a tutor, so he can learn an extra *daf* of Gemara.) Yes, you can afford it. Why? Because no matter what you pay, Hashem says, "I will foot the bill."

In fact, it makes sense that these expenses are on Hashem's "bill," so to speak. For *Chazal* say, "A person has three partners

33. *Beitzah* 15b.
34. Ibid 16a.

[in his formation]: HaKadosh Baruch Hu, his father, and his mother."[35] Each of these partners contributes his portion. The father provides the bones and sinews; the mother — the skin, flesh, and hair; "and HaKadosh Baruch Hu gives him a spirit and soul."[36] Thus, when the child needs food or clothing, who buys it? His father and mother, since they formed his body. And when he needs to learn Torah, who pays? Hashem, Who gave him his soul. The *neshamah* belongs to Hashem; He pays for its expenses.

And just as Hashem pays for Torah study, He pays for Shabbos expenses, including Shabbos clothing. This is Hashem's day, so everything goes on His account.

Let us illustrate this principle with an allegory about the wealthy, legendary Baron Rothschild. Let us imagine: One fine day, the baron approaches a caterer and says to him, "In one month I will be making a wedding for my only daughter. I want it to be an unforgettable evening. The reception must be exquisite, of course, as befits Baron Rothschild — and I want you to cater it."

"I am very honored," the man stammers, "but I don't think it's within my means to throw such a lavish affair."

"Do you think the expenses will be on your bill?" replies the baron. "Surely not. Just buy whatever you need. Go to all the butchers, the fish stores, the bakeries, etc., and select the finest delicacies. Make special orders if necessary, and put everything on my bill. Prepare a sumptuous meal, for which you will be handsomely rewarded. But don't forget — you're not paying for anything, so don't scrimp on anything. This is my banquet — the banquet of Baron Rothschild!"

On *erev Shabbos,* Hashem turns to every Jew and says,

35. *Niddah* 31a.

36. Ibid.

"Tomorrow is My day. You are My guest, and I am asking you to be My caterer. Keep in mind that all the meals on this day are My meals, and prepare them accordingly!"

The Jew replies, "But I don't think I can manage to prepare a meal befitting the King of the Universe."

Hashem answers, "I didn't mean that you should pay! I will pay Myself. You just go buy whatever you want. *Borrow on My account, and I will pay.*"

And so it is. We can splurge for Shabbos, even if our finances are tight. As mentioned, however, a person must establish a practical framework within which to fulfill this mitzvah, since there is no end to what may be bought, baked, etc. The *Mishnah Berurah* says one shouldn't "borrow on Hashem" wildly, lest he ultimately transgress the laws of financial honesty. We should not buy things beyond our lifestyle, acting as if we *really* were commissioned by "Baron Rothschild." The main thing is to know you're preparing everything for Hashem. He ordered the meal, so try to "compliment" Him as best you can.

The same applies to how we dress for Shabbos. When a person looks through his wardrobe, trying to decide what to wear for a certain occasion, he takes into account whose company he will be in. If he'll be among very distinguished people, he dresses accordingly. If he realizes he has only tatters and an important occasion is coming up, he considers buying himself a new outfit. So it is with Shabbos: We should keep in mind Whom we're dressing up for. We're like *Kohanim,* ministering before Hashem in dignified, priestly garments.

And the same goes for our Shabbos candlesticks. Shouldn't they be as nice as possible, like the Menorah in Hashem's home, the Beis HaMikdash?

Awe of the Beis HaMikdash and Shabbos

It is a positive Torah mitzvah to be in awe of the Beis HaMikdash, as it says, *"You shall fear My Mikdash."*[37]

Sefer Yere'im states that there is a mitzvah of being in awe of Shabbos as well.[38] In fact, this awe is not just a mitzvah but a living reality, as we see from the following halachah:

> If a person purchased food from a vendor who is unreliable regarding the taking of *ma'aser*, and the person forgot to take *ma'aser* from [this food] before Shabbos or Yom Tov, what should he do? He should ask the vendor whether *ma'aser* was taken. If the vendor says *ma'aser* was taken from it, the person may rely on this and eat it. This is because the awe of Shabbos is upon the *am ha'aretz*, so he doesn't sin on Shabbos.[39]

During the week, we may not rely on the word of a vendor who's an *am ha'aretz*. But on Shabbos, we believe him when he says he took *ma'aser*. For on Shabbos he won't lie, because he is afraid of Shabbos.

This is the awe of Shabbos, similar to that of the Beis HaMikdash. On Shabbos (as in the Beis HaMikdash) there are so many things we must be careful of. So many minor details entail major prohibitions. Thus, we have a mitzvah of "fearing" Shabbos. This is not a negative, paralyzing fear. It is a positive, sobering one, which encourages us to watch what we're doing on Shabbos. Someone who walks around on Shabbos with an easy, carefree attitude, as if he has nothing in the world to be concerned about, is liable to transgress the halachos of Shabbos.

37. Rambam, *Hilchos Beis HaBechirah* 7:1.

38. *Siman* 410.

39. Rambam, *Hilchos Ma'aser* 12:1.

On the other hand, people sometimes get nervous and pressured on Friday because so many things must be taken care of before Shabbos. Surely the fear of Shabbos is not meant to ruin the enjoyment of Shabbos. But we should know that the tension of *erev Shabbos* is rooted in the mitzvah of fearing Shabbos. And this mitzvah is actually an aspect of fearing Hashem, which is the most exalted level a Jew can attain. *Sefer Yereim* states that it is not Shabbos itself (or the Beis HaMikdash itself) that we are to fear—it is He Who commanded us regarding them!

The Fragrance of the Incense

In the Beis HaMikdash there was a golden *mizbei'ach*, on which it was a mitzvah to offer *ketores* twice a day. Eleven spices, the finest in the world, were ground very finely and placed on glowing coals. This *ketores* produced a wonderful fragrance. The fragrance was so strong that *Chazal* say:

> Women as far away as Yericho didn't need to use perfume because of the fragrance of the *ketores*. A bride in Yerushalayim didn't need to [perfume] herself because of the fragrance of the *ketores*.[40]

In Temple times, many millions of people poured into Yerushalayim during the *regalim*. There were all kinds of stores there, but none sold perfume. The air was so full of the heady fragrance of *ketores* that it was impossible to smell any other scent. *Sefer HaChinuch* explains that this phenomenon was designed to increase appreciation for the beauty of the Beis HaMikdash. People saw that not only was the Mikdash the most impressive building in the world, but even its fragrance was always special.

40. *Yoma* 39b.

The Fragrance of Shabbos

We've described the fragrance of the Beis HaMikdash. This has always brought me to wonder: What is the special fragrance of Shabbos? (Indeed, according to the Ari *z"l*, it's customary to smell fragrant myrtle branches on Shabbos, but not all follow this custom.)

I would like to tell a true story. This story was originally told by R' Simcha Wasserman, *zt"l*, who served as a rabbi in Los Angeles, and was the son of R' Elchanan Wasserman, *zt"l*.

There was a family of *ba'alei teshuvah* in Los Angeles who had returned to Torah due to R' Wasserman's efforts. Their oldest son reached the age of bar mitzvah, and they decided to celebrate the Shabbos of the bar mitzvah in a hotel because they had many relatives and friends. Since the hotel was out of town, they wrote on the invitation that whoever could not remain in the hotel for the entire Shabbos should not come, and they should instead participate in a bar mitzvah reception during the week. They emphasized that people were requested not to drive on Shabbos.

R' Wasserman was not able to come to the bar mitzvah for Shabbos. Friday morning, he called the family to wish them "mazel tov" and apologize for being unable to attend. Then the rabbi asked the mother if she had prepared a cholent for Shabbos. "Pardon me, Rabbi, but our friends don't know what cholent is," she replied. "We're serving cold food for lunch, including the meats and side dishes."

R' Wasserman said, "I'd like you to make a cholent nonetheless." Of course, she did as the rabbi requested.

Shabbos morning, a car stopped at the hotel, and a middle-aged couple stepped out. They entered the hotel, and suddenly the woman froze and said to her husband, "I can't take it. Let's get out of here right away!" Before the parents of the bar mitzvah boy could even greet them, they disappeared.

On *motza'ei Shabbos* the family called the couple to ask what had happened, and they were told an amazing story.

The woman who'd walked out was a Holocaust survivor. Taken from her home at age six, she spent a few years in the camps. At the end of the war she emigrated to America, where she'd built her home. She remembered nothing of her childhood in Poland—not her father or mother, not Shabbos, and no other sign of Jewishness —and this complete break with her past had distressed her all her life. Psychologists and psychiatrists had tried to help her without success.

But on this fateful Shabbos, when she'd entered the hotel and smelled the cholent, suddenly everything came back to her as if it had just happened. What was the story? She had been seized from her home in Poland on Shabbos, as the aroma of cholent filled the house. So when she smelled the cholent in the hotel, everything came back: all the childhood memories of her warm, beloved home. She was simply overwhelmed.

I heard that this couple became true *ba'alei teshuvah,* and recently their daughter married a *yeshivah bachur.*

Such is the power of the smell of cholent, and this is indeed an amazing story. Still, I would not call this aroma the special "fragrance of Shabbos." So what is this special fragrance?

I think that the special "fragrance" of Shabbos is *shalom bayis*. It is written in the *sefer Tomer Devorah*[41] that one shouldn't express anger on Shabbos, even when according to halachah it would be permitted or even proper to do so, as is sometimes necessary for the sake of *chinuch*. (Of course, this means not real, inner anger, but rather an external show of it.) We shouldn't be angry on Shabbos, because "The world is sweetened by the aspect of *oneg* [*Shabbos*], and there are no judgments on Shabbos." Anger is fire, and *Chazal* compare getting angry on Shabbos to

41. *Tomer Devorah,* chap. 2.

lighting a fire,[42] about which is written. *"You shall not kindle fire in all your dwelling places on the Shabbos day."*[43]

There should be a nice atmosphere in the home on Shabbos. There should be a feeling of peace and tranquility. During the twenty-four hours of Shabbos, the atmosphere should be pleasant, because we are in the Beis HaMikdash, so to speak.

Maintaining this high level of domestic harmony on Shabbos is challenging. A non-observant Jew once confided to me: "I'm at work all week long, and my wife isn't home much either. We meet only on Shabbos, and then the fights start."

This is not what Shabbos is supposed to be. Shabbos is meant to unify the family. There is a specific halachah of *shalom* on Shabbos. The greeting of "*Shabbat shalom*" is not a product of modern Hebrew. It has its source in *Chazal*:

> When Shabbos commences, one says, "*Shalom*." And when it departs, one says, "Shabbos is not a day for crying out... dwell in *shalom*."[44]

When we desist from our work on Shabbos, it is in a spirit of peace and tranquility. This is the beautiful "fragrance" of Shabbos. This is the special atmosphere that fills the home.

And why is Shabbos the time for a special halachah of *shalom bayis*? Every person is unique. Husband and wife come from different backgrounds, and when they come together to build a home, their differences naturally create certain conflicts and power struggles. The husband says, for very good reason, that it should be like this. And the wife says, with very good reason, the opposite. This creates problems. When Reuven is Reuven and Rachel is Rachel, it's hard to have real *shalom bayis*.

42. *Tikkunei Zohar, Tikun* 48.

43. *Shemos* 35:3.

44. *Shabbos* 12b.

But on Shabbos, we lose our personal identity, so to speak. There is no Reuven and no Rachel; there is only Hashem. We eat at Hashem's table. We are His guests. Usually, husband and wife don't fight when they are guests. In their own home, he is the master of the house, and she is the mistress. They feel they're on their own turf and can be themselves. But when visiting others, neither of them is the head of the household, and thus they unite.

This may be compared to two candles who are arguing over which of them sheds more light. When they're taken outside into the sunlight, the argument ceases. For in relation to the sun, candlelight becomes insignificant.

"And No Man Shall Be in the Ohel Mo'ed..."

When we come home on Friday night, we greet the angels and say, "*Shalom aleichem malachei ha-shareis...*" and we conclude, "*Tzeischem l'shalom....*" First we greet the angels and then say goodbye to them. This is surprising: Why do we ask the angels to leave? Let them stay. Are they bothering anyone?

The Chofetz Chaim explains that we are saying *shalom aleichem* to the angels of Shabbos and *tzeischem l'shalom* to the angels of the week. This is similar to Yaakov's dream with the ladder, where the angels of Eretz Yisrael went up, and the angels of *chutz la'aretz* came down to escort him further.

There is another answer to this question, based on our comparison to the Beis HaMikdash. When a *Kohen* offered *korbanos* in the Temple courtyard, other people were permitted to be present. But when he would enter the *Kodesh HaKodashim,* the Torah commands, "*And no man shall be in the Ohel Moed when he enters to atone in the holy place, until he exits.*"[45]

45. *Vayikra* 16:17.

The Midrash tells us that even angels were not allowed to be present:

> He entered the *Kodesh HaKodashim,* and the ministering angels fled from him. *"And no 'man' shall be in the Ohel Moed when he enters"* — this refers to the ministering angels, about whom is written (*Yechezkel* 1:10), *"And the likeness of their faces was the face of a 'man.'"*[46]

The moment in which the *Kohen Gadol* entered the *Kodesh HaKodashim* was very special. Hashem was alone with His beloved nation. This intimate moment required absolute privacy. Therefore, even the angels, with all due respect to their greatness and holiness, had to leave.

When we leave shul on Friday night, angels escort us home. We come home and find the Shabbos table set. We stand and say to the angels: "*Shalom aleichem... bo'achem l'shalom... barchuni l'shalom....*" And then we say to them, "My dear angels, we are about to recite Kiddush and begin the Shabbos meal. This is the meal of Hashem. At this meal, '*No "man" shall be in the Ohel Mo'ed.*' Therefore we bid you goodbye: '*Tzeischem l'shalom*!' The time has come for you to leave, because this is a moment when Hashem is alone with His beloved people, and even angels cannot be present at this holy time."

4. PRACTICAL GUIDELINES FOR SHABBOS

Fill the Day with Content

Now let us examine the practical level and talk about how to implement this wonderful idea that Shabbos is like the Beis HaMikdash.

Many of us wonder what to do on Shabbos. How exactly should we spend this precious day? In the winter, when the days are short, the problem is not so pressing, as Shabbos is

46. *Yalkut Shim'oni, Iyov* 908.

over before we know it. But on long, summer afternoons, we have more trouble. The children are bored, and sometimes we ourselves don't know how to keep busy.

This problem brings us to one of the striking contradictions of Shabbos. On the one hand, Shabbos is the greatest and most wonderful day of the week. On the other hand, no mitzvah in the Torah can seem so devoid of *kedushah* as Shabbos. Even *b'nei Torah* who learn full-time all week long sometimes find Shabbos rather empty. They visit, they eat, they nap a few hours, and the day just goes by. While Yom Tov seems to be full of *kedushah,* Shabbos tends to be empty — unless we fill it with content.

The six weekdays are naturally full of qualitative activity. Some men go to work, others to *kollel,* some wives go to teach and others do other things, but everyone is busy. And on Shabbos, all this blessed activity comes to a stop. Thus, Shabbos by definition seems empty. We don't work, we don't go to school; we don't do much of anything. If we fill Shabbos with *kedushah,* it will become the greatest and holiest day. But if we leave it empty, that is exactly what it will be.

So we ask: What should we be doing on Shabbos?

A Mirror

To answer this question, let us compare Shabbos to the Yomim Tovim. It is written, "*Six days shall you work and do all your labor, and the seventh day is Shabbos to Hashem, your God.*"[47] What is this verse telling us? Simply speaking, it says that the six weekdays are a time of doing. "*Six days shall you work....*"

The Vilna Gaon explains it differently.[48] He says the verse hints at the six Yomim Tovim: the first days of Pesach, the last days of Pesach, the first days of Sukkos, the last days of Sukkos,

47. *Shemos* 20:8–9.

48. Cited ad loc. in *Ohel Yaakov al HaTorah,* by the Dubner Maggid, in the gloss at the bottom of the page.

Shavuos, and Rosh Hashanah. On these days, it is permitted to do the work of cooking and of carrying objects from domain to domain — *"Six days shall you work and do all your labor."* But *"the seventh day is Shabbos to Hashem, your God"* — Shabbos is different. On Shabbos these *melachos* are forbidden.

What is the basic difference between Shabbos and Yom Tov? Each holiday has a special mitzvah, while Shabbos does not. Pesach has matzah, Rosh Hashanah has shofar, Yom Kippur has fasting and *teshuvah,* Sukkos has sukkah and *lulav.* All these mitzvos are like an engine that generates *kedushah.* Matzah is called *nahama dimehemnusa,* the bread that brings a person to *emunah.* The sound of the shofar penetrates the depths of our *neshamah* and affects us. And so on.

Shabbos has none of these. The very word "Shabbos" is derived from the word *shevisah,* "cessation from activity." If we were to define the essence of Shabbos, we would point to this word. It is an absence of everything else; a cessation of the activity that preceded it.

Yom Tov is compared to a picture; each one has its own beautiful scene. But Shabbos is like a mirror — it has no content of its own. Shabbos is a day on which the whole world stops — no plowing, no cooking, no writing, etc. And when everything stops, what's left? Hashem! On this day, there's no world. There's only Hashem. Therefore, the mirror of Shabbos reflects Hashem. That is why we say that Shabbos is the day of Hashem.

And that is why Shabbos has so many intricate halachos. In order to fulfill the mitzvah of *lulav,* you just need to pick up a *lulav.* Shaking it in six directions adds to the mitzvah, but the basic Torah requirement is fulfilled the moment you take the *lulav* into your hand. Whereas on Shabbos, every move we make is complicated. For twenty-four hours, we must pay attention to everything we do. We make a salad, open the refrigerator, turn on the tap, want to pull off a paper towel...everywhere we turn it's Shabbos, Shabbos, and again Shabbos. And not just in the kitchen and the living room. When we go outside, we again encounter Shabbos: the complex laws of transferring objects from domain to domain. And so it is with virtually every move we make on Shabbos.

Hilchos Shabbos surround and permeate our lives because Hashem surrounds everything and fills everything. We live this reality on Shabbos. There is nothing but Shabbos; there is nothing but Hashem. The entire world ceases to exist, and we are now with Hashem alone, since there *is* nothing else. In this way, the numerous restrictions of Shabbos allow us to break free of the bounds of ordinary, mundane reality. Today, we are not just human beings living in the everyday world. We are transformed and uplifted to a whole new plane of reality in which we are alone with Hashem.

Kedushah of Shabbos Comes from Hashem

Virtually every type of *kedushah* we know of is "man-made." The *kedushah* of Eretz Yisrael was produced by Yehoshua bin Nun. Then it was lost during the Babylonian exile and reproduced by Ezra HaSofer. The *kedushah* of the Beis HaMikdash was created by Shmuel HaNavi and Shlomo HaMelech. How were they able to produce this *kedushah*? In order for a material thing to be filled with *kedushah,* it requires a Jew to come and dedicate it to *kedushah.* This is true for Eretz Yisrael, for the Beis HaMikdash, and for *korbanos*.

The same holds true for the Yomim Tovim. Their *kedushah* is generated when the Jews declare the new month, which happens when the Sanhedrin accepts the witnesses who've seen the new moon.

The Ritva uses this principle in a novel way, by explaining a passage in the Talmud[49] as follows: One year the Gentile authorities forbade the Jews to fast on Yom Kippur. What did the Sanhedrin do that year? When the time for Rosh Chodesh came, the Sages didn't declare the new month. Since they never produced the *kedushah* of Rosh Chodesh, that year there was no Yom Kippur. Neither was there Rosh Hashanah or Sukkos. We see from here that the *kedushah* of all these holidays is produced by the Jewish People.

But there is one *kedushah* that Hashem produces all by Himself: that of *Shabbos Kodesh*. Shabbos was created by Hashem alone, at the beginning of Creation. It is *zeicher l'ma'aseh Bereishis* — a remembrance of Hashem's original act of Creation.

What are the ramifications of where the *kedushah* comes from? If it depends on us, then we must create a fitting receptacle for the *kedushah*. Thus, each holiday has its special mitzvah, its receptacle for the *kedushah* of the day. And it's our responsibility to make that receptacle. But when Hashem Himself gives us the *kedushah,* and it all depends on Him, there's no need for such preparation on our part.

The Gemara[50] recounts that Turnus Rufus asked R' Akiva how he knew that that day was Shabbos. R' Akiva answered, "The Sambatyon River proves it." All week long it threw up stones, but on Shabbos it rested.

Let us ask: Does the Sambatyon observe the other mitzvos as well? Does it put on tefillin or eat matzah on Pesach? Assumedly not. So why does it choose to keep Shabbos? The answer is that all the other mitzvos are things for *us* to do. We put on tefillin; we eat matzah. We create the *kedushah* of Yom Tov. But Shabbos comes to us from Hashem: He *gives* us

49. *Chullin* 101b.
50. *Sanhedrin* 65b.

Shabbos as a gift. Thus, the Sambatyon River feels Shabbos too. All of Creation feels Shabbos. Because it comes from Hashem.

Implementing Zachor and Shamor

All of this leads us back to our question: What should we be doing on Shabbos? How can we attain the *kedushah* of Shabbos?

There are two things we need to do on Shabbos:

The first is to remember Shabbos, to know Shabbos is here — *Zachor.* If we are unaware that Shabbos is here, nothing will help. Let's say a *chasan* doesn't know the *kallah* is present. In such a situation, they cannot rejoice together! Knowing Shabbos is here means being aware that this day can grant us greatness and closeness to Hashem more than any other time.

The second thing we need to do is guard Shabbos — *Shamor.* We must guard this special time alone with Hashem from the disturbance of weekday influences. Shabbos is our private audience with Hashem, and this privacy must be protected. *Chazal* tell us that a non-Jew may not keep Shabbos and is put to death if he does. Why? What did he do that was so terrible? The Midrash explains that he is invading the privacy of the King and Queen, who are sitting together.

Guard Shabbos so it will be just for you and Hashem. The world is gone and has ceased to exist, so forget about your mundane, weekday life with all its routine activities. You are now alone with Hashem, in *Olam HaBa*!

Shabbos has one positive mitzvah and one negative mitzvah. The positive one is, *"Remember the day of Shabbos."*[51] And the negative one is, *"Guard the day of Shabbos."*[52] This second mitzvah means not to desecrate Shabbos, and we will now

51. *Shemos* 20:7.
52. *Devarim* 5:11.

explain its significance.

As mentioned, the word "Shabbos" is derived from *shevisah,* "cessation from activity." During the six days of the week, Hashem did His work. On the seventh, He ceased; He rested from His work. What does this mean? Was Hashem tired and in need of a day of rest?

It says in the Gemara[53] that Hashem created the world by uttering the Hebrew letters *yud* and *heh.* With the *heh,* Hashem created the entire universe as we know it. With the *yud,* He created *Olam HaBa.* All Hashem did was pronounce two letters. Even a human being wouldn't be tired out by such work, even if he uttered the letter *heh* all day long. So what does it mean that Hashem "rested" after creating the world?

The answer is that *shevisah,* cessation from work, does not mean rest. It means stopping. For six days Hashem created a world. On the first day, the heavens and earth. On the second day, He divided between the upper waters and the lower waters. On the third day, vegetation and trees; on the fourth, the luminaries of the sky; on the fifth, fish and birds; and at the end, on the sixth day, animals and man. During these six days Hashem was busy, so to speak, creating and forming. But on the seventh day Hashem stopped creating and returned to His state of greatness. He said, so to speak, "I am not here anymore. I am returning to My state of greatness."

That is the meaning of Shabbos—*shevisah.* For six days we live within the world. We go out to do business, we toil to earn a living, etc. Of course we also pray three times a day, but our prayers comprise only the *kedushah* that is within our world. On Shabbos, we leave our world. We return to Hashem and to *His* world. Just as Hashem stopped creating and returned to His state of greatness, on Shabbos we cease to live within the world

53. *Menachos* 29b.

and we return to our true greatness.

It would seem that Shabbos has additional significance in our generation. In previous times a person would get up in the morning and go out to the fields and pastures. How great and deep was his world? How interesting was this world of cows and chickens? It wasn't so hard for him to disconnect from the world.

Nowadays, Shabbos is so important. The modern world exerts such a grip on us that it's hard to disengage from it. Shabbos gives us the ability and the opportunity to shake off the world around us, with all its media and communication and nonsense, and connect ourselves to Hashem.

In short, on Shabbos, we don't have to *do* anything. Our job on this day is to disconnect from the world, from our occupations and hobbies, and live in seclusion with Hashem. The only thing that interests us is *kedushah*.

And that is the meaning of the halachos of Shabbos, which tell us not to plow, plant, build, write — all the forms of creative work — *meleches machsheves*. What do we do on Shabbos? *Zachor v'shamor.* We remember what Shabbos is and are careful not to ruin its beauty.

Shabbos is like the week of *sheva berachos*. During these days the *chasan* and *kallah* don't go to work; they just live together. On Shabbos we live with Hashem. How? By spending time with Him privately and not being involved with any matters other than *kedushah*. To live in Hashem's house, to eat at His table, to understand that the clothes we wear on Shabbos are priestly garments.

If we remember that it is Shabbos, and we live with Shabbos, there is no level of greatness that Shabbos cannot take us to. As we say in davening, *Uveirachto mikol ha-yamim v'kidashto mikol ha-zemanim.* It is the most blessed and holy day of all.

But when we lack a true appreciation of it, Shabbos is the emptiest day of all. Let us return to the allegory of the *chasan* and *kallah*. If they don't love one another, if they aren't getting along—and surely if they aren't even aware of each other's existence—they cannot develop a meaningful relationship. Even twenty-five years together won't help.

Many people have already spent hundreds of *Shabbosos* with Hashem, and they've even said, *"Bo'i kallah, bo'i kallah,"* but they still don't realize in Whose house they're living. They remain unaware of what greatness they're experiencing. That is why, one Shabbos after another, they have a sense of emptiness.

The Torah tells us, *"Remember the day of Shabbos."* Know in Whose house you're living. Be aware of Who is with you, in Whose honor you're lighting candles, for Whom you are setting the table, for Whom you're cooking and baking, for Whose sake you are putting on Shabbos clothes.

And the Torah also tells us, *"Guard the day of Shabbos."* Don't disturb Shabbos. Don't bring a newspaper into Shabbos, don't talk politics on Shabbos. We say in Shabbos morning prayers, *"Ba-yom ha-shevi'i his'alah v'yashav al kisei kevodo."* This means, "On the seventh day, He elevated Himself and sat on His throne of glory." On Shabbos we are elevated, in the Beis HaMikdash!

If a person enters the Beis HaMikdash and understands this is Hashem's house, he can reach a level akin to prophecy. Whereas a person who enters the Beis HaMikdash without knowledge of its true nature, will see nothing but the technical performance of animal sacrifice. What benefit will such a person derive from this sacred place?

Shabbos Kodesh is a Beis HaMikdash. But we must remember that today is Shabbos. During these twenty-four hours, while we sit at the Shabbos table, we must remember Whose guests we are.

The thing that ruins Shabbos most is to sit around and engage in empty talk, secular reading, and other vanities. Such activity desecrates Shabbos. It's as if the Shabbos weren't even here. We must remember Shabbos, prepare for it as befits

Hashem's honor, and greet it properly when it arrives. And when Shabbos departs, we must take leave of it as respectfully as possible. If we say goodbye nicely to Hashem, He will come again. But if we keep checking the clock to see if Shabbos is over yet, and when the time comes we sigh with relief, who says He'll want to visit us again?

If we don't ruin Shabbos, everything will fall into place. For Shabbos contains within it infinite greatness, infinite love, and infinite *deveikus* to Hashem. This is Shabbos's gift to each and every one of us. If we truly want it, it is ours.

"סולם מוצב ארצה וראשו מגיע השמימה"

5

Shabbos Connects Us to the World of Kedushah

Shabbos Nurtures the Rest of the Week

SOMETIMES SMALL THINGS CAN have a big effect. *"The beginning of an argument is like opening a hole in the dam."*[1] There is a big dam holding back a vast body of water. If you poke a little hole in it, the whole dam will collapse. It might take a while, but in the end it will happen.

There are certain weak points in our observance of Torah and mitzvos, little "holes" that can wreak havoc on our spiritual life. We need to search for them and seal them before trouble strikes.

Conversely, there are small things that have great potential for bringing us blessing and plenty, yet they are often blocked. One of the important foundations of Jewish life is that Shabbos is a fountain, a *ma'ayan,* of blessings. It is the great source of all blessing. This reality was imprinted in the world at the time of Creation.

Hashem created our world during the six days of Creation. This reality has a tremendous, indestructible power, for Hashem took an oath regarding it: *"For all the days of the earth there will*

1. *Mishlei* 17:14.

be sowing and reaping and cold and heat and spring and fall and day and night; they shall not cease."[2]

There are a great variety of things in this world that are constantly changing, but what Hashem established at the time of Creation will never change. As Shlomo HaMelech said, *"What was is what will be."*[3]

Part of the world's basic nature is that it is built from six days and then one. And that one day is the core of the other six, and that day is Hashem's day. This is the way the world works — it is a natural law, and there is no way around it.

With this in mind, we can better understand something that seems so puzzling. Many people devote their lives to Torah study. Precious *kollel* men and yeshivah students invest so many hours and put so much effort into their learning and *Yiddishkeit*, and they do it with a genuine yearning to grow and advance in their *avodas Hashem*. Yet the results are sometimes less than hoped for. These people often undergo considerable downfalls and crises. They invest so much effort and goodwill but don't see as much success. Why is this? What's behind this mystery?

In my opinion, one of the main reasons is that we are not connected enough to the basic source of all success. We do not tap into the power source that generates true spiritual growth. This source is none other than *Shabbos Kodesh*.

Hashem created the six weekdays in a way that their main source of *kedushah* is from Shabbos. Where does our strength to daven and learn all week come from? From where do we draw our vitality on Sunday, Monday, and Tuesday? It all comes from Shabbos. And this fountain of blessing is virtually closed to many of us. Many of us have almost no idea how to even approach it.

2. *Bereishis* 8:22.

3. *Koheles* 1:9.

The Weakest Day in Avodas Hashem

Sure, we all keep Shabbos. But with a little understanding and effort, our whole Shabbos can be transformed completely, producing amazing results.

It is no secret, that for many of us, Shabbos is the weakest day in our *avodas Hashem*. This is true even of people whose entire week is spent in Torah study. Let's take a practical look at the matter: During the week everyone has a schedule. Within a typical yeshivah/*kollel* schedule, there are about four hours of learning in the morning, another four in the afternoon, and about two at night. This is a lot of time to sit and learn. And besides this, there is davening. All in all, the day is packed with Torah and *avodas Hashem*.

The same is true of working men. A Jew goes out and works long and hard to keep him and his family going, and to send his children to learn Torah. Besides that, he sets regular times in his daily schedule for learning Torah. All in all, he is busy with mitzvos from morning to night.

And then Shabbos comes, and everyone's whole daily schedule of learning and mitzvos comes to a halt. Let's take a look at how someone's Shabbos can go by without his really doing anything particularly uplifting. (You may or may not identify with certain parts of this description.)

On Shabbos evening, Yankel is exhausted from a hard week and goes to sleep early. It is a long, winter night, and he doesn't wake up until almost twelve hours later. He realizes he's a little late for the minyan, but after all he can still catch up if he skips some of the extra *Pesukei d'Zimrah* of Shabbos, so he runs to shul. During the Torah reading, he peruses some of the *parashah* sheets laying around the shul, looking for a nice *vort* he can say at the table, and before he knows it, davening is over. He chats with a friend for a few minutes and then is back home.

The meal is not quite ready yet, so after a quick Kiddush over cake, Yankel sits down on the couch and glances at the

Shabbos section of the newspaper. He relaxes until the meal begins. The cholent is even more delicious than usual, so he can't resist a second helping. Yankel is then overcome by drowsiness — probably because of the long week. He mumbles his way through *Birkas HaMazon* and heads for bed.

A few hours later Yankel is on his way to Minchah, feeling a little groggy from his long nap. Then comes *seudah shelishis,* at which he sings a couple of *zemiros* because there are still a few minutes until Ma'ariv.

How could the precious day of Shabbos just float by like that? What's going on here?

When Shabbos Begins, the Slack Begins

It is written in Torah sources that at midday on Friday, the *kedushah* of Shabbos starts to set in. Amazingly enough, that is exactly when things begin to unravel for many of us. Just when the first bells of *kedushah* begin to ring, things start going downhill.

It is truly remarkable. Every Friday at 12:30 P.M., what happens? The *beis midrash* empties out. The last *seder* of the week is over. And that's when the situation begins to deteriorate. It is most unfortunate that this occurs at the moment about which we could say, *"The voice of my Beloved is knocking — 'Open for Me, My sister, My wife, My dove, My perfect one.'"*[4]

To be honest with ourselves, how much time do we really need to prepare for Shabbos? Everyone knows that in the winter the days are short, and in the summer the days are long, yet people seem to make the same Shabbos preparations and learn the same number of hours all year round. Where does the time go? It just evaporates — because a feeling of slackening sets in as Shabbos approaches.

4. *Shir HaShirim* 5:2.

In my opinion there is a crucial point here. It's not a matter of proper time management on *erev Shabbos* and Shabbos; that's not really the issue. It's much more than that. Here is one of those little holes responsible for a person's entire downfall. If a *ben Torah* would grab hold of *Shabbos Kodesh* from beginning to end and fill it with meaning, he wouldn't just gain one more day. He would access a great fountain of *kedushah*.

We are all aware that the Yomim Nora'im are not just a ten-day period that comes and goes. We know that these important days open up the gates for us for the entire year to come. Similarly, if we knew how to take advantage of what *Shabbos Kodesh* has to offer, our lives would be transformed.

This One Enters the Realm of That One

I will now try to explain why I think Shabbos is spiritually the lowest day of the week for many of us.

Let us consider the connection between *kodesh* and *chol*. When we recite the Havdalah prayer when Shabbos comes to a close, we express a very deep concept: "*He Who divides between the sacred and the mundane, between light and darkness, between Yisrael and the nations, between the seventh day and the six days of the week.*"

Some things are as far from one another as east is from west. The World to Come is far from this world, Heaven is far from earth, the sacred is far from the mundane. Each is unlike the other and in opposition to it.

Yet Hashem made things sequential. Shabbos follows the week. The days of *Mashiach* follow this world. There is something which connects these two different things, and this connecting element enters the realms of both things it connects.

Picture a chain composed of rings. Every two rings are connected to one another via a third ring, which enters the space of both. Another example is a bridge spanning a river. To connect one side of the river to the other, the bridge must touch both.

We live in this world, and the Messianic era is yet to come. We think that one fine day there will be an abrupt switch. This world will stop, and right away the days of the *Mashiach* will start. This is true, but we must know that these days seep into our world and vice versa. As explained in the previous chapter, when *Mashiach* comes all the nations will join forces to fight him. This battle is called the War of *Gog u'Magog*. It is a seeping of the troubles of our world into the Messianic age.

Conversely, in this period of *ikvesa d'Meshicha,* the days preceding the coming of *Mashiach,* there is a tremendous *siyata di'Shemaya,* because the light of *Mashiach* seeps into our world.

This is all because of the connecting element, which enters both worlds and thus links them.

Hashem created the universe with two parts — Heaven and earth: *"The heavens are heavens for Hashem, and He gave the earth to the sons of men."*[5] Heaven is the place of *kedushah*. That is where the angels sing praises before Hashem, and the *serafim* and *ofanim* call out, *"Kadosh, Kadosh, Kadosh...."* It is a world of *kedushah*. The world we live in, on the other hand, is the mundane world of earth, a place of ordinary, physical life.

Shabbos and the Beis HaMikdash Are the Bridges

Certain "ladders" bridge the world of *kedushah* and our mundane world. One of these was the Beis HaMikdash. It connected the Heavenly world above and the ordinary world in which we live.

The Beis HaMikdash had a puzzling quality. On the one hand, a visitor could think he was in a very ordinary place. If we took pictures inside the Beis HaMikdash, what would we see? *Kohanim* up to their ankles in blood, slaughtering and quartering animals, flaying the hides and eating vast amounts

5. *Tehillim* 115:16.

of meat. And piles of fat and entrails smoking on the Altar.

Probably the closest parallel in our times is what we do on Pesach night. Imagine a person ignorant of Jewish customs peeking in the window and observing us reclining at the table, downing glasses of wine in two gulps, and gobbling up giant crackers, our cheeks bulging as we swallow as fast as we can. He definitely would not think we were doing anything holy. Yet we know how much *kedushah* the Seder has. It is one of the holiest events of the year.

So it was with the Beis HaMikdash. It had its mundane appearance, but other aspects showed that the Beis HaMikdash was completely otherworldly. There were ten ongoing miracles. And in the *Kodesh HaKodashim* was the *Aron HaKodesh,* which *Chazal* tell us took up no physical space.[6] The *Aron* was two and a half *amos* wide, and the *Kodesh HaKodashim* was twenty. If someone went in there with a tape measure, however, he would find that from one side of the *Aron* to the wall were ten *amos,* and from the other side of the *Aron* to the wall were ten *amos*. So where was the *Aron*? The answer is that it took up no space. The Beis HaMikdash was simply not of this world!

The Beis HaMikdash was a ladder whose top was in the world of *kedushah,* above this world, and whose bottom was in our world below. If the Beis HaMikdash were only a Heavenly place of miracles and angels, it would be irrelevant to our world. It wouldn't help us at all. No human being could enter and benefit from it. But it was not that way; it was a ladder.

Let us imagine a Jew visiting the Beis HaMikdash. He expects to enter an awesomely holy place. He takes a cautious step through the gate, his heart pounding with fear, and he thinks, "Who knows what's going to happen to me?" He progresses another step, and another, and amazingly enough he is

6. *Megillah* 10b.

still alive. He walks around a little in the Temple courtyard and meets a *Kohen* hurrying to his service.

"Excuse me, sir," he asks fearfully, "what is your name?"

"Yankel," the *Kohen* answers.

"You're Yankel? I thought you were the angel Gavriel!"

"No, I'm a regular person, just like you."

When a person entered the Beis HaMikdash, at first he would see only *Kohanim, Leviyim,* and *Yisraelim*. As he progressed, he encountered higher and higher levels. He would come to the Main Altar, which stood in the Temple courtyard. A *Kohen* could go past that through the *Ulam* and into the *Heichal,* which contained the Menorah, the Shulchan with the *lechem ha-panim,* and the Incense Altar. At the far end of the *Heichal* he would see the thick curtain beyond which lay the *Kodesh HaKodashim* — the part of the Beis HaMikdash that actually penetrated the Heavenly world of *kedushah*. Here was the head of the ladder between Heaven and earth.

We now come to a question: What business did the *Kohen Gadol* have entering the *Kodesh HaKodoshim*? Isn't Heaven a place for angels, not men? In fact, *Chazal* ask this question:

> *"And no man shall be in the Tent of Meeting..."* (*Vayikra* 16:17). Said R' Abbahu: And was the *Kohen Gadol* not a man? Rather, it may be understood according to what R' Pinchas said: When the spirit of *kedushah* rested upon the *Kohen Gadol,* his face glowed like a torch [and he was not a man at that time]. As it is written (*Malachi* 2:7): *"The lips of the Kohen shall guard knowledge... for he is an angel of Hashem of Hosts."*[7]

It was forbidden for any human being to be present when the *Kohen Gadol* entered the *Kodesh HaKodashim* on Yom Kippur. Indeed, he wasn't there either — he was transformed into an angel. The Beis HaMikdash was a ladder whose feet were on

7. *Vayikra Rabbah* 21:12.

earth and whose head protruded into Heaven above. To perform its function, it had to reach from the mundane to the holy.

And what about *Shabbos Kodesh*? Upon entering Shabbos, one seems to be in a completely mundane realm. He eats, he sleeps. Nothing looks so special here. But it is a ladder, and if he knows how to climb it, he can reach Heaven. He can cross the bridge and enter the world of *kedushah*.

Reach Heaven — or Remain with Nothing

The weekdays are part of this mundane world, which Hashem has filled with meaning through His Torah and mitzvos. Each day has its special mitzvos, its special qualities and greatness.

What about Shabbos? Its meaning is unlike that of other days. Shabbos's meaning is the very fact that it penetrates Heaven. With ordinary weekdays, our job is to fill them with *kedushah*. We set aside times for Torah learning, we involve ourselves with various mitzvos, etc. We know what to do. But when it comes to Shabbos, we're at a loss. Who knows how to climb this ladder? Shabbos is imbued with a power no other day has, yet if we don't know what to do with it, we'll remain below, grounded in this mundane world. That is how Shabbos ends up being the emptiest day of the week.

The following analogy illustrates this syndrome:

A person needs to eat, wherever he is. So when he goes on a trip, he packs a sandwich and a water bottle, so he'll have something to eat on the way. But if a person is home and feels like eating, and he starts searching his knapsack for his sandwich and water, he won't find them. The bag is empty. Why? Because the home is the source of all food. This is where all the sandwiches and water bottles come from. Here he has a fridge full of food! But if he doesn't realize he needs to open the fridge, he'll remain hungry.

Every Jew, whether sitting in the *beis midrash* or working

for a living, is doing a mitzvah. *"Man was born for labor."*[8] So it is all week long. But this changes when Shabbos arrives, since Shabbos is a day of rest. On this day, there is a *kedushah* of a completely different level. On Shabbos we don't subsist on a "sandwich." We don't live on what we've packed with effort and careful planning to keep us going while we're far from home.

On Shabbos we're home. We're standing right at the source of it all. If a person knows where to look for *kedushah* on this day, if he knows how to access it, he can reach even to Heaven. All the gates are open on this day. But if, on Shabbos, he tries to live as he does all week, he'll run into trouble. He won't find even a sandwich to eat, so to speak. He'll be completely empty-handed.

As we've said, Shabbos is the fountain of a person's vitality for the whole week. Someone whose Shabbos is empty will lack the vitality he could have had. If he learns all week nonetheless, it's thanks to the fact that he at least observes the halachos of Shabbos. But someone who desecrates Shabbos, *chas v'shalom,* has lost everything. He has blocked the fountain of Shabbos. He has severed a vital artery and is now cut off completely from *Yiddishkeit.*

If our weekdays are lackluster, falling short of expectations, one of the main reasons is our ignorance of the secret of how to grab hold of the greatness of Shabbos. Shabbos cannot be treated like every other day; it has a special form of service, which calls for greatness.

We won't go into detail in this chapter, but the main point is that we must put effort into making Shabbos meaningful. Whoever does so opens up a mighty fountain from which he'll drink all week long. It will transform his life. But if someone just slides through *Shabbos Kodesh,* treating it as a day off on

8. *Iyov* 5:7.

which he eats cholent, he is missing out on all the beauty and power of this day. If we don't make our Shabbos meaningful, it will naturally be the weakest and lowest day of the week.

Erev Shabbos and *motza'ei Shabbos* deserve our attention too, as they connect Shabbos and the weekdays, leading us into and out of Shabbos. They bridge the mundane week and the *kedushah* of Shabbos.

Actually, most people regret how little they take advantage of these holy times. But they tell themselves that other things are a lot more important. They fail to realize that these holy times hold the key to all their spiritual success.

Living Shabbos

What should we do on Shabbos? How can we utilize this day and make it meaningful?

In truth, this is a broad topic, but we'll mention just two points now:

1. We need to guard Shabbos, taking care not to desecrate it.
2. Above all, we need to remember that today is Shabbos.

On a long Shabbos afternoon or evening, if we just sit and idly chat, we desecrate Shabbos. The very fact that we forget today is Shabbos is a desecration of Shabbos! All the more so if someone reads a book—even stories of tzaddikim—just to pass the time, for he is unaware that today is Shabbos. This person is not living Shabbos, and that's considered desecrating Shabbos.

For these twenty-four hours, let us try to live with the Shabbos as much as possible. Let us be *Shabbosdik,* filling the time with learning, with *kedushah*. This doesn't mean we have to jump to high *madreigos*—there's no need for that. The *madreigos* come from Hashem, from Shabbos itself. All we have to do is, *"Open your mouth wide, and I will fill it."*[9] If we just live with the reality that now it's Shabbos, and we realize we're drinking from the great fountain of Shabbos, everything will be as it should. Someone who lives *Shabbos Kodesh* is penetrating the world of *kedushah,* as if he had entered into the holiest places of the Beis HaMikdash.

Now let us discuss guarding the Shabbos. We can understand this concept by comparing it to the Beis HaMikdash. There was a lot of guarding in the Beis HaMikdash. There were partitions and curtains, and all the doors were guarded, lest strangers entered. This was an important aspect of the Beis HaMikdash and is a very interesting point. How many hours a day were *korbanos* actually being offered there? From the morning until the early afternoon. At two o'clock the Beis HaMikdash was already closed. The service of the *korbanos* did not last the whole day, and the Beis HaMikdash was not just a place for bringing *korbanos.*

So what did they do there twenty-four hours a day? They guarded. They lived within the Beis HaMikdash, in partitions within partitions, guarding it day and night. A Jew who entered there knew very well that he was now in the Beis HaMikdash.

And so it is with Shabbos. This is the time to sit in the *beis midrash,* to learn, to daven, to say Tehillim, to do various other things that show appreciation and honor of Shabbos — not to engage in empty activities and sit around talking nonsense. That ruins the beauty of it all. We must guard the *kedushah* of Shabbos as the *Kohanim* guarded the Beis HaMikdash.

Let us pay special attention to *erev Shabbos* as well. A person must make sure to fill these hours with content. It needn't be something unusually lofty or special; just do something spiritually valuable with the time. If you're a *yeshivah bachur* or a *kollel*

9. *Tehillim* 81:11.

man, you can go to the *beis midrash* and continue with your regular learning, or you can pick a different topic to learn. I have no doubt that someone who devotes this time to learning will become a *gadol b'Yisrael*!

I was taught by one of my *rabbe'im* about a certain *gadol* who sat and learned every *erev Shabbos* and continued learning all Shabbos. And that was how he became great. Surely there are people who became great through different ways, but this is one definite way to succeed: *erev Shabbos*, Shabbos, and *motza'ei Shabbos*.

Someone who does this will see worlds open up before him. He'll merit tremendous *siyata di'Shemaya* in every way, because he'll be blessed by *Shabbos Kodesh* itself, which is the fountain of all blessing.

לימוד התורה בשבת

6

The Innermost Neshamah of Shabbos

A Holiday's Illumination Lies in Its Torah

CHAZAL TELL US ABOUT the special light that filled the world at the beginning of Creation.[1] With it, Adam HaRishon could see from one end of the world to the other. But Hashem hid this wonderful light, lest the evil generations use it, as it says, *"And from the wicked their light was withheld."*[2] It is stored away for the tzaddikim.

Torah sources say that this special light is hidden in the holidays. When a holiday comes, the light shines forth and illuminates a person's *neshamah*. That's why the holidays are called Yomim Tovim, "good days," since it is written about this light: *"And God saw the light that it was good."*[3] During the rest of the year, this light is hidden in the Torah.

There are many stories about *gedolei Yisrael* who by virtue of their great Torah learning were able to see from one end of the world to the other. This is because someone who delves deeply into the Torah discovers within it the same light that

1. *Bereishis Rabbah* 12:6.
2. *Iyov* 38:15.
3. *Bereishis* 1:4.

enlightened the eyes of Adam HaRishon.

Each Yom Tov has its special *masechta* that speaks of its nature and halachos. *Chazal* tell us that Moshe Rabbeinu enacted a special decree that the Jewish people should study the day's topics on the appropriate day.[4] They should learn the halachos of Pesach on Pesach, the halachos of Shavuos on Shavuos, and the halachos of Sukkos on Sukkos. This is because the Yom Tov's essence is hidden within its *masechta*. The holiday's light lies in its special Torah, and that's why almost every holiday has its own *masechta*. (Shavuos lacks its own *masechta* but has a certain connection with *Maseches Shevuos*. This is a topic to be discussed at another time.) Thus we have the *masechtos* of *Rosh Hashanah, Yoma, Megillah, Pesachim,* and *Sukkah*. And Shabbos has two *masechtos*: *Shabbos* and *Eruvin*.

We could say that the day's special *masechta* is the *neshamah* of the day.

Body, Soul, and Innermost Soul

We all know a person is composed of two parts: body and soul. The physical body is built mainly of bones. Inside the body resides the *nefesh*, the life force. The *nefesh* is kept alive by the blood, as it says, "*For the blood is the nefesh*."[5] We could say that the body frames the *nefesh* and *neshamah*.

But if we look a little deeper, we'll discover that a person has an additional part. There is the body, the *neshamah*, and the "*neshamah*'s *neshamah*." This reality is described in various ways. Sometimes it is called *nefesh, ruach, neshamah*. And sometimes it's called *guf, nefesh, ruach*. Both descriptions mean essentially the same.

The main point here is that the body is the person's outer

4. *Megillah* 4a.
5. *Devarim* 12:23.

form: his arms, legs, eyes, ears, etc. And inside the body is a life-giving spirit, which constitutes the inner personality. And inside *that* is the "*neshamah*'s *neshamah.*" This is the person's conscience, his sense of *kedushah,* which moves him to strive to transcend his natural capabilities.

The mitzvos are also composed of several parts. Simply speaking, there are three parts: the body, the *neshamah,* and the *neshamah*'s *neshamah*. But on a deeper level, the mitzvos have five parts: act, speech, thought, will, and joy. These are as follows:

The act of the mitzvah, the *ma'aseh ha-mitzvah,* is the external part. The others are internal, each within the preceding. Thus, joy is the innermost part of the mitzvah. The holy Ari *z"l* made a well-known remark that all the great *madreigos* he reached, all the profound understanding of Torah he attained, were thanks to doing mitzvos with *simchah*. His joy in a mitzvah was tremendous. As David HaMelech said, "*I rejoice over Your words like someone who finds great riches.*"[6] The Ari *z"l* would delight in a mitzvah the way an ordinary person would rejoice in finding a great treasure.

These five parts are the full structure of a mitzvah. When a person comes to do a mitzvah, he should do it in all its parts:

1. The act (*ma'aseh*): the external, physical deed.

2. Speech (*dibbur*): usually the *berachah* or words of Torah that are pertinent to the mitzvah.

3. Thought (*machshavah*): one's *kavanah* to fulfill his halachic obligation.

4. Will (*ratzon*): one's inner desire to serve Hashem.

5. Joy (*simchah*): one's happiness over the fact that he has merited serving his Creator.

6. *Tehillim* 119: 162.

These are the five parts of a mitzvah, corresponding to *nefesh, ruach, neshamah, chayah,* and *yechidah.*

We Attain the Innermost Soul through Torah Study

The Yomim Tovim and other holy times have three parts too. There's the external part—the mitzvos of the holiday—such as eating matzah, sitting in the sukkah, reading the megillah, etc. Then there's the *neshamah,* the spiritual benefit we gain from the holiday. And there is a third, deeper part: the *neshamah*'s *neshamah.*

The *neshamah* of the holiday lies in its *tefillah,* and the *neshamah*'s *neshamah* is in its Torah study. This includes any Torah learned that day but specifically the *masechta* devoted to the topics and halachos of the day. Simply speaking, Moshe Rabbeinu decreed the study of the day's topics on the appropriate day so we would know how to conduct ourselves on the holiday. But there's a deeper point here: The essence of the holiday is found within the *masechta* that discusses its topics and halachos.

We attain the *neshamah* of Shabbos only through *tefillah.* Some people mistakenly think Shabbos is not really a time of prayer, since on this day we don't make requests for our personal needs. But the opposite is true—Shabbos is a special time of prayer. We connect with the inner nature of Shabbos through its *tefillos.* That's how we attain the *neshamah* of Shabbos.

The Shabbos prayers are worded differently from the weekday prayers. Instead of requesting, "*Selach lanu,*" etc., on Shabbos we request, "*Sab'einu mituvecha.*" The latter relates to matters of *Olam HaBa* and is much loftier than our requests on weekdays.

And what about the *neshamah*'s *neshamah,* the innermost soul of *Shabbos Kodesh*? This we attain through study, mainly of *hilchos Shabbos* and *maseches Shabbos.* Thus, on Shabbos there is special importance to Torah learning in general and to learning *maseches Shabbos* specifically.

The Very Life of Shabbos Is in Maseches Shabbos

First let us consider the nature of *Seder Mo'ed,* which includes *maseches Shabbos.* On its simplest level, *Seder Mo'ed*—as opposed to the other six *sedarim* of *Shas*—deals with life itself. We can understand this point by comparing *Seder Mo'ed* to *Seder Nashim,* for example. *Chazal* say, "Any man who has no wife has no joy, blessing, and goodness."[7] A man without a wife is incomplete. He lacks a lot of very important things. Still, at least he's alive. Thus, while *Seder Nashim* discusses an extremely important topic, it doesn't deal with life itself.

And so it is with *Seder Kodashim* and *Seder Taharos.* They deal with holiness and purity, which greatly enhance and enrich our lives. But without them, a person is still alive.

But *Seder Mo'ed* is different. It deals with a Jew's very life. For this reason, the whole section of *Shulchan Aruch* that includes the holidays is called "*Orach Chayim*—the way of life"—how to be alive. Perhaps this is a sharp statement, but in my opinion only someone who has completed *Seder Mo'ed* can be called alive!

We all try to observe the halachos of *Seder Mo'ed.* But we all know that, practically speaking, it is virtually impossible to keep Shabbos without knowing *hilchos Shabbos.* And without learning *maseches Shabbos,* it's almost impossible to know the halachos of Shabbos properly.

According to what we've said, when a Jew wakes up in the morning and says, "*Baruch Attah Hashem...v'tzivanu al netilas yadayim,*" his true life lies in *maseches Berachos.* And if he wants his Yom Tov to really be a Yom Tov, he must learn its *masechta,* be it *Pesachim, Sukkah,* or whatever. Or he can learn *maseches Beitzah,* which is called *Maseches Yom Tov.* And the true life

7. *Yevamos* 62b.

of *Shabbos Kodesh* is to be found in *maseches Shabbos*. It's a big *masechta,* quantitatively and qualitatively. The author of *Eglei Tal,* a famous work on the *melachos* of Shabbos, wrote in his introduction that just as Shabbos is equivalent to the entire Torah, learning *Maseches Shabbos* is equivalent to learning the entire Torah! It's a wonderful *masechta* whose topics relate to all areas of life in minute details — and it connects a person to Hashem.

The Importance of Knowing Hilchos Shabbos

The following story illustrates the special importance of learning the halachos of Shabbos.

The city in which R' Yehoshua Leib Diskin served as rabbi heard that the Emperor was coming for a visit. Needless to say, the residents made extensive preparations for this important event. The head of the city's Jewish community looked forward to personally greeting the Emperor. This man was Torah-observant but not very learned, although he was wealthy and a leading property owner.

R' Diskin told him, "I don't think it's a good idea for you to be here when the Emperor arrives."

"But I'm the head of the community!" he replied, insulted. He decided not to listen to the rabbi.

The Emperor came and toured the city. There was a hospital the Jews had built, and they showed him the beauty of the building. The Emperor said, "I don't think those windows fit so well. They should have been built differently."

The head of the community replied, "Yes, honorable Emperor, this is true, but we thought that for certain reasons it would be better to make them this way."

They continued on to another building. There too, the Emperor commented on how it should have been built. And the head of the community replied similarly, "Yes, we thought of that, but we decided it would be better like this because..."

As soon as he'd finished speaking, an officer grabbed him

and threw him in jail.

"What's going on?" the man asked in total shock.

The officer explained, "Don't you know the law that when the Emperor says something, he is not to be contradicted? One should reply, 'You're right, Your Highness, and we shall do accordingly.'"

After he was released from jail, the head of the community approached R' Diskin and asked him, "How did you know I would run into trouble with the Emperor? Do you have *ruach ha-kodesh*?"

R' Diskin replied, "It wasn't *ruach ha-kodesh.* It was simply because I knew that you are not learned enough to be familiar with the ways of royalty. I feared that if you spent time in the presence of the Emperor, you would err."

Let us consider what the *Mishnah Berurah* wrote in his introduction to *Hilchos Shabbos*: "The illustrious author of *Urim V'Tumim* has testified in his work *Ya'aros Devash* that it's absolutely impossible to avoid the prohibitions of Shabbos without learning all the laws properly and very carefully."

This is because Shabbos is the day we are in the presence of the King, and a person unfamiliar with the King's ways cannot spend time in His presence. The laws are very complicated, and an ignorant person will surely stumble.

Masechtos Shabbos and Eruvin Form a Ladder

According to the way the *masechtos* are ordered in *Shas,* after we conclude *Shabbos* we begin *Eruvin,* which is also about the laws of Shabbos. In truth, if *Eruvin* weren't also about Shabbos, we couldn't bear to separate ourselves from *maseches Shabbos,* since it's such a special *masechta* and is connected to the innermost *neshamah* of Shabbos itself. And we can't relate to Shabbos without learning the *masechta* that speaks about it. Together, these two *masechtos* form a ladder — we first learn *Maseches Shabbos* and then we go on to *Maseches Eruvin*.

The basic prohibitions of Shabbos, found in *Maseches Shabbos,* come from the Torah, while the laws of *eruvin,* found in *Maseches Eruvin,* are Rabbinic. This might lead us to consider the laws found in the latter *masechta* secondary. But *Chazal* teach us:

> When Shlomo HaMelech enacted the decrees of *eruvin* and of *netilas yadayim,* a Heavenly voice came out and said (*Mishlei* 23:15, 27:11), *"My son, if your heart is wise, My heart will also rejoice. ...Be wise, My son, and gladden My heart; for then I can answer those who humiliate Me."*[8]

We see that the Rabbinical decrees are especially beloved by HaKadosh Baruch Hu. There are actually three parts to the Torah, as implicit in the verse, *"That which I did not command, or speak, nor did it enter My heart."*[9] Rav Elchanan Wasserman, *zt"l,* explained this verse as referring to the Written Torah, the Oral Torah (also received at Sinai), and the Rabbinical decrees. "Speak" refers to what Hashem spoke to us. "Command" refers to what Hashem revealed to Moshe Rabbeinu. And "enter My heart" refers to the Rabbinical decrees, which Hashem neither spoke nor commanded, but they are His inner will.

The latter may be compared to a father who asks his child for water, and the child brings him wine instead. The wine pleases the father much more than the water, although the water was requested, and the wine wasn't. The child was wise enough to understand the inner will, hidden deep within his father's heart.

Therefore, the first stage is to learn *Maseches Shabbos,* which contains the speech and commands of Hashem. Afterward, we

8. *Shabbos* 14b.
9. *Yirmeyahu* 19:5.

learn *Maseches Eruvin,* which contains what is hidden deep within Hashem's heart, so to speak. This is why Hashem said about the Rabbinical decree of *eruvin, "My heart will also rejoice."*

Furthermore, Hashem said, *"Then I can answer those who humiliate Me."* If the nations of the world argue that the Jewish people have also sinned and thus are no better than any other nation, Hashem has a powerful reply ready for them. He will say that the Jews have a wonderful and unique quality that makes them deserving of His love: They fulfill even matters that are hidden within His heart, so to speak. *Maseches Eruvin* expresses this quality.

On *Shabbos Kodesh,* let us strengthen our Torah learning in general, and that of *hilchos Shabbos* and *Masechtos Shabbos/Eruvin* in particular. This study will enable us to tap into the innermost *neshamah* of Shabbos, connecting ourselves to the source of all blessing.

תלמיד חכם בבחינת שבת

7

The Beis HaMikdash, Talmidei Chachamim, and Shabbos

The Special Quality of a Talmid Chacham

As we know, the Beis HaMikdash was where the *Shechinah* rested, and any Jew who entered its gates was surrounded by *kedushah*.

And just as in the Beis HaMikdash, so it is on *Shabbos Kodesh*. On Shabbos we are enveloped and surrounded by *kedushah*. Yet some people find Shabbos constricting and confining, and they wonder why it has to be that way. The answer is that the beauty of Shabbos lies in the fact that it surrounds us. It's like the Beis HaMikdash where we are in the presence of the King. For the twenty-four hours of Shabbos, we live surrounded by HaKadosh Baruch Hu.

There is something else that has similar qualities to those of Shabbos and the Beis HaMikdash. The Zohar says that a *talmid chacham* embodies an aspect of Shabbos. In previous generations, when a great rav and *talmid chacham* would come to town, the locals would greet him dressed in their Shabbos clothes. These were not necessarily their nicest clothes, but they were Shabbos clothes. For example, a Chassid had a very old *shtreimel* that he would wear on Shabbos, and he also had a brand new weekday hat. His weekday hat actually looked better and was more respectable than the old *shtreimel*, but what did he wear when the great rav arrived? The *shtreimel*.

This is because a *talmid chacham* is called "Shabbos," for he's also like the Beis HaMikdash, as we will explain.

"As If All Your Work Were Done"

First of all, let us discuss what Shabbos is.

The word "Shabbos" comes from the root *shevisah*, meaning cessation. The *Shulchan Aruch*[1] rules that on Shabbos one should consider all his work to be finished.

It is written, "*Six days shall you work and do all your labor*."[2] "How can a person do all his work in six days?" asks the *Mechilta* in *parashas Yisro*. And it answers: "Cease from labor *as if* all your work were done." This *Chazal* implies that on Shabbos we should put all our mundane, weekday concerns out of our minds. We should feel as if everything were taken care of, and we have nothing to concern ourselves with other than living in Hashem's presence.

I once saw this halachah observed in its full sense. A number of years ago, in the shul where I davened, there was a very rich man who supported many *yeshivos*. One Friday, a few minutes before candle-lighting, he heard news of a financial step the government had just taken that caused him a staggering loss. I kept my eye on him all Shabbos, and it was amazing—you couldn't tell anything had happened. He went home and made Kiddush, the next morning he davened just like usual, he looked the same and behaved just the same. After Ma'ariv of *motza'ei Shabbos*, he went home and made Havdalah—and then began to feel distressed.

This man was not a rabbi or a leading Torah scholar. He was a simple, ordinary Jew. But on *Shabbos Kodesh*, business

1. *Orach Chayim* 306:8.
2. *Shemos* 20:8.

simply did not exist. He fulfilled the halachah of "all your work is done." This halachah expresses the nature of Shabbos, which is like the Beis HaMikdash. The Beis HaMikdash is the special place where we live with Hashem, and Shabbos is the special time when we live with Hashem.

The Talmid Chacham Is the Heart of Klal Yisrael

What does it mean that a *talmid chacham* is like Shabbos?

Many halachos governing behavior in the Beis HaMikdash apply also to Shabbos and to a *talmid chacham*. On Shabbos we have halachos of how to dress and what we may speak about, as derived from the verse, "*You shall honor it by not... seeking your own needs or speaking of the forbidden.*"[3] And so it is with a *talmid chacham*, who is obligated to wear special clothing. When a *yeshivah bachur* walks in the street, we can see that he is wearing the clothing of a *talmid chacham*. Similarly, a *talmid chacham* speaks and eats differently from an ordinary Jew.[4]

All these halachos stem from the strict requirements that apply to a *talmid chacham*. Just as in the Beis HaMikdash, where we know that any deviation from the proper procedure can be disastrous, and just as on Shabbos, where the smallest mistake in matters of *melachah* is very serious, so it is with a *talmid chacham*.

Chazal say: "Any *talmid chacham* with a grease stain on his garment is liable for the death penalty."[5] Why is he treated so strictly? What is so terrible about having a stain on his shirt? It is because a *talmid chacham* is like Shabbos and the Beis HaMikdash. His entire being is dedicated to learning Hashem's

3. *Yeshayahu* 58:13.
4. See Rambam, *Mishneh Torah, Hilchos Talmud Torah.*
5. *Shabbos* 114a.

Torah. The Beis HaMikdash was the heart of the world, *Shabbos Kodesh* is the heart of the mitzvos, and the Torah we learn is the heart and mind of *Klal Yisrael*. This is why *talmidei chachamim* are subject to especially stringent halachos.

On Shabbos We're Alone with Hashem

The term "Beis HaMikdash" means a "house" of *kedushah*. What is the purpose of a house? *Chazal* convey to us how highly Hashem values a house:

> Not like Avraham, for whom it is written, "mountain," as it says (*Bereishis* 22:14), *"As it is said this day, on the mountain Hashem will be seen."* And not like Yitzchak, for whom it is written "field," as it says (ibid., 24:63), *"And Yitzchak went out to pray in the field."* Rather, like Yaakov, who called it "house," as it says (ibid., 28:19) , *"And he called the name of that place 'the house of God.'"*[6]

This teaching of *Chazal* expresses the different approaches taken by the *Avos*. What is the right way to achieve a personal connection and relationship with Hashem? Avraham chose the way of the "mountain," Yitzchak, the way of the "field," and Yaakov, the way of the "house." And Hashem cherished the way of the "house" above all.

Obviously, it is impossible to build a relationship with Hashem in the street or the park, as this relationship requires privacy. If a person spends his time in the street, this surely will not help him grow to be an outstanding *talmid chacham* and *yerei Shamayim*. But Avraham Avinu maintained that climbing to the top of a high mountain and separating himself from the impurity of his surroundings granted him sufficient privacy with Hashem.

Yitzchak Avinu disagreed: A mountain is not enough. True, there are not very many people on top of a mountain;

6. *Pesachim* 88a.

nevertheless, it is an area open to all who wish to enter. What we need is a field, because a field is private property. That is why *"Yitzchak went out to pray in the field."* He felt that in order to be alone with Hashem and build a relationship with Him, a field is needed.

Yaakov Avinu countered that even the privacy afforded by a field is insufficient to build a proper relationship with Hashem. What we need is total privacy—that of a house. A house is one hundred percent private. No one comes in without knocking, even when the door is unlocked. This is because everyone knows that a house is a private place and no one may enter unless granted permission by the master of the house.

Hashem agreed with Yaakov Avinu: *"Rather, like Yaakov, who called it 'house.'"* Here, Yaakov Avinu taught us something very important. To build a relationship with Hashem, *deveikus* itself is not enough. The *deveikus* needs complete privacy. Not like Avraham's mountain, and not like Yitzchak's field, but like Yaakov's house.

In order to build a true relationship with Hashem, we need a house of *kedushah*. In other words, we need a Beis HaMikdash. In the Beis HaMikdash, we lived with Hashem in *kedushah* and *taharah*. And on Shabbos, we live alone with Hashem, undisturbed by the world and its mundane concerns. And living with Hashem is also the quality of a *talmid chacham.*

Extending Greetings on Shabbos

I was once asked by a non-observant Jew: "How can it be that phoning my mother on Friday night just to wish her a good Shabbos is forbidden? In what way does this desecrate the Sabbath?"

I answered him: "There is a certain *masechta* in *Shas* that is called *Middos*—Measurements. It details all the measurements and all the areas in the Beis HaMikdash. It doesn't say anywhere in this *masechta* that there was a phone in the Beis HaMikdash. And I assume that even in the Third Temple, may it speedily be built, there won't be a phone."

Then I explained to him why the Beis HaMikdash has no phone. Imagine you're meeting with an important person, and in the middle of the conversation you see a friend walk by. Will you interrupt the conversation to call out, "Hey, Moishe, how are you doing? What's new?" That would be insulting to the important personage you are meeting with.

Now imagine you are standing in the Beis HaMikdash in the presence of HaKadosh Baruch Hu. Would you interrupt this sublime meeting with Hashem to talk about some other matter?

The following sheds light on what it means to live in Hashem's presence on Shabbos. "The Sages permitted greeting on Shabbos, only out of necessity."[7] As mentioned, our speech on Shabbos is limited—to the point that we are barely permitted to extend greetings to people we meet. What's so terrible about greeting a friend? The answer is that just as we wouldn't interrupt a meeting with an important person to say hello to a friend, so it is on Shabbos, when we are in the presence of Hashem. If *Chazal* hadn't permitted us to do so, we would not take our minds off Hashem even to greet others.

Completely Dedicated to Hashem

This is the nature of a *talmid chacham* as well. A *talmid chacham* is a Jew who lives with Hashem and reflects Hashem in all aspects of his life. For him, there is nothing other than Hashem and His Torah and mitzvos.

A *talmid chacham* is not measured by the number of pages of Gemara he has memorized. Neither is he measured by the number of hours per day that he devotes to learning. A *talmid chacham* is measured by his dedication to Torah learning.

7. *Yerushalmi, Shabbos* 15:3.

> The stones of a person's house and the beams of a person's house testify about him, as it says (*Chavakuk* 2:11), *"For a stone will cry out from the wall, and a beam will answer it."*[8]

Chazal are telling us that when a person arrives in the next world, the walls of his house will testify about him. Admittedly, his walls were there to see what he did even when no one else was, but it would seem to me that our children also are capable of testifying quite a bit about us! Sometimes, a small child innocently reveals something very significant that was said or done in the house.

I remember that when I was about ten years old, my friend said something I'll never forget. He told me that his little brother had come home from school after learning about how Hashem had spoken to the *Avos* and the *Nevi'im,* and he asked their mother, "Why doesn't Hashem speak to Daddy? He learns whenever he has time!" Their father worked in diamond polishing. He would go to work early in the morning and return late in the afternoon, but he learned at every opportunity. His little boy didn't understand why Hashem did not speak to Daddy, too.

Then my friend said something unforgettable: "I hope my child will say that about me, too!"

This father represents what a *talmid chacham* is. Although he was a working man, he was totally dedicated to Torah learning. He learned whenever he could, whenever he had the opportunity. It's a matter of dedication.

Chazal tell us a *talmid chacham* is like Shabbos. Shabbos means disconnecting ourselves from the material world in order to live in the presence of Hashem. This is the nature of a *talmid chacham* as well.

Shabbos is like the Beis HaMikdash, like a *cheder yichud*

8. *Ta'anis* 11a.

in which we are alone with Hashem. *"And You did not give it, Hashem, our God, to the nations of the world. And You did not bequeath it, our King, to the worshippers of idols."*[9] A non-Jew may not enter our private area of *Shabbos Kodesh*. If he wants to fulfill other mitzvos, he may go right ahead. He is welcome to do all the mitzvos, but not Shabbos. When Shabbos arrives, it is the time of, *"May He kiss me with the kisses of His mouth."*[10] On Shabbos, we're with Hashem alone.

And so it is with a *talmid chacham*. If a person wants to devote his life to Hashem and be a *talmid chacham*, it is not so important exactly how many pages of Gemara he learns a day, or how brilliant he is. What matters is how dedicated he is, how *"Shabbosdik"* he is, how much privacy he has with Hashem.

A Talmid Chacham's Heart

Shlomo HaMelech advises us: *"More than you guard anything, guard your heart."*[11] Why? *"Because from it come the sources of life."*[12] A person guards his eyes, his face, his body. But, above all, he should guard his heart, for it is the source of his very life.

Not long ago, I was in Chile, South America. There is a Jewish school there with a thousand pupils, and its cafeteria serves pork. Not only that, seventy-five percent of the teachers there are non-Jews. And this is called a "Jewish" school!

I was also in Los Angeles. There are about thirty thousand Israelis living there, and the intermarriage rate is approximately thirty-five percent. And there are other places where the rate is eighty percent!

Who is responsible for all of this?

9. The Shabbos morning *Amidah*.

10. *Shir HaShirim* 1:2.

11. *Mishlei* 4:23.

12. Ibid.

In my opinion, everything follows the heart. It's not a problem of the toes or the fingers or any other part of the body — it's a heart problem. The heart must be pure. Sometimes, a person's hands or face get dirty, but the heart remains clean, pure, whole, protected, and holy. Everyone knows that a medical procedure performed on the heart has to be precise down to the millimeter. This is because the heart is a crucial and extremely sensitive organ. It is the source of life.

Back to our question: Who is responsible for the sorry spiritual state of Chile's schoolchildren and Los Angeles' lost Israelis? I suggest that we point the finger at ourselves, who are devoted to Torah study. The *talmidei chachamim* are the heart of *Klal Yisrael*. We, who sit and learn in the *yeshivos* and *kollelim*, influence everything that happens around the world.

We know that the whole world received its blessing through the Beis HaMikdash. We know that the six days of the week receive their blessing through *Shabbos Kodesh*. In the same way, each generation receives its blessing through its *talmidei chachamim*. The Beis HaMikdash was a hothouse of Torah, a hothouse of *kedushah*. And this is the true definition of a *talmid chacham* as well: a Jew who is nothing but Torah and *yir'as Shamayim*. He speaks like a *talmid chacham*, he thinks like a *talmid chacham*, he eats like a *talmid chacham*, and he walks like a *talmid chacham*. In short, every detail of his behavior testifies that he is a Jew who lives with HaKadosh Baruch Hu.

We all keep Shabbos, *baruch Hashem*, but what is Shabbos's main message? We must dedicate this day completely to Hashem. On this day, it is as if we enter the Beis HaMikdash and eat at Hashem's table. We become Hashem's guests, so to speak. Hashem pays for all the Shabbos expenses, since this is His day and we are His guests.

And so it is with a *talmid chacham*. Everyone dedicated to Torah learning at one time has tasted the experience of, "*His palate is sweet, and He is all delight."*[13] But this is not enough. He must be a Shabbos Jew, a Beis HaMikdash Jew, inside the House of Hashem!

"If I Am Not for Myself, Who Will Be for Me?"

Unfortunately, there are not enough *talmidei chachamim* of this type, who dedicate their entire being to Hashem and His Torah. We know how great and precious is the mitzvah of bringing merit to *Klal Yisrael*. There are more and more people returning to Torah and mitzvos, and we all do our best to encourage our fellow Jews to improve their ways. It is surely a great mitzvah to show concern for others. Who among us would not gladly utilize an opportunity to influence people to return to Torah?

But in truth there is only one person we can influence and make into a good Jew and a *talmid chacham*: ourselves! Yes, we're responsible for our family members and those around us. But when it comes down to it, Hashem entrusted us with our own souls. A person is responsible primarily for himself. Only he can correct and improve his ways.

Hashem says to us, so to speak, "I placed a precious Jewish *neshamah,* which belongs to Me, in your hands. Please treat it properly and dedicate it to Hashem." This is the essence of a Jew, and it's actually the only thing we truly have.

We are fortunate to have been greatly blessed by Hashem. We have nourishing food to eat, we have beds with sheets and pillows to sleep on, we have supportive families, and much more. What can we give Hashem in appreciation for all we have received? Only ourselves.

If we dedicate ourselves to living in the presence of Hashem, to being Jews dedicated to Shabbos, and building a

13. *Shir HaShirim* 5:16.

Beis HaMikdash for Hashem within our hearts, we will secure bountiful blessings for ourselves and the entire Jewish people. Guarding the *kedushah* of Shabbos has never been more important than in our generation. This is because there have never been so many distractions. Privacy with Hashem has never been so hard to come by. Due to modern communication and media, our lives are filled with all that happens around the world.

A *talmid chacham* is like Shabbos. If you want to be a *talmid chacham,* then be *Shabbosdik,* at least on Shabbos itself. "*Zachor es yom haShabbos l'kadsho.*" On Shabbos we are meant to be sanctified and special.

Fortunate is he who connects himself to Shabbos, which is "blessed above all the days and sanctified above all the times." It is the fountain of everything we want and need.

השבת - מעין עולם הבא

8

On Shabbos, the Truth about the World Is Revealed

"The Heart of Those Who Seek Hashem Will Rejoice"

THE CHOFETZ CHAIM HAS a wonderful *mashal* on our subject.

A wealthy man had a son who reached marriageable age, and a *shadchan* arrived with a proposition from the father of a certain eligible young lady. They spoke about the proposed *shidduch,* analyzed it from all possible angles, and in the end nothing came of it. A while later, the son of the wealthy man became engaged to a young lady from a different family.

When the wealthy man sat down with his assistant to address the wedding invitations, the assistant suggested that one be sent to the father of the first young lady, who was turned down. The wealthy man retorted, "Just because he *wanted* to be related to me doesn't make him related!"

So it is in our world, says the Chofetz Chaim. Just because a person wants to be related doesn't make him related. But when a person wants to be related to Hashem, so to speak, to develop a personal relationship with Him, he's already related! Hashem promises: *"The heart of those who seek Hashem will rejoice."*[1] This

1. *Tehillim* 105:3.

promise applies to anyone with such a desire. Even if he's still seeking and hasn't found Him yet, he is promised the joy of a relationship with HaKadosh Baruch Hu.

Likewise, anyone who devotes time to learning about Shabbos is in the category of "those who seek Hashem."

A World That's Completely Good

Shabbos Kodesh is the heart of *Klal Yisrael*. If we want to describe a Jew connected to Jewish tradition, we say he's a "*shomer Shabbos*." We could say he's a believing Jew, he keeps kosher, or we can use many other descriptions. But we describe him as a "*shomer Shabbos*" — because when a Jew keeps Shabbos, that says it all. Shabbos is the essence of a Jew.

Why is Shabbos so important that it is considered the essence of a Jew?

Shabbos is called *mei'ein Olam HaBa,* which means, "like the World to Come."[2] We don't know exactly what *Olam HaBa* is, for the simple reason that we were never there! But let us ignore the words "to Come" for a moment and focus on the "World." When *Chazal* described Shabbos with the wonderful expression of *mei'ein Olam HaBa,* they taught us that Shabbos is a different world, completely different from the world known to us.

Each person views this world differently. And even the same person will look at it differently at different stages in his life. For many people it's a beautiful world. For others it's a sad world. Some say it's cruel or confusing. Clearly this world contains joy as well as sadness, beauty and grace as well as sickness and suffering. It's hard to describe exactly what this world is, but one thing is for sure: Through our eyes, we don't see this world as completely good.

2. See *Berachos* 57b.

When it comes to *Olam HaBa*, however, we don't have such trouble describing it. We characterize *Olam HaBa* in *Birkas HaMazon* as *"yom shekulo tov."* The world of *Olam HaBa* isn't varied; it's all good! It has no sadness, sickness, or stupidity. Rather, *"The earth will be filled with knowledge of Hashem as the water fills the sea."*[3] It is a world of wisdom, *kedushah*, greatness, and closeness to Hashem.

Hashem created two worlds, this one and the next one, and they are totally different from one another.

Hashem Is in Our World

Now let us ask: Where are these two worlds? Our instinctive response is that this world is the one we're living in now, and *Olam HaBa* is where we'll live in the future. But this is a big mistake.

The Gemara recounts, in *Berachos* 48a, that when Abbaye and Rava were children, they were sitting before Rabbah and learning from him. Rabbah asked them, "Whom do we bless?" They answered, "Hashem!" Then he asked them, "And where is Hashem?" Rava pointed to the ceiling, and Abbaye went outside and pointed to the sky. Rabbah said to them, "Both of you will be great scholars."

We will not go into this Gemara in depth, clarifying the *machlokes* between Rava and Abbaye when they were children. But there is one point I would like to bring out: Why did *Chazal* tell us Abbaye and Rava were children? Why is this detail significant to the story?

We may assume that even as children, Abbaye and Rava were very wise. Nevertheless they were children. So when they were asked where Hashem is, they pointed upward. But if they would be asked this question at an older age, they would point neither to the ceiling nor to the sky. They would say, "Hashem

3. *Yeshayahu* 11:9.

is here, with us." They pointed upward because the greatness of Hashem is expressed in the heavens above, in all their grandeur and beauty. But Hashem is surely here as well—within our world.

Likewise, it's incorrect to say that this world is now, and *Olam HaBa* will be in the future. They're both here now!

On Shabbos We See the World as It Is

This point is actually what Shabbos comes to teach us.

Imagine a person sitting in a dark hall, watching a horror show. He is the kind of person who takes everything too seriously. He forgets he's just watching a show, and he thinks someone is really chasing after him and trying to kill him. He's scared to death! Suddenly the lights go on in the hall, and he sees that it was just a show. He calms down and returns to the true reality of life.

This is *Shabbos Kodesh*. All week long, a person lives in the world as it appears to be, with all its terrifying aspects. Until, suddenly, Shabbos arrives and he sees the truth in front of his eyes. Not the truth of the future, but that of the present!

It is written, *"Then our mouths will be filled with laughter."*[4] It doesn't say we will be filled with joy, but with laughter. We'll be laughing and laughing. What's the joke?

Imagine a person walking in the dark, and he sees a pair of piercing, green eyes staring at him from under the brush. He is too terrified even to scream. Suddenly he hears a meow, and a black cat escapes, running for her life. He bursts out laughing, "Wow, what a joke! It was just a cat…"

"Then our mouths will be filled with laughter." We'll look back at all the problems we had and say, *"Baruch Attah Hashem... HaTov v'HaMeitiv."* Really, everything was wonderful, just fine.

4. *Tehillim* 126:2.

When will we do this? *"Then."* In the future, in *Olam HaBa*.

Chazal tell us that Shabbos is like *Olam HaBa*. This day enables us to view the world as it truly is. *Shabbos Kodesh* is completely good—here, in *our* world. Yom Tov is disconnected from our world, but Shabbos is not—it's the seventh day of the week. The world has six directions. There are the four sides—north, south, east, and west—plus the top and bottom. That makes six, corresponding to the six weekdays. And the center, the *neshamah* of it all, is the seventh, which corresponds to *Shabbos Kodesh*.

Shabbos is the day on which we can appreciate what kind of a world we live in. And its primary halachah is *shevisah*, "cessation from work." When we reach a state of "all your work is done," all problems are solved.

No Worries on Shabbos

When Shabbos departs, we recite, *"Vihi no'am"* and *"V'Attah kadosh,"* and we partake of the *Melaveh Malkah* meal.

Torah sources explain that by escorting out Shabbos in this way, we retain its *kedushah* the whole week. In our world, blessings are divided into two categories: *gashmiyus* and *ruchniyus*. The way to hold on to the blessings of *gashmiyus* for the whole week is by eating *Melaveh Malkah*. And the way to hold on to the blessings of *ruchniyus* for the whole week is by reciting, *"Vihi no'am."*

It is important to know that Shabbos is not just another day of the week. On the contrary—all our success in this world on any day of the week depends on our closeness to Hashem. And this depends on Shabbos, as we shall explain.

The Rambam writes, "The power of thought that Hashem granted us is what connects us to Him."[5] When we think

5. *Moreh Nevuchim* 3:56.

about Hashem, we are actually with Him. And when we think about something else, we simply disconnect from Hashem.

In other words, if a person has *bitachon* in Hashem, he's connected to Him and lacks nothing. As it says, "Even a wicked person who repents and trusts in Hashem will be surrounded by *chesed*."[6] Shabbos is a flowing fountain of *bitachon*. If we utilize this fountain and draw from it a generous supply of *bitachon* for the coming week, then the whole week will be like Shabbos, and we'll lack nothing.

To illustrate this point, let us imagine a very poor man. He has only a few dollars to his name, perhaps enough to buy bread and milk for his children. What does he do? He goes out and buys a lottery ticket. To his great surprise, he wins first prize: ten million dollars.

He doesn't even have money for bus fare to get to the city where his prize is waiting. So he borrows ten dollars from a friend. Now he is sitting hunched in a corner on the bus, in his tattered clothing, tired and hungry, arousing the pity of all who see him. But is he truly pitiable? Not at all. He's a very wealthy man! In his pocket he's still poor, but in his mind he's rich.

Nearly everyone worries about financial problems of some sort. But imagine someone whose father comes to him with a bank statement from his account that shows an enormous credit, with seven zeros. His father says to him, "Whenever you need, you should know there is plenty here. Just take!" This person now feels quite different. If his father has placed ten million dollars at his disposal, he no longer has financial problems.

This is what *Shabbos Kodesh* is. It's a day when the phone is disconnected, the banks are closed, and it's forbidden to think about problems. "All your work is done." Hashem tells us, so to speak, "You should know the whole world belongs to Me."

6. *Vayikra Rabbah* 15:3.

Suddenly the truth is revealed before our eyes, and we realize that our Heavenly Father has a tremendous fortune — the world and all it contains — and it's all designated for us!

Bitachon Brings Deliverance

I once heard a wonderful explanation of a story in *Tanach* from R' Chaim Shmuelevitz, *zt"l*:

> The king of Aram battled against Yisrael. He discussed with his ministers, saying, "My camps will be in such and such a place."[7]

This passage recounts how the king of Aram sent his warriors to a certain location to ambush the Israelites. It then relates how Elisha HaNavi warned the king of Israel not to pass by that place, as the warriors of Aram were lying in wait for him there. The king avoided that location and was saved from trouble. This happened several times, and the king of Aram became very upset. He wanted to know who the spy was, who was revealing all his military secrets to the enemy!

His ministers explained to him that there was no spy. Elisha had *ruach ha-kodesh* and knew even what the king said in private — and he revealed it to the king of Israel. Upon hearing this, the king of Aram wanted Elisha taken alive. He ascertained Elisha's whereabouts and at night, he surrounded the town with a large brigade.

The next morning, Elisha's attendant was shocked to discover they were in dire straights. Elisha told him:, *"Do not fear, for those on our side are more numerous than they are."*[8] Hashem opened the attendant's eyes, and he saw the brigade of Aram surrounded by a vast army of angels standing on the hills, equipped with fiery horses and chariots capable of quickly

7. *II Melachim* 6:8.
8. Ibid., 6:16.

obliterating the enemy.

Then Aram attacked. Elisha prayed they should be struck by blindness, and he thereby escaped capture.

Asked R' Chaim Shmuelevitz: Why did Hashem send the army of angels if in the end they didn't do anything and played no role in the miracle? He answered that from here we learn a very important lesson. As long as Elisha's attendant was afraid, no miracle could take place. *Bitachon* was lacking. When he said in fear, *"Alas, my master, what shall we do?"* the forces of Divine deliverance were paralyzed.

The first thing Elisha had to do was calm his assistant and show him the truth: Hashem was protecting them — the enemy couldn't touch them! When Hashem saw that the assistant trusted in Him and no longer feared the enemy warriors, then Hashem could act on his behalf and save him.

This is what Shabbos is all about. It is a day that fills us with *bitachon*, and we realize Hashem is here with us right now and has only the best in store for us. In other words, *Shabbos Kodesh* reveals to us the way we should view this world, and in that light we proceed to live the rest of the week.

Iyov's Mistake

This idea that Hashem is here with us in this world is actually the foundation of the entire book of *Iyov*.

This book tells an amazing story. Iyov was a great *tzaddik*, as Hashem Himself testifies in the beginning of the book.[9] Iyov was also wealthy and prominent. He did a lot of *chesed* and gave a lot of *tzedakah*.

Once, on Rosh Hashanah, when the world was being judged, Satan came before Hashem and argued that if Iyov was put to the test, he wouldn't pass. Hashem gave Satan permission to

9. *Iyov* 2:3.

test Iyov by taking away his property and his family, but He warned him not to afflict his body. Indeed, Iyov lost all his children and all his wealth. Yet he remained a *tzaddik* and didn't speak against Hashem.

The next Rosh Hashanah, Satan came again. This time Hashem said to Satan, "*Have you noticed My servant Iyov? There is no one like him in the world. He is perfected and upright; he is God-fearing and turns away from evil. He still maintains his perfection. You incited Me to destroy him for no reason!*"[10]

But Satan claimed that there was still no proof of Iyov's righteousness: Anyone would give all his property to save his life. Satan then said, "*Now if You send forth Your hand and afflict his bone and flesh, he will surely blaspheme You to Your face.*"[11]

Hashem gave Satan permission to afflict Iyov's body but not to take his life. And Iyov suffered terribly. The result was that Iyov cursed the day he was born. Iyov's three friends came to console him and speak to him. Indeed they spoke at length, carrying on deep discussions with Iyov over the course of ten chapters.

His friend Elifaz claimed Iyov must have sinned; otherwise, why would Hashem send suffering upon him? But Iyov denied having sinned. He insisted, and rightly so, that he was a complete *tzaddik* and had done nothing wrong.

His friend Bildad claimed Hashem must intend to bring Iyov great goodness in the end; it was worthwhile for him to suffer now, so he would have it good in the future. Iyov replied that in the end he would die; how many years did he have left to live? Therefore, future fortune could never make up for his present suffering. Iyov's friend Tzofar also put forth a claim, as explained there.

10. Ibid.
11. Ibid., 2:5.

So they argued back and forth. No one succeeded in overcoming Iyov's brilliant and powerful replies. Iyov exalted Hashem, describing His glory and might at length. Finally, Hashem Himself came and answered Iyov. And we still don't understand exactly what Hashem answered him.

Where did Iyov's mistake lie? Iyov knew he was a *tzaddik*, and therefore he was perturbed by his seemingly unjust suffering. He couldn't accept or understand his being afflicted so. His arguments sound very convincing! Where was he making a mistake?

Every living being has a life span. Ants live a few months.[12] And what is the life span of a human being? Seventy, eighty, perhaps even a hundred twenty years.

But in truth, the life span of a human being is eternity! When Hashem created Adam HaRishon, He created him to live forever. After Adam sinned, however, he needed to be cleansed of his sin. He had to return to the dust from which he was formed, so he could arise for *Techiyas HaMeisim* as pure as when he was originally created—in order to live forever. Eternity is the true life span of a human being.

Iyov denied *Techiyas HaMeisim* and eternal life. He reasoned as follows: Living for eternity means living a spiritual life in *deveikus* with Hashem, Who is the eternal Source of life. But how can I live that way? Hashem is exceedingly great and sublime (as Iyov himself so eloquently described), and we're so small. How can we achieve *deveikus* with the Almighty? So if I can't achieve eternal life, I'll live only seventy or eighty years, or at most a hundred twenty. If so, why must I suffer so much?

Many people suffer greatly. If we knew we would live for a hundred million years, and the first eighty years would be full of suffering, we probably would be willing to make the

12. *Devarim Rabbah* 5:2.

investment. Iyov's mistake was that he thought he would die after eighty years or so rather than living eternally, since no one can live in a state of total *deveikus* with the Almighty.

How did Hashem set Iyov straight? *"Hashem answered Iyov from the storm."*[13] Hashem was telling him: You see? I can speak to you. I'm capable of lowering Myself from the highest Heavens in order to be in direct contact with you.

Then Iyov understood everything. A personal relationship with the *Ribbono shel Olam* is possible! At that point, Iyov had no more questions. He understood that even a hundred years of suffering is worth it, if the rest of eternity will be spent in *deveikus* with the *Ribbono shel Olam.*

Shabbos Is a Precious Time Spent Alone with Hashem

This is the message of Shabbos. We say on Shabbos, *"And You gave us, Hashem, our God, in love...."* Shabbos is a world of love. We realize Hashem loves us; He's close to us. He's here with us right now. We need to appreciate what a wonderful world we live in!

Accordingly, we can understand why *chillul Shabbos* is such a severe sin. Let's say a man comes home and insults his wife. This behavior is surely improper and even cruel. But one remark won't necessarily destroy their *shalom bayis*. Perhaps she'll just ignore his comment.

Now let's say that at the most delicate moment—for instance, when the *chasan* is in the *cheder yichud* with his *kallah,* expressing his love for her—she replies, "I don't care if you love me, and I don't want to be close to you. In fact I think you're disgusting!" Such an outburst will severely damage their married life, if not put an end to it.

Shabbos is the moment of connection and love between

13. *Iyov* 38:12.

Hashem and us. The whole world disappears; it ceases to exist. The *chasan* and *kallah*—Hashem and *Klal Yisrael*—are in the *cheder yichud* together, so to speak. If at this exalted moment we show Hashem we don't care about His love, we don't want to be close to Him, and *Olam HaBa* doesn't interest us, this is a stark denial of Hashem. It is a most grievous sin. For Shabbos comes to teach us the wonderful message that we live in *Olam HaBa,* in Hashem's embrace.

We must receive this wonderful message and take it with us throughout the week. In this way we can live here, in this world, in the embrace of HaKadosh Baruch Hu.

נרות שבת - הארת חושך העולם הזה

9

Shabbos: A Flash of Light in the Darkness of This World

We Enter the Kedushah of Shabbos by Lighting Candles

HOW IMPORTANT IS THE mitzvah of Shabbos candles?[1] We can answer this question by comparing it with other mitzvos and noting which one of them takes precedence:

> Rava said: It is clear that if a person must choose between Shabbos candles and Chanukah candles, Shabbos candles take precedence. This is because of *shalom bayis*.[2]

This statement shows how important and precious Shabbos candles are. They take precedence over Chanukah candles, which are quite important themselves. Chanukah candles publicize a miracle. Publicizing a miracle is basic to our *emunah* and expresses our belief in *hashgachah pratis* and in Hashem's closeness to us. This would seem to be the most important thing, as the Ramban writes, "The purpose of all the mitzvos is [to

1. This translation employs the word "candles" merely as a convenient and familiar term. It doesn't mean to imply that candles are preferable to oil lights.

2. *Shabbos* 23b.

strengthen] belief in our God…and this is the purpose of all Creation."[3]

Nevertheless, Shabbos candles take precedence. What gives them such tremendous significance? True, as *Chazal* said, Shabbos candles enhance *shalom bayis,* as it's unpleasant to be in the dark and trip over things. And *shalom bayis* is definitely a matter of paramount importance. But Shabbos candles do more than merely spare us from sitting in the dark on Friday night.

As mentioned, the word "Shabbos" comes from the word *shevisah,* meaning "cessation." When Shabbos arrives, everything else turns to nothing and ceases to exist. During the six weekdays, the world follows the natural order of things, but when Shabbos commences, everything stops. The natural order ceases to function, and the only thing that exists is Hashem's glory. Shabbos reveals Hashem's Oneness. On this day we realize that *ein od milvado* — there is nothing besides Him.

This is why *melachah* is forbidden on Shabbos. In truth, there is no prohibition of working hard on Shabbos, as long as we don't do any *melachos*. For instance, most views permit carrying heavy tables from one place to another. On Shabbos we are forbidden to do only those thirty-nine creative acts that were employed in building the Mishkan, which is called a "miniature world." Any act that builds the world is forbidden on Shabbos. This is the way things run on Shabbos: The entire world is negated, and only Hashem exists.

And what causes the world to be superseded by Shabbos? This isn't really a question. The Gemara[4] states that Shabbos is a fixed entity, from the beginning of time. Hashem created the world in such a way that it is preeminent for six days, that's when we work, but on the seventh day it is "*Shabbos for Hashem,*

3. See Ramban on *Shemos* 13:16..

4. *Chullin* 101b.

your God."[5] It happens automatically. Technically, however, we see that Shabbos is brought in by lighting Shabbos candles. This indicates that Shabbos candles play a significant role in the great changeover between this world and the world of Shabbos.

This World Is Darkness

Shabbos is the absolute opposite of the weekdays, as we say in Havdalah, "*He Who divides between the sacred and the mundane, between light and darkness....*" In fact, "light and darkness" aptly describes the difference between this world and the next:

> "*You make darkness...*" (*Tehillim* 104:20). This is this world, which resembles night.[6]

What is "darkness"? Let's say a man enters the *beis midrash* in the middle of the night to look for a certain Gemara. The electricity is off, there's no moonlight, and it's totally dark. He starts to feel along the walls with his hands, trying to figure out what part of the bookcase he's near, but he can't find the *sefer* he's looking for. Would it be correct to say that when it became dark that evening, all the books simply flew out the window, and now there's nothing there? Surely not. The books are all there, right in front of his eyes, just as they are in the middle of the day. It's just that in the dark he doesn't see what's right there in front of him.

This demonstrates to us that the difference between light and dark is not whether something exists or not. What is there in the light is there in the dark too. The difference has only to do with the person: In the dark he can't see what's there.

This world is "dark," and the next world is "light." The truth is that *Olam HaBa* is here right now, spread out right in

5. *Shemos* 20:10.
6. *Bava Metzia* 83b.

front of us. The whole difference between this world and the next is that in *Olam HaBa,* a person sees the truth, while here in this world, the darkness conceals it.

Olam HaBa is nothing more than a revelation of Hashem's Oneness. The truth is that His Oneness is spread out before our eyes. Hashem's existence, the fact that *"His glory fills the world,"*[7] is the most revealed thing there is.

Let's say we notice a big, fancy chandelier hanging from the ceiling in the middle of a *beis midrash.* We know very well that, at some point, someone must have hung it there. This is perfectly obvious to us. It is also obvious that whoever hung it there could not have been a quadriplegic, since hanging a large, heavy chandelier from a high ceiling requires a certain amount of physical agility. We can also assume that he had at least a minimal knowledge of electricity.

If this is so with one chandelier, it is even clearer when we look around the world and try to understand who formed the sun and stars. The same is true when we consider the human body and ask ourselves who invented the eye or the brain. The reality that's right in front of us proves Hashem's greatness and demands that we subjugate ourselves to Him.

Nonetheless, even though Hashem's existence is so obvious, people are still in the "dark." They don't sense that they're under Hashem's *hashgachah pratis* and that their *parnasah* comes only from Him.

One day, walking down the street, I saw a man exerting himself to pick up heavy rocks and then put them back down. I asked him, "What are you doing—exercising?" He was surprised by my question: "Surely not; I'm working for my *parnasah.* Don't you know that no one earns money unless he works?"

7. *Yeshayahu* 6:3.

One morning at Shacharis I noticed a Jew rush out of the shul right after *Kedushah,* pick up a heavy toolbox, and zoom away in his vehicle, looking for work. This is actually a very strange thing to do, since the world has a Creator Who controls everything that happens. No one can make a living himself without Hashem. No one can make more money than Hashem decided to give him, no matter how hard he works. Working is merely a penalty we must pay in order to get the *parnasah* that's coming to us anyway. True, we must pay the penalty, but why run around like a maniac to do so?

The explanation of the above two stories is that the darkness of this world is so deep that it conceals even the most glaring truth. The *sefer Chovos HaLevavos*[8] tells a story of a pious Jew who sailed to a faraway country to seek *parnasah.* On the way, a non-Jew asked him what god he served. The Jew started to describe the greatness and power of Hashem. The non-Jew looked at him and said, "But you're traveling in order to earn a living. Can't your God supply you with a livelihood in your own place?" The pious Jew was seized with embarrassment in the face of this simple but piercing question, and he immediately turned back to seek his *parnasah* in his hometown.

Before he encountered the non-Jew, this pious Jew was in the "dark."

Shabbos Illuminates the Darkness of This World

The light and *kedushah* of Shabbos peaks on Shabbos afternoon at the time of Minchah. Nevertheless, we enter the gates of *kedushas Shabbos* when we light candles on Friday afternoon.

When Shabbos arrives and we light the candles, we "turn on the lights," so to speak, and suddenly we see everything in

8. Introduction to *Sha'ar HaBitachon.*

front of us. On Shabbos we don't have to struggle and sacrifice to achieve spirituality. Our common sense simply begins to operate. When a candle is lit, a person sees the reality before his eyes. This changes the whole way he looks at himself and his surroundings. Shabbos is nothing more than a moment of light. It is on that day that we see the truth and realize that going to work is all a façade, nonsensical to the extreme. The Torah reflects this truth, the truth of Shabbos, through the thirty-nine *melachos* that are forbidden on that day.

This reality that is revealed on Shabbos calls for special halachos. For instance, we have a prohibition of "*daber davar*." We may not speak on Shabbos as we do during the week.[9] It is told in the *Talmud Yerushalmi*[10] that R' Shimon bar Yochai's elderly mother would speak a lot on Shabbos, and when he commented to her that it was Shabbos that day, she would immediately be quiet.

Another special prohibition on Shabbos is that of reading *shtarei hedyot*:

> *Shtarei hedyotos,* which include documents of debt and financial accounts and letters between friends, are forbidden to read. Even perusing them without reading them out loud is forbidden.[11]

It is well known that this prohibition includes reading the newspaper, even just the news articles.

It is clear why these things are forbidden. Even if a person is interested in reading about news and politics, will he do it in the *beis midrash*? Surely not. This is because the *beis midrash* is a *beis Hashem,* and it's not fitting to read such nonsense there. If he wants to read the newspaper, he goes outside next to the

9. *Shabbos* 113b.
10. *Shabbos* 15:3.
11. *Shulchan Aruch, Orach Chayim* 307:13.

street vendor and reads it there.

When a person is in the middle of the *Shemoneh Esreh,* will he pause to read a newspaper or talk politics? *Chas v'shalom.* He will do so only after he takes his three steps backward and takes leave of Hashem, saying, so to speak, "*Ribbono shel Olam,* goodbye! That's it — I'm no longer in Your world."

But all this is on an ordinary weekday. On *Shabbos Kodesh,* a person's eyes are opened, and he sees the world the way it really is. He recognizes the true reality, that "*the whole earth is full of His glory.*" And he understands that appropriate behavior does not come to an end at the exit of the *beis midrash.* A *beis midrash* is a *beis Hashem,* and Hashem exists outside too, just as He does inside! When we daven the *Shemoneh Esreh,* we're standing before Hashem. Is it possible that after taking three steps, we part with Hashem and say goodbye?

Surely it doesn't befit the holiness of Shabbos to read a newspaper or sit around talking about meaningless topics. But this isn't the only reason behind the prohibition. It is also because Shabbos is a day when our mind works clearly and perceives things as they are. Our eyes are opened, and we see clearly the truth — that Hashem is here before us.

The moment we light Shabbos candles, all the halachos of Shabbos apply to us.[12] For this is a moment of light; this is what initiates Shabbos. As we mentioned before, candle-lighting time is not the peak of Shabbos. As Shabbos goes on, the level of *kedushah* steadily rises. But the light of the Shabbos candles causes us to open our eyes and see the truth. We realize Who created the whole world. We recognize Who sustains it and pumps life into it every single moment.

When this happens, and a person knows he's in the presence

12. According to halachah, this applies only to women, who accept Shabbos through candle-lighting.

of the great Creator, he realizes he has no need at all to work! At that moment he is forbidden to do the thirty-nine *melachos*. All the halachos of Shabbos are initiated by the Shabbos candles, by the moment of light.

Alef Dalet Nun Yud

The Oneness of Hashem means that He is the only thing that exists, and "there is nothing besides Him" — *ein od milvado*. There are actually three, progressively deeper understandings of "*ein od milvado*."

The simple understanding is that there is a world, and Hashem is the One Who runs it. Let's explain what this means. Take a person who's highly talented and motivated, has ample means at his disposal, and works hard day and night (and he even knows how to lie and cheat a little when necessary). What will be with him? According to the way of the world, this fellow stands a good chance of becoming wealthy and successful. Now take a person without brains, backing, or determination to succeed. Where will he end up? Doing menial jobs here and there.

Let's say a child doesn't feel good, *chas v'shalom*, and his parents take him to the doctor. Usually, in accordance with the way of world, if the parents are poor, they go to a clinic, wait for hours in the waiting room, and finally are received by a harried doctor who prescribes something that may or may not help. But if the parents have some money, they make a private appointment with a leading doctor, and the child gets the treatment he needs.

This is the reality of the world known as *olam ha-sheker* — the world of untruth, the world of darkness. In truth, the "way of the world" is nothing but an illusion. Why? Because the world has a Master. Only He makes the decisions, and only He provides a person with health, livelihood, etc. These things come from Hashem, not from the "way of the world." Every normal person understands that he won't get anywhere by trying to outsmart the *Adon HaKol*, and the true key to success is doing His will.

This is the simple understanding of *"ein od milvado."* The Divine Name that expresses this understanding is י-ה-ו-ה א-ד-נ-י. In other words, Hashem (Whose Name is י-ה-ו-ה) is the אדון over all. He is the Master of the world.

Elokim

The second, deeper understanding of *"ein od milvado"* is as follows:

The world we see with our eyes owes its very existence to the fact that Hashem pumps life into it at every moment. For it is written, *"And You give life to all."*[13]

This may be compared to a person who cannot breathe on his own and is hooked up to artificial respiration. The machine constantly pumps life into his body. So it is with the world. At every moment, Hashem sustains it and enables it to continue to exist. Without Hashem's life-giving force, the world would instantly revert to nothingness.

According to this understanding as well, there is such a thing as the world. But the true nature of the world's existence is that Hashem is constantly giving it life. Its very existence depends on His continual input.

The Divine Name that expresses this understanding is י-ה-ו-ה א-ל-ה-י-ם. In other words, Hashem is the "בעל היכולת ובעל הכוחות כולם—Omnipotent and All-Powerful." The word א-ל-ה-י-ם denotes strength. Thus this Divine Name expresses the idea that Hashem has all the power and strength, as He is the constant Source of all the forces that exist. All strength emanates from Him.

13. *Nechemyah* 9:6.

Hashem Is the World's True Reality

The third and deepest understanding of *"ein od milvado"* is that the world does not really exist at all. Rather, Hashem's Oneness fills and encompasses all of Creation. The existence of the world is not an independent reality — it is nothing more than an expression of the Divine will. Therefore, there is no existence or reality other than Hashem. This is the true meaning of *"ein od milvado."* But this concept is very deep and the *sefer Nefesh HaChayim* states that we cannot properly understand this idea and are not allowed to speak about it at length.[14]

Since this level of understanding is so difficult to attain, the Divine Name that expresses it is י-ה-ו-ה א-ה-י-ה. The word א-ה-י-ה is in future tense. Thus this Divine Name means, "I will reveal Myself in the future." Someday we'll understand it all.

When Hashem told Moshe Rabbeinu to go down to Egypt and bring the Jews out of slavery, Moshe asked which Divine Name he should use when informing them of the coming redemption. Hashem answered him, *"So should you say to the Israelites: 'א-ה-י-ה sent me to you.'"*[15]

Hashem was saying to them: Right now you can't understand the meaning of My Name. But someday you'll merit that understanding.

Shabbos Is a Moment of Light

Shabbos Kodesh teaches us these three ideas:

1. Hashem is the Master of the world. That's why we don't work on Shabbos. He provides us with what we need, and only He decides how much we'll receive, so we won't gain anything by working harder than we need to.

14. *Sha'ar* 3, chap. 6.
15. *Shemos* 3:14.

2. It is written, "*On the seventh day,* א-ל-ה-י-ם *finished all the work that He did.*"[16] This teaches that Hashem is א-ל-ה-י-ם, the Source of everything that exists. He created the world and continues to sustain it every moment.

3. It is written, "*And He ceased on the seventh day from all the work that He did.*"[17] On this day, Hashem brings the existence of the world to a halt. Not only is He the Master of the world and the One Who sustains it, but on this day, everything else ceases to be. There is no reality other than Hashem. This is the literal meaning of "there is nothing besides Him."

If we add up the *gematrios* of these six Divine Names—י-ה-ו-ה א-ד-נ-י, י-ה-ו-ה א-ל-ה-י-ם, י-ה-ו-ה א-ה-י-ה—they total exactly 250, which is the *gematria* of נר, "candle."[18] For when we light Shabbos candles, the truth that's in front of us all week long is suddenly revealed. "The lights go on." It was there all along; we just didn't see it. Hashem is the Master over all, He sustains it all, and "there is nothing besides Him."

This is what Shabbos expresses, and this gives rise to the prohibition of *melachah*. For when the Shabbos candles illuminate our eyes, we see that going to work simply makes no sense at all.

But there's another message Hashem communicates to us through *Shabbos Kodesh*. During the week, many people hurry to their jobs. Before Shacharis is even over, you can already see them racing down the street, lucky to gulp down a cup of coffee and a bite to eat before they're off to work. There is simply no time for more. The morning's quick bite keeps them going until lunch, and even then, many people still have no time to sit

16. *Bereishis* 2:2.

17. Ibid.

18. י-ה-ו-ה א-ד-נ-י 65 + 26 = 91; י-ה-ו-ה א-ל-ה-י-ם 86 + 26 = 112; י-ה-ו-ה א-ה-י-ה 21 + 26 = 47. All together, 91 + 112 + 47 = 250.

down to a proper meal. They just gobble up another bite and get going again. What can they do? They have to make money; they have to finish the job. People are so busy making a living that they hardly have time to eat.

That's how it is on the weekdays. But when Shabbos arrives, Hashem says to us, so to speak, "Today, you are invited to eat with Me." When we sit at Hashem's table, there's no such thing as a coffee and a quick bite. We're served wonderful dishes: For first course, we might have challah, gefilte fish, and salads. For the second course, hot soup. For the main course, chicken and side dishes. And then dessert. All the delicacies are brought out. Why? What happened?

It's very simple. When you're sitting with Hashem, you lack nothing. Hashem tells us, "All your work is done." Now you can eat.

Thus, Shabbos is a moment of light in every way—even physically.

Chanukah Candles

The uplifting feeling of Shabbos is wonderful. But it lasts only until *motza'ei Shabbos*. After we recite Havdalah, everything changes. We go from the splendid light we so enjoyed on Shabbos back to the darkness of the weekdays. It seems as if we leave behind life as a holy Jew and return to ordinary human existence.

There are several ways in which we can bring the *kedushah* of Shabbos into the weekdays. One way is, "*Remember the Shabbos day to sanctify it.*"[19] During the week, we should remember the *kedushah* of Shabbos.

Another way is by having the *Melaveh Malkah* meal on *motza'ei Shabbos*. This carries the material aspects of Shabbos into *motza'ei Shabbos* and thus into the weekdays.

19. *Shemos* 20:7.

Yet another way is by reciting *"Vihi no'am"* on *motza'ei Shabbos,* which carries the spiritual aspects of Shabbos into the weekdays. In *"Vihi no'am"* we pray to be saved from the formidable spiritual dangers we face during the week: *"Upon the lion and the viper you shall tread; you shall trample the young lion and the serpent."*

All these practices are like glimmers and sparks of the holiness of Shabbos within the weekdays. But in the end, Shabbos is light and the weekdays are dark. If so, it seems we hardly benefit from the *kedushah* of Shabbos. It's like someone who goes into a diamond mine, fills his pockets with precious, glittering jewels, and then loses them all. All he has left is a little diamond dust in his pockets. When Shabbos or Yom Tov is over, the person goes back to the way he was before. How much does he have left of *Shabbos Kodesh* or of the wonderful holiday that just passed? How much remains of the uplifting experience of Yom Kippur, for instance?

That's why we have Chanukah.

The Chanukah candles radiate the holy light of Shabbos in the weekdays as well. The following Gemara hints at this idea:

> The *Shechinah* never descended below...for it is written (*Tehillim* 115:16), *"The heavens are heavens for Hashem, and He gave the earth to the sons of men."* But how could it be said that the *Shechinah* never descended below? It is written (*Shemos* 19:20), *"And Hashem descended on Mount Sinai."* When the *Shechinah* descended, it remained ten *tefachim* above the ground.[20]

Ten *tefachim* create a separate domain. If the *Shechinah* hovered ten *tefachim* above the ground, it never really came down to earth, because it remained in a separate domain. This is reflected in the halachos of Shabbos as well. The *reshus ha-rabbim*

20. *Sukkah* 5a.

extends only ten *tefachim* high. But the *reshus ha-yachid* extends upward without limit, reaching "even to the heavens."

Shabbos Kodesh reveals to us the reality that the world is the *reshus ha-yachid* of Hashem. It is all His alone, because "there is nothing besides Him." Therefore, the Shabbos candles are placed on the table or in another place higher than ten *tefachim*, beyond the *reshus ha-rabbim*, for this is the position from which they can shed light. Once a week, a Jew "visits" Hashem's *reshus ha-yachid*, so to speak. He sees the truth that Hashem is *yachid b'olamo*, alone in His world. But during the week, a Jew is in the *reshus ha-rabbim*. He's in the dark.

Then comes Chanukah and teaches us that with those same candles — with the same enlightened view of the world that we have on Shabbos — we can illuminate the darkness of the weekdays. We can bring the reality of *ein od milvado* into our daily lives. For in truth, the message of Shabbos is not limited to that day alone. It applies just as well during the week.

The preferred position of the Chanukah candles is below ten *tefachim*, because something below ten *tefachim* is in the domain of this world, the *reshus ha-rabbim*. It is "down-to-earth," so to speak. Thus, the Chanukah candles radiate the light of Shabbos from within the reality of this world, illuminating our lives in a way that even Shabbos cannot. This is because on Shabbos we are in the *reshus ha-yachid* of Hashem, the reality of *Olam Haba*.

Let us do all we can to take the true reality that reveals itself on Shabbos and bring it into the weekdays — to live with the recognition that "there is nothing besides Him."

„כולה שלך – שותפים"

10

Three Mitzvos—and Our Partnership with Hashem

Three Mitzvos that Belong Exclusively to the Jewish People

Chazal tell us that the Greek rulers banned three mitzvos: Shabbos, Rosh Chodesh, and *bris milah*.[1] Why these three?

Only these mitzvos are off limits for non-Jews. Regarding mitzvos in general, we cannot stop a non-Jew who wants to fulfill them:

> If a non-Jew wants to perform one of the other mitzvos of the Torah in order to receive reward, we do not prevent him from doing so according to halachah. If he brings a *korban olah,* we accept it from him. If he gives *tzedakah,* we accept it from him.[2]

If a non-Jew wants to be a Jew's guest on Seder night and eat matzah, we may teach him that he should eat a *kezayis* within the specified time if he wants to fulfill the mitzvah. And he will even receive reward for his good deed! So it is with the other mitzvos: mezuzah, tefillin, tzitzis, etc. A non-Jew may

1. See *Otzar HaMidrashim,* p. 185.
2. Rambam, *Mishneh Torah, Hilchos Melachim* 10:10.

fulfill them and receive reward.

But he may not keep Shabbos. If he does so, he incurs the death penalty,[3] although execution is not meted out by Sanhedrin. Shabbos is a mitzvah that's off limits for non-Jews. In fact, the non-Jewish mind cannot quite grasp how keeping Shabbos is even possible. Gentiles have a hard time believing that Jews really keep all those difficult halachos, as illustrated by the following Gemara:

> I was told by Issor the convert: "When we were non-Jews, we said that the Jews probably don't keep Shabbos. For if they kept Shabbos, we would find many money purses in the streets! [Because there are always money purses dropped in the street, and if the Jews keep Shabbos, they may not pick them up. Where are all those purses?]"[4]

Rosh Chodesh is another mitzvah that's off limits for non-Jews. Regarding the mitzvah of Rosh Chodesh, the Torah says, "*This month shall be for you.*"[5] This means that the *beis din* alone can establish Rosh Chodesh and declare it holy. The creation of Rosh Chodesh is the exclusive domain of the Jewish people. The Midrash describes what happens in Heaven on Rosh Hashanah, which is actually the Rosh Chodesh of the month of Tishrei:

> The ministering angels gather together and say to HaKadosh Baruch Hu, "When is Rosh Hashanah?" He answers them, "Why are you asking Me? Let's go ask the Rabbinical court…."[6]

Rosh Chodesh—and along with it, the entire year's cycle of

3. *Sanhedrin* 58b.
4. *Avodah Zarah* 70a.
5. *Shemos* 12:2.
6. *Yalkut Shimoni, Tehillim* 831.

holidays—is in the hands of the Jewish people. In fact, *Chazal* say that even natural phenomena such as the rate of a child's physical maturation are subject to the *beis din*'s decision about whether to add a month to the year. Thus, if there's an extra Adar a little girl will mature physically one month later.[7]

All this shows how Rosh Chodesh is a realm to which non-Jews have no connection. It belongs to Jews alone.

What about *bris milah*? It, too, is exclusive to Jews. For there is much more to this mitzvah than the mere surgical procedure. Thus, if a non-Jew undergoes circumcision without converting, he remains an *areil* ("uncircumcised"), i.e., it doesn't count as *bris milah*. He hasn't changed a bit.

Accordingly, the Mishnah states that someone who vows not to benefit from *areilim* may benefit from all Jews, even if they didn't yet undergo *bris milah*.[8] But he may not benefit from non-Jews, even if they're circumcised! This is because the verse says, *"All the nations are areilim...."*[9]

This verse teaches us that the nations of the world are by definition considered *areilim*, no matter what they do, since they have no connection to the mitzvah of *bris milah*. A Jew, on the other hand, is automatically considered *mahul* ("circumcised"), even if he hasn't yet undergone *bris milah*.

Thus we see that these three mitzvos—Shabbos, Rosh Chodesh, and *bris milah*—express the essence of what makes a Jew special and different. We will soon see exactly what this essence is.

7. See *Yerushalmi, Sanhedrin* 1:5.
8. *Nedarim* 31b.
9. *Yirmeyahu* 9:25.

The "Contradiction" between Shabbos and Rosh Chodesh

Shabbos expresses a single, wonderful message: *shevisah*. Everything ceases. The world belongs a hundred percent to HaKadosh Baruch Hu. All week long, a person can go out into the big, wide world and be active. He can conduct business, he can seek out the best medical treatment, he can take care of all sorts of things. Once Shabbos comes, everything ceases. Then the truth is unveiled; the world belongs totally to Hashem. This point is emphasized by the prohibition of *melachah*. We stop doing everything, and the only thing left is Hashem.

And what about Rosh Chodesh? It seems to express exactly the opposite; it shows the ultimate importance of our actions. The entire world depends on Torah. And only Jews have the ability to make decisions in Torah, such as when Rosh Chodesh will be. This demonstrates the control that we have over the world, thereby establishing that the world belongs one hundred percent to us!

It seems that Shabbos and Rosh Chodesh are at odds with each other. There is a certain argument between them, so to speak. Shabbos says everything belongs to Hashem, and Rosh Chodesh says everything belongs to the Jewish people. How can we resolve this argument?

"It's All Mine" versus "It's All Yours"

To understand the conflict between Shabbos and Rosh Chodesh, let us consider the conflict described in the first Mishnah of *Bava Metzia*.

Two people enter *beis din* while holding onto opposite ends of a single garment. One claims, "It's all mine," and the other voices the same claim: "It's all mine." What is the halachah in such a case? The Mishnah says the garment should be divided between them; each one gets half.

Now let's put a new twist on this well-known Mishnah and have the people claim, "It's all yours." Each one claims the garment belongs fully to the other person! What is the halachah in such a case? Before we get carried away speculating about it, let us note that the Midrash actually tells of such a story.[10]

Alexander the Great went to visit the king of Katzia, whose land lay beyond the mountains of darkness. The king greeted him bearing copious gifts of gold and silver, but Alexander refused them, saying he had enough gold and silver in his own country. He explained to the king that the purpose of his visit was to observe how monetary cases were judged in the land of Katzia. The king of Katzia consented to his request.

This is the case that came up: Two men came before the king. The first claimed: "I bought a field, and while plowing it I discovered a buried treasure. But the treasure doesn't belong to me, since I bought only a field and not a treasure. Thus, I maintain that I should return the treasure to the one who sold me the field."

The second man countered as follows: "When I sold him the field, I sold it with all its contents. Thus, the treasure belongs to him, not me."

(Note that each was saying, "It's all yours.")

How did the king of Katzia rule in this case? He asked the first man if he had a son, and the second man if he had daughter. When both answered *yes*, the king ruled that the son and daughter should marry and take the treasure as a wedding gift.

Noticing Alexander's perplexed expression, the king asked him, "Did I not judge correctly? How would you have ruled?"

Alexander responded that he would have killed them both and taken the treasure for the royal storehouse.

The king then asked him, "Does it rain in your land? Does the sun shine?"

Alexander answered, "Yes."

10. *Yalkut Shimoni, Tehillim* 727.

The king of Katzia further inquired whether there were farm animals in Alexander's country. When Alexander answered that indeed there were, the king commented that it must be only in the animals' merit that the sun shines and rain falls there.

Competition Keeps the World Going

Before we get back to Shabbos and Rosh Chodesh, let's try to understand where Alexander the Great was coming from. His legal decision seems quite out of place. Why should these two fine men be killed and robbed? Bear in mind that Alexander the Great of Macedonia was not a greedy savage. After all, he'd come all this way just to study property law in Katzia's supreme court, and he'd even turned down a handsome gift of gold and silver!

In truth, Alexander's ruling reflected great wisdom. Every society is composed of people who say, "It's all mine." The welfare of society depends on this type of competition.

Take a rug, for example. It was made by someone who wanted to make a profit, not take a loss. The same goes for a loaf of bread. Who worked the field, who marketed the grain, who baked the dough? People who wanted to make more money, obviously. Everything depends on competition. It is essential for the proper functioning of society.

Alexander understood this point. Therefore, he disdained people who didn't care about themselves, who didn't seek their own gain but instead said, "It's all yours." He considered them dangerous to society. Someone driven to become rich will build a factory and manufacture clothing, or he'll market food products, etc. But two people who say, "No, you take it," are espousing an alien ideology. If this trend spread throughout society, in the end there wouldn't even be bread to eat. Everything would fall apart, and people would be left grazing like animals…

A subversive ideology such as this constitutes rebellion against the kingdom and all it stands for. Thus, argued

Alexander, the fitting sentence is execution of the rebels and confiscation of their property by the state.

How to Deal with the "It's All Yours" Attitude

Now let us understand why the king of Katzia disagreed with Alexander's ruling.

Indeed, the king was not at all perturbed by the attitude of the two men. We can explain by returning to the Mishnah in *Bava Metzia*.

When two people fight over a garment, there are two ways they can fight. The first is where each says, "It's all mine." The second is where each says, "It's all yours." If they fight the first way, the halachah is that the garment should be divided, in which case each gets only half — and half a garment might not be worth much. But what does the halachah dictate if they fight the second way? From the Midrash about the king of Katzia, we see that both people should receive the whole garment. This is because they are not taking anything away from the other, rather they are both giving.

And how may we practically implement such a ruling? By their becoming partners. Thus, the king ruled that the two men should become in-laws. Through the marriage of their children, they would jointly benefit from the whole treasure. To the king of Katzia, the "it's all yours" way of fighting is vastly superior.

Now let us return to the argument between Shabbos and Rosh Chodesh. Shabbos says: Everything belongs to Hashem. Rosh Chodesh says: On the contrary, the Jewish people were given the power to make decisions affecting the functioning of the world. In other words, through Shabbos we're saying to Hashem, "It's all Yours." And through Rosh Chodesh, He's saying to us, "It's all yours."

We find a similar argument expressed in *Shir HaShirim*.[11]

11. 1:15.

Hashem says to us, "*You are beautiful, My dear companion.*" And we say to Hashem, in the next verse, "*You are beautiful, my Beloved.*" We say, "*Shabbos Kodesh!* Everything is Yours." And Hashem says, "Rosh Chodesh! Everything is yours."

What is the resolution of this argument? *Bris Milah.* A *bris* is a covenant, a partnership. Through *bris milah* we become partners with Hashem and live together with Him in unity. This way, Hashem has everything, and we have everything too, so to speak.

How does this arrangement work?

We know very well how this works in everyday life. A husband and wife have two ways to live together. According to the first way, he says, "Look how hard I'm working and what I do for you." And she says, "Look what efforts I make and how much I help you." In other words, he says, "It's all mine," and she says, "It's all mine."

In such a case, he takes half and she takes half. The home is divided, and each has "half a garment." The ones who suffer the most are the children, who are being pulled by each parent in a different direction.

And then there's the second way: He says, "It's all yours. I know everything is in your merit." And she says, "It's all yours. I know that only your efforts are keeping us going." According to this way, no one is trying to take anything away from anyone. Thus, they live in harmony and unity. In the end, they both have everything.

This arrangement is called a *bris*.

Jointly Running the World

There is a *bris,* a covenant of love, between Hashem and the Jewish people. Let us take a look at how it works. We say to Hashem, "*Shabbos Kodesh!* The whole world is Yours." And Hashem says to us, "Rosh Chodesh! I have placed the Torah in your control, and the world is yours."

As we have explained, the "it's all yours" approach necessitates that the two parties become partners. If so, how do we live together with Hashem and run the world "jointly," so to speak? Hashem, in His unfathomable wisdom, created the world in such a way that it is one hundred percent His *and* one hundred percent ours.

Take rain, for instance. Rain is one of the most important things in the world. Rain falls from the clouds and is one hundred percent from Hashem. A person cannot go up with a bucket and draw water from the clouds. He has to sit and wait for Hashem to make it rain. This holds true not just for rain but for most of the important things in the world. Health, *parnasah,* and satisfaction from one's children are all things a person cannot attain by himself. Everything belongs to Hashem. This is Hashem's part.

On the other hand, although Hashem is the One Who sends the rain, what determines whether or not He'll send it? *"And if you surely hearken to My commandments... I will give the rain of your land in its time."*[12] This passage, from the second paragraph of the Shema, tells us: If you're righteous, rain will come. And if not, *"He will stop up the heavens...."*[13] So who brings the rain? We do! Our actions determine whether or not the rain will come.

We see that we have a wonderful partnership with Hashem. He brings the rain. But we decide for Him, so to speak, whether or not to bring it—through the mitzvos we do or fail to do. So to whom does the running of the world belong? One hundred percent to Hashem and one hundred percent to us.

Let's take another example. On Rosh Hashanah, Hashem opens His book, in which He records everything we will or

12. *Devarim* 11:13–14.
13. Ibid 11:17.

won't receive in the coming year—health, happiness, satisfaction, *parnasah,* etc. Every dollar we earn, every headache—it was all written down by Hashem Himself on Rosh Hashanah. And no person can add a single word to what was written.

But what does Hashem write? Only what we dictate to Him, so to speak. If we say, "*Zochreinu l'chayim... v'chosveinu b'sefer hachayim,*" if our prayers express a true desire for closeness with Hashem, and if we renounce our sins by saying, "*Ashamnu, bagadnu,*" then Hashem will inscribe for us everything good. But if we are half-hearted and lukewarm toward Hashem, then He'll write something else.

This is a wonderful partnership we have with Hashem. He writes down everything, and we dictate to Him what He writes. We say, "It's all Yours," and He says, "It's all yours." The world is His, and the world is ours. This is thanks to the *bris* we have with Hashem, as expressed by the mitzvah of *bris milah.*

We have now answered our original question: The Greek rulers banned the three mitzvos of Shabbos, Rosh Chodesh, and *milah* because these mitzvos express the essence of what makes a Jew special and different. And what is this essence? The *bris* with Hashem!

Prayer and This World

The true *bris,* the true relationship between us and Hashem, comes about mainly through *tefillah.* Besides being a mitzvah, *tefillah* is actually our program for life in this world. *Chazal* describe *tefillah* as *chayei sha'ah,* the life of this world.[14]

But Torah is called *chayei olam,* the life of the World to Come. This is because every word of Torah we learn is so precious that it cannot be translated into payment in this world.

This may be compared to a person traveling through the

14. *Shabbos* 10a.

Negev on a scorching summer day. He is hot and thirsty. Finally he sees a roadside stand where vendors are selling cold drinks. The traveler approaches the stand and asks how much a bottle of soda costs. The vendors tell him, "Five shekels." But all he has is a diamond worth over a hundred thousand dollars. He asks them if maybe they have change for his diamond, but they smile and say they don't have quite that much cash on hand just now…In the end he leaves as thirsty as he came. He has no way to translate his wealth into a cold drink.

That is what Torah is like. Every word of Torah we learn is put away for the wonderful day when its greatness and eternity will be revealed. But until then, we cannot benefit from its reward.

Prayer, in contrast, is the framework for life in this world. As we explained above, this world belongs one hundred percent to Hashem. This is very important to know. He didn't divide up the world between us and Him. Hashem didn't say, "Half the world is yours, and the other half is Mine. You go out to work, and I'll give you *siyata di'Shemaya,* and together we'll build the world." That's not how Hashem created His world!

That is, in fact, the approach of the nations of the world. They say a person needs to work hard, and he also needs *mazel.* In other words, they're saying, "Half is mine, and half comes from a supernatural power." But Jews know this is a mistake. The world belongs completely to Hashem. This point is crucial! The reason we go out to work is only because Adam HaRishon was penalized for his sin.

And we have a day that teaches us this. On this day we eat, drink, and enjoy. And we don't work, because Hashem gives us everything. That day is Shabbos.

But Hashem says to us, "True, the world is Mine. But how do I run it? Out of love for the Jewish people! Come, let's establish a *bris*. I will run the world according to the extent of our unity and harmony." And this *bris* is upheld through prayer.

In the *Kuzari*, R' Yehudah HaLevi compares the three daily prayers of Shacharis, Minchah, and Ma'ariv to breakfast, lunch, and supper. Why do we eat breakfast? To live. Why do we eat lunch? Because breakfast is already digested, and a person needs to continue to live. And so it is with supper. This is what the *Kuzari* is saying: Prayer sustains us in this world just like breakfast, lunch, and supper.

But nowadays there is a new concept: snacks! You can grab a snack almost any time—between meals, even in the middle of the night. I think this could be a good idea for prayer, too. Grab a little bit of prayer during the day or night, for prayer is the essence of our life in this world. It expresses our relationship with Hashem.

Prayer is simply a matter of communication. If a person wants to communicate with his friend, he phones him. If the friend sees the caller's number displayed and doesn't want to answer, there's no way the caller can get through. His friend needs to answer the phone, and then they can talk freely.

Here we come to a point that must be understood very clearly. With whom does Hashem want to communicate? Whose "phone call" is Hashem interested in answering? People commonly think Hashem wants to communicate with the righteous, not the wicked. But David HaMelech has a different answer: *"Hashem is close to all who call to Him; to all who call to Him truly."*[15] Hashem wants to communicate with whomever earnestly calls out to Him. Whether Hashem answers a call or not does not depend on the caller's righteousness. What is truly important is that the person is seeking closeness with Hashem. Whoever seeks closeness will surely find it.

This is the greatness of prayer. It is our means of

15. *Tehillim* 145:18.

communicating and relating. It is how we establish a *bris* with Hashem. We must always keep in mind that the world is built upon Shabbos, Rosh Chodesh, and *bris milah*. Hashem says, "The world is yours." And we say, "Everything is Hashem's." In the end we establish a *bris* and jointly run the world.

"לקטו לחם משנה"

11

Friday Links Shabbos's Kedushah to the Weekdays

Lechem Mishneh and Friday

ONE OF THE UNIQUE characteristics of Shabbos is that everything is double. Shabbos has a double *korban,* a double portion of manna, a double punishment for desecrating it, and a double reward for keeping it.[1]

At every Shabbos meal we say *ha-motzi* over two loaves of bread, *lechem mishneh,* as a remembrance of the double portion of manna that fell for *b'nei Yisrael* each Friday in the *midbar.* As we know, this double portion was to suffice for Friday and Shabbos.

If we think about it for a moment, the mitzvah of *lechem mishneh* on Shabbos doesn't seem to make much sense. When did the double portion of manna fall? On Friday. It didn't fall on Shabbos, and in fact, by the time Shabbos came, no one had a double portion of manna anymore, because they had eaten their first portion on Friday! Eating *lechem mishneh* on Friday would be strange, but eating it on Shabbos is even stranger.

We are not the first to address this question.[2] But here we will offer an answer that brings out a deeper level of meaning

1. *Yalkut Shimoni, Beshalach* 261.
2. See *Sifsei Chachamim* on *Bereishis* 2:3.

and sheds light on the special nature of the sixth day of the week—Friday.

As mentioned by the Ramban,[3] the seven days of the week correspond to the seven *middos* of Hashem, and these seven *middos* are alluded to in a well-known verse: "*Yours, O God, is the greatness and the power and the glory and the victory and the majesty, for all that is in Heaven and on earth is yours. Yours is the sovereignty....*"[4] These *middos* include *chesed, gevurah, tiferes, netzach, hod*—and the sixth *middah* is *yesod,* as hinted at by the above words, "For all that is in Heaven and on earth."

What is this *middah* of *yesod*? The Zohar explains "*for all that is in Heaven and on earth*" as meaning, "unified in Heaven and on earth." In other words, the sixth *middah* unifies Heaven and earth. Since Friday, the sixth day of the week, corresponds to this *middah,* we learn that the special quality of Friday is to unify the sacred with the mundane.

What does it mean to unify Heaven and earth—to unify the sacred and mundane?

There is a relationship called a partnership. If a business man wants to market a certain product, he chooses a partner. One partner works in Bnei Brak, and the other in Jerusalem. At the end of the month, the two partners make an accounting and divide the profits equally between them. The one who works in Bnei Brak profits from the sales made in Jerusalem, and vice versa. For when two people merge, each has what belongs to the other. But when they don't merge, each has only what is his own.

The world is divided into two realms: *ruchniyus* and *gashmiyus,* otherwise known as Heaven and earth. The distance separating Heaven and earth is tremendous. They seem so far apart

3. *Bereishis* 1:3.

4. *I Divrei HaYamim* 29:11.

and so different from one another. But there is a *middah* that unites them.

This *middah,* called *yesod,* causes Heaven to become Heaven and earth combined. And similarly, earth becomes earth and Heaven combined. In other words, *gashmiyus* becomes *gashmiyus* and *ruchniyus* together, and so too with *ruchniyus.*

Getting back to the subject of *lechem mishneh,* when *b'nei Yisrael* were in the *midbar,* a double portion of manna fell for them every Friday. This was their food for Friday and Shabbos together. They would eat half of the double portion on Friday and the other half on Shabbos. Due to this unique partnership, mundane Friday became partners with sacred Shabbos.

Even though, technically, there was a separate portion for each day, there was still a partnership because both Friday and Shabbos had a part in the *lechem mishneh.* Each had a part of the combined whole, which contained both the sacred and the mundane.

Jews and Yesod

When a Jew eats cholent on Shabbos, it's not just a physical act. On Shabbos, the *gashmiyus* is *ruchniyus,* and the *ruchniyus* is *gashmiyus.* Furthermore, *ruchniyus* penetrates Friday, and thereby penetrates the other weekdays as well. Although Friday is mundane and Shabbos is sacred, the Torah gave us the opportunity to unify the weekdays with Shabbos through the *middah* of *yesod,* which unifies *gashmiyus* and *ruchniyus* for the entire week. This unification is expressed by *lechem mishneh.* On Shabbos we say *ha-motzi* over two loaves: one for Shabbos, and one for the weekdays. This signifies that Shabbos includes both *ruchniyus* and *gashmiyus.*

When a Jew eats, although it is a mundane action, there is also a spiritual aspect to it. So it is when a Jew learns Torah. Although it is a spiritual act, it influences the physical realm as well.

Chazal say, "Torah weakens a man's strength."[5] What does this mean? The Vilna Gaon explains that only at the beginning of a man's learning session does the Torah weaken him. As he continues to learn, it gives him extra strength and enables him to continue learning further with increased energy Thus, from *ruchniyus* a person receives physical strength!

The Chofetz Chaim once met an elderly lady who had seen the Vilna Gaon in her youth. He asked her what the Gaon had looked like. The old lady replied that the Gaon had appeared to be on the heavier side. The Chofetz Chaim was puzzled: How could the Gaon have been heavy when he ate only a *kezayis* of bread each day? The answer is that *ruchniyus,* Torah learning, gives a person physical robustness as well.

This expresses the special character of Friday. It is a day that unifies the *kedushah* of Shabbos with the mundane weekdays. It sanctifies the rest of the week. Thanks to Friday, the *kedushah* of Shabbos not only illuminates our *ruchniyus,* it penetrates our *gashmiyus* as well.

Yosef the Unifier

This *middah* of *yesod,* of unifying Heaven and earth, is the special *middah* of Yosef HaTzaddik. This is the innovation in *avodas Hashem* that Yosef brought into the world: the ability to unify *gashmiyus* and *ruchniyus.* This is what he accomplished by successfully withstanding his great *nisayon.* He showed that through *gashmiyus,* a person can become a holy tzaddik. This is in fact what happens when a person overcomes the influence of *gashmiyus,* as Yosef did — the *gashmiyus* turns into *ruchniyus* for him. Through passing his *nisayon,* Yosef merited rulership and sanctity, for he unified Heaven and earth.

Friday is what integrates these two worlds. And here lies

5. *Sanhedrin* 26b.

the difference between a Jew and a non-Jew. For a non-Jew, there is a tremendous gap between *ruchniyus* and *gashmiyus*. They are cut off from one another. When he eats, he is totally physical, and when involved in matters of the spirit, he is totally otherworldly and saintly.

The *middah* of *yesod* expresses a Jew's true character. When a Jew eats, he is spiritual. And when he learns Torah, he connects to the Torah so profoundly that it is not just a spiritual matter for him; he actually enjoys it.

This idea is expressed by a verse written about *b'nei Yisrael*'s leaders at Mount Sinai: *"They gazed upon God, and they ate and drank."*[6] *Targum Onkelos* explains that they were so happy over their *korbanos*, which Hashem had graciously accepted, that they felt as if they had eaten and drunk. For them, sitting in the *beis midrash* was like sitting at a banquet.

For a Jew, Heaven and earth are not cut off from one another. Learning Torah is *geshmak*: It's tasty and enjoyable! Among the foundations of *Yiddishkeit* are two important factors: A person should truly enjoy his learning and that even when he is involved in *gashmiyus* he shouldn't disconnect from *ruchniyus*.

Friday is preparation for Shabbos. On the one hand it is a mundane day, and on the other hand it is completely sacred. It is a special day of *kedushah* that unifies Heaven and earth. Thus, it is especially important to learn Torah on Friday and not let this precious day slip through our fingers. It is a great loss for us to treat the crucial time of Friday as if it were a "day off" from *avodas Hashem*. By properly appreciating and utilizing Friday, with its unique *middah*, we can unify Heaven and earth!

6. *Shemos* 24:11.

שלש קדושות בשבת

12

Three Ascending Levels of Kedushah on Shabbos

Three Stages

THE *KEDUSHAH* OF SHABBOS is like a ladder with three rungs. As Shabbos goes by, we climb the ladder to higher levels. There is Friday night, Shabbos morning, and Shabbos at Minchah, each with its own unique character and *kedushah*.

There are various ways of describing these three levels, or times, of *Shabbos Kodesh*. One way is through the special names of the Shabbos meals. In the *zemiros* we call the Friday night meal *"chakal tapuchin kaddishin."* We call the morning meal *"Atika Kaddisha,"* and *seudah shelishis* we call *"ze'eir anpin."*

These names hint at the special character of these three times. The deeper meaning of these names is beyond us, but we'll focus on bringing out the unique aspect of *avodas Hashem* that is called for during each of these times.

There is another way to describe these three times. If we look at the Shabbos prayers, we'll see that at night we recite the passage of *Attah kiddashta,* while in the morning we recite *Yismach Moshe,* and in the afternoon, *Attah Echad*. Shabbos is surely unique in this way: the text of the Amidah changes from prayer to prayer. On weekdays, and even on Yom Tov, the Amidah for the three regular prayers stays essentially the same. Only on Shabbos does it change like this, for Shabbos has three unique times and levels.

We could compare these three prayers, and the levels they represent, to the stages of a wedding. Shabbos night is like the first stage of the wedding, the *kiddushin* (when the *chasan* gives the *kallah* the ring). Thus we recite *Attah kiddashta,* which comes from the same root as *kiddushin*. Shabbos morning is like the second stage of the wedding, the *simchah* of the wedding celebration. Thus we recite *Yismach Moshe,* from the same root as *simchah*. And Shabbos afternoon, with Minchah and *seudah shelishis,* is like the *yichud* of the couple.[1] Thus we recite *Attah Echad,* from the same root as *yichud*.

The *Tur* compares these three times to the three key *Shabbosos* in history — the Shabbos of Creation, the Shabbos of the giving of the Torah, and the Shabbos of *Mashiach*.[2] Friday night corresponds to the Shabbos of Creation, Shabbos morning to the giving of the Torah, and Shabbos afternoon to the time of *Mashiach*.

These are truly amazing matters! Let us try to understand them a little.

The Sun and the Rain

The *sefer Chovos HaLevavos* contains a section called *Sha'ar HaBechinah,* "The Gate of Discernment," which describes how to discern Hashem's wisdom and greatness in the world.

The first chapter teaches that Hashem's wisdom is essentially one. But as it expresses itself in the world, it divides into the many individual phenomena Hashem created. About this is

1. Although the couple usually spends a short time alone in the *yichud* room before joining the wedding celebration, the full significance of *yichud* takes place only after the celebration, when the couple goes home to be alone with each other.

2. *Tur, Orach Chayim* 294.

said, *"You made all of them in wisdom."*[3]

There are two ways to discern Hashem's wisdom and greatness in the world, and *Chovos HaLevavos* offers an allegory for each.

The first allegory concerns the sun. Although its light is essentially one, when it passes through a prism it divides into the various colors of red, yellow, blue, etc.

The second allegory involves rain. Although rain is essentially one substance, when it waters a garden it produces flowers of many different colors and plants of various kinds.

The *nimshal* is that Hashem's wisdom is one and it is the source of everything. But as we perceive it in the world, it divides into a wide variety of phenomena.

Two Ways to Find Hashem

There are two ways to find Hashem in our world. The first is that which the Rambam describes:

> What is the way to attain love and fear of Hashem? When a person considers Hashem's wonderful and great deeds and creatures, and discerns from them that Hashem's wisdom is infinitely deep, he immediately loves Hashem and praises Him and is possessed by a great desire to know Him.[4]

The Rambam is saying that by looking at what Hashem created, and by thinking about it, a person can come to love and fear Hashem as well as have faith in Him. Indeed it is written:, *"The heavens tell God's glory."*[5]

The second way to find Hashem in our world is described in the following Midrash:

3. *Tehillim* 104:24.
4. *Mishneh Torah, Hilchos Yesodei HaTorah* 2:2.
5. *Tehillim* 19:2.

> Why does it say (*Devarim* 6:6), *"And these words will be... on your heart?"* Because it says (ibid. 6:5), *"You shall love Hashem, your God,"* but we don't know how to attain love of Him. Thus Scripture says, *"And these words will be... on your heart."* Place these words [of Torah] on your heart, for they bring you to recognize Him Who spoke and created the world, and to cleave to His ways.[6]

This Midrash is saying that through learning Torah we can recognize Hashem and come to love Him.

Thus we have the two principal ways of recognizing Hashem. The first is through the physical world Hashem created, and the second is through the Torah. Both bring us to recognize Hashem's existence and greatness. Both reveal His glory.

What is the difference between Hashem's glory as proclaimed by the physical world and His glory as revealed through learning Torah? This is what *Chovos HaLevavos* is telling us with the two allegories mentioned above.

Someone who walks through a forest and sees all kinds of lush plants and blooming flowers of various colors knows for sure that it rained recently. He has no doubt about it, because these things cannot grow without water. He doesn't see the actual rainwater, but from seeing what grew, he figures that there must have been rain.

A person's discernment is of a different type when he sees light that passed through a prism and broke up into various colors. Indeed, the light he sees is no longer what it once was. It went through changes; it was filtered out from its pure, original state and changed into colors. Nevertheless, he sees the light itself.

This is the difference between seeing Heaven's glory in the physical world and seeing it through the Torah. Seeing it in

6. *Yalkut Shimoni, Va'eschanan* 839.

the physical world means that anyone with even minimal intelligence can see how wonderful and miraculously complex the world is. Heaven and earth, sun and moon and stars, the marvels of the human body—all these bring him to understand that an awesome God must have created this amazing universe. And this understanding brings him to love and fear the great Creator and to have faith in Him. But he still hasn't seen Hashem. About the physical world is said, *"The heavens tell God's glory."*

It's different with someone who learns Torah. *Nefesh HaChayim*[7] explains at length how Hashem and His will are one and Hashem and His word are one. As *Chazal* put it, "The Torah is *HaKadosh Baruch Hu*." In a certain sense, through a certain prism, the holy Torah allows a person to see Hashem Himself!

Night and Day

Returning to the topic of the three time periods of Shabbos, let us now try to understand the difference between Friday night and Shabbos day. Generally speaking, *Shabbos Kodesh* is the time when we can perceive Hashem's existence, since Shabbos expresses the fact that the world was created. Therefore, someone who wants to find Hashem can find Him on Shabbos.

The Shabbos night meal is called *"chakal tapuchin kaddishin,"* as we say in the *zemiros*. Literally translated, this means "orchard of holy apples." When we see apples growing in an orchard, we know someone planted apple seeds there. Likewise, if holy apples grow in the orchard, holy apples must have been planted there.

On Friday night we recite *Va'yechulu*, declaring that on the Shabbos of Creation, Hashem completed His act of creating the

7. *Nefesh HaChayim*, sec. 4.

world. When we declare that He completed His act of creating, we're really saying that He is the One Who created it all, and He runs it to this day. In other words, we find Hashem through the *chakal tapuchin kaddishin,* through the physical world He planted and created.

Shabbos morning reflects a higher level: the Shabbos of the giving of the Torah.[8] This is something completely different! Here we see Hashem Himself, so to speak. We discern Hashem's existence not merely from the fact that the physical world must have a Creator, that the field must have a planter. That was the *chakal tapuchin kaddishin* of Friday night. The meal of Shabbos morning, however, is called "*Atika Kaddisha,*" as we say in the *zemiros*. Literally translated, this means "the Holy Ancient One." In other words, we are now talking about Hashem Himself. We're seeing Hashem Himself, so to speak, as we do through the Torah. This level is what we call *kabbalas p'nei Shechinah.*

The difference between Friday night and Shabbos morning is like the difference between seeing a painting and recognizing that a painter must have been involved, and seeing the painter himself reflected through a lens. With the second way, the actual painter is seen. On Friday night we see the physical world and thereby learn of the existence of the Creator. But on Shabbos morning we see Hashem Himself, so to speak, reflected through a lens.

And why on Friday night do we say *Attah kiddashta,* whereas on Shabbos morning we say *Yismach Moshe*? The following parable brings out the point.

Once, a great king was about to marry a young maiden. This maiden, while preparing for the wedding, became possessed by

8. According to all views, the Torah was given on Shabbos. See *Shabbos* 87a and Rashi ad loc.

fear. She heard of the king's greatness, his strength, the incredible power he wields. She could hardly go on; she kept fainting.

But this was only until she entered the *chuppah*. The moment she saw the shining face of her *chasan*, the moment she saw him smile at her lovingly, her joy overcame her fear, and she was calm.

So it is with the Jewish people. When they recognize Hashem through His great and awesome acts of Creation, they are seized by a tremendous fear of Him. But when they see Hashem Himself, so to speak, their joy overcomes their fear.

On Friday night we concentrate on *Attah kiddashta*. We focus on *kedushah* and fear of Hashem. We see the awesome universe He created and understand how exceedingly great and awesome the Creator Himself must be. This brings us to fear Him. When Shabbos morning comes, we see Hashem Himself, the shining radiance of His face, so to speak. The fear is now replaced by tremendous joy, and we recite *Yismach Moshe*.

Fear and Love — Night and Morning

Although the preceding thoughts are lofty matters, they have a practical application, as we will explain.

On Friday night we work mainly on *emunah*. At night, a person cannot see — he needs *emunah*. It is written, "*Your emunah is at night*."[9] We understand what is behind things, but we don't actually see it. This is *emunah*.

Shabbos morning is a time of joy. *Yismach Moshe b'matnas chelko*. We rejoice over the portion Hashem has given us, at seeing Hashem Himself, so to speak. On Shabbos morning we feel the joy of *Ashreinu mah tov chelkeinu*, of *kabbalas p'nei Shechinah*.

Although there is *kabbalas p'nei Shechinah* on Friday night too, it's not the main point then. This point is emphasized primarily

9. *Tehillim* 92:3.

on Shabbos morning. In other words, on Friday night there's more fear of Hashem, and on Shabbos morning there's more love of Hashem.

Friday night is a time of *avodah,* while on Shabbos day we actually perceive the *kedushah* of Hashem, so to speak. We are in the Beis HaMikdash. When we experience *kabbalas p'nei Shechinah,* in which Hashem shows us such a shining and smiling face, there is such grandeur, such *deveikus* and *kedushah*! We have no choice but to behave differently. A prince doesn't wallow in the street.

There is another way to describe the difference between Friday night and Shabbos morning. Two kinds of people don't speak *lashon ha-ra.* The first is the one who refrains because he learns *sefer Chofetz Chaim* and is aware of the severity of the sin and its great punishment. He achieves this through *avodah* — study and introspection. The second is the one who simply finds *lashon ha-ra* nauseating. Though he rarely opens *sefer Chofetz Chaim,* he cannot understand why anyone would want to speak badly about others. This is like Shabbos day, where the change in our behavior is intrinsic, influenced by our feelings, which have changed due to our enhanced perception of the *kedushah* of Hashem.

Getting to the Afternoon

Let us now try to understand the difference between Shabbos morning and Shabbos afternoon. As mentioned, the morning meal is called *"Atika Kaddisha,"* whereas *seudah shelishis* is called *"ze'eir anpin."*

The term *Atika Kaddisha* (the Holy Ancient One) refers to Hashem, as it is written, *"And the Ancient of Days sat, His garment white as snow."*[10] The "garment" in this verse refers to

10. *Daniyel* 7:9.

the thirteen *middos* of *rachamim*. *Middos* are refered to as "garments." If we want to gain some rudimentary knowledge about a person, first we take note of how he dresses. Simply speaking, someone who dresses like a Jew is a Jew, and someone who dresses like a non-Jew is a non-Jew. Garments express inner qualities.

Hashem has a "garment," so to speak, that expresses His *middos*. This garment is the thirteen *middos* of *rachamim*. One of these thirteen *middos* is *erech apayim*. It is the opposite of the *middah* called *ketzar apayim*, or *ze'eir anpin*. The *middah* of *erech apayim* represents tremendous compassion.

Erech apayim means "slow to anger." What is the significance of this *middah*? Although Hashem does not waive any sin, and everything is recorded and remembered, He is very slow to anger. He patiently waits and waits, looking forward to the sinner's *teshuvah*. This patience expresses infinite compassion. *Erech* is one, and *apayim* (a plural noun) is two, so together they're three. Three is a *chazakah*. This implies that Hashem's compassion is a *chazakah*; it continues forever. This is the aspect of *Atika Kaddisha*, of Shabbos morning.

Shabbos afternoon is the third and highest level of Shabbos. It is the time of *seudah shelishis*, which is called *ze'eir anpin*. This is puzzling, for *ze'eir anpin* is a lower level than *erech apayim*. If *seudah shelishis* is the peak of Shabbos, why do we go down a level?

The reason seems to be as follows. The *middah* of Shabbos morning, *erech apayim*, expresses tremendous compassion. But if Hashem ran the world only with *erech apayim*, the world would fall apart. Indeed, after thousands of years, the wicked would be punished. But in the meantime Hashem would patiently wait and wait, and the unbridled evil of the wicked would destroy the world!

That is why *middas ha-din* exists—to prevent the wicked from destroying the world. It is the *middah* of *ze'eir anpin*, or "quick to anger." If Hashem were too quick to anger, the world would surely be destroyed. But if Hashem were too slow to anger, the world would still be in danger of falling apart. Thus, Hashem blends quickness to anger with slowness to anger, and the result is: *"He is patient but He collects what is due to Him."*[11] This blend of *rachamim* and *din* constitutes the basis of how Hashem runs the world.

Chesed Overcomes Din

The *middas ha-din* expressed in *ze'eir anpin,* "quick to anger," is actually a great *chesed.* This we see from *Chazal*'s teaching in *Gemara Shabbos.*[12] Hashem tells the *Avos,* "Your children have sinned," hoping the *Avos* will speak up in defense of the Jewish people and protect them from punishment. Avraham fails to defend them, and so does Yaakov. But Yitzchak defends them valiantly. He makes elaborate calculations proving that the percentage of time they spend sinning doesn't call for punishment.

What are *Chazal* teaching us? And why did Yitzchak succeed where the others failed?

Hashem was saying to the *Avos*: "Now it is a time of *din.* Later will come a time of *rachamim,* but now—in the framework of *din*—what do you have to say in defense of the Jewish people, to protect them from punishment?" The *Avos* were in a quandary. Avraham answered, "My *middah* is *chesed.* But in truth, without *chesed,* there really is no way of escaping the *din.*" And Yaakov answered, "My *middah* is *rachamim.* But without this *middah,* there indeed is no escape."

Then Hashem asked Yitzchak what he had to say. Yitzchak, whose *middah* is *din,* had an answer! He argued cogently in the Jews' defense, showing how they may be judged favorably even

11. *Bereishis Rabbah* 67:4.

12. 89b.

according to *middas ha-din*. The percentage of time they spent sinning was relatively small, and Yitzchak said he was capable of "paying" for it if necessary: "For I have offered my very life before You" (by *Akeidas Yitzchak*).

Let's say we come to a father and say, "Look, your son did such and such." The father won't respond, "Take it easy on him, just let him go." Instead he looks for a way to justify his son, claiming the boy isn't really guilty. (Actually, it's not just fathers who do this. People are constantly doing the same to justify themselves. "You know why I came late for davening? The baby cried all night because of an ear infection, and I was too exhausted to get up...")

Since Yitzchak's *middah* is *din*, he acted as a good father does and looked for a way to justify his children according to *din*. He didn't say a single word about mercy, about going easy on them. He simply argued that if we take an objective look at the numbers, we will see that his children do not deserve punishment. When the Jewish people heard Yitzchak's calculations, they understood that he had saved them according to *din*. And the above-mentioned *Chazal* goes on to say that they exclaimed to Yitzchak, *"You are our father! Avraham didn't know us, and Yisrael didn't recognize us."*[13]

Yitzchak then pointed to Hashem. He responded, "It's not I; it's Hashem. Hashem's *rachamim* is so great and all-pervasive that even the *din* itself produces *rachamim*. There is a type of *rachamim* that offers an alternative to *din*, and there is another type that overpowers the *din* from within the *din* itself." The Jews then exclaimed, *"You, Hashem, are our Father and Redeemer...."*

The best illustration of this point is the person who comes up with the most intelligent and brilliant proofs that he is right.

13. *Yeshayahu* 63:16.

He thinks of fifty different reasons to justify himself. And he really is right. How did this come about? Because he loves himself so deeply, he is right according to the *din*.

Yitzchak Avinu was right in what he argued. Yitzchak expresses the true meaning of *middas ha-din*. And he explained that he didn't do it; rather, the *chesed* of Hashem, which is so powerful, overcame the *din* from within the *din* itself. This expresses the true meaning of *din*: it's actually a great *chesed*.

The truth is that Hashem sees no evil; He is totally *chesed*, as it is written, *"He is pure of eyes and doesn't see evil."*[14] Hashem doesn't see any sin — He judges everyone favorably. But when we don't judge favorably, then Hashem doesn't either. When we speak badly about people, then Hashem looks at us in a bad way.

From Seudah Shelishis into the Week

Essentially, Shabbos is a time of pure *rachamim*, of *erech apayim*. So why does it conclude with *ze'eir anpin*? Because as soon as we recite Havdalah, the *erech apayim* must cease. Unending, unlimited mercy cannot continue into the weekdays. The world wouldn't survive that way!

That's why we have the special time of *seudah shelishis*. This is a time of *yichud,* of oneness, as we say in Minchah on Shabbos, *"Attah Echad v'Shimcha echad."* This expresses the absolute Oneness of Hashem. We say, so to speak, "Hashem, Your *rachamim* is so powerful that it includes even *ze'eir anpin*. Even *ze'eir anpin* comes to the Shabbos table." Through the Shabbos Minchah prayer, we turn *middas ha-din* into *rachamim,* by means of *kedushas Shabbos*. In this way the *rachamim* of Shabbos can be continued and brought into the week.

What does this mean, practically?

14. *Chavakuk* 1:13.

It means that on Friday night, we should focus on seeing the power of Hashem as reflected in the world He created. This is a time to be filled with fear and awe of Hashem. It is a time of *yirah* and *avodah*. Shabbos day, in contrast, is a time to feel joy and *deveikus*. It is a time of great spiritual elevation, of forgetting about the world and everything in it. There is no world! And Shabbos afternoon, at Minchah time, a person starts to think to himself: Soon the weekdays will be here again. Havdalah will bring an end to *kedushas Shabbos*. And then, what benefit will remain from all the spiritual elevation I experienced on Shabbos? I should work on myself and correct my shortcomings. How can I improve myself?

Let's say a person tends to speak *lashon ha-ra*. On Friday night he says to himself, "That's it. No more *lashon ha-ra* for me — I'm finished with it." On the one hand, this is a very beautiful decision. On the other hand, it's worthless, because as soon as he says "*HaMavdil bein kodesh l'chol*" he'll be back to his old tricks as if nothing happened.

That's why we have *seudah shelishis* — a time when we start to return to the weekdays, so to speak. At this time, *rachamim* and *din* blend. We are no longer caught up in the excitement of *Shabbos Kodesh*, which disconnects us from the state conducive to sin. At the time of Minchah and *seudah shelishis*, we begin connecting to what's coming next, so to speak. *Kedushas Shabbos* starts working on our shortcomings and spiritual declines. We start truly correcting things and setting them right.

This is why Shabbos afternoon corresponds to the Shabbos of the time of *Mashiach*, whereas Shabbos morning corresponds to the Shabbos of the giving of the Torah. The difference between these two historic *Shabbosos* lies in the fact that right after the Shabbos of the giving of the Torah, the sin of the golden calf took place.

At Mount Sinai we saw Hashem, so to speak, "*You saw how*

I spoke to you from the heavens."[15] This was a supremely exalted moment. *B'nei Yisrael's* souls flew from their bodies. But then they made the golden calf! The experience of standing at Mount Sinai and hearing Hashem speak didn't do much to lift their spiritual level over the long run. A person can jump up high, but he comes right back down to where he started, continuing to do exactly the same things.

The Shabbos of the time of Mashiach will rectify the sin of the golden calf. It will perfect the world. This is the nature of *seudah shelishis*: It is the time that straightens out our lives. It is the time when we utilize *kedushas Shabbos* to think about how our Torah learning is, how our davening is, how our *avodas Hashem* is, and what can be improved. This is the purpose—and beauty—of the *kedushah* of Shabbos.

Ra'ava DeRa'avin

In Torah sources we find that *seudah shelishis* is called the time of *ra'ava dera'avin,* the "will of wills." *Ra'ava* is Aramaic for *ratzon,* which means a person's will—i.e., what the person wants. What does "will of wills" mean?

The whole world expresses the will of Hashem. However, Hashem's will is not always the same. Here Hashem wants suffering, and there He wants joy. Here prosperity, and there poverty. All these are the wills of Hashem. In its practical expression, each will differs from the next. Thus we may ask: What is the one will that underlies and motivates all the various wills that exist? What is the "will of wills," the *ra'ava dera'avin*?

Chazal tell us, "Everything Hashem does, He does for the best."[16] This means that one will gives rise to all the wills: Hashem's will to bestow goodness! Because of Hashem's will

15. *Shemos* 20:18.
16. *Berachos* 60b.

to bestow goodness, He punishes here and enriches there. Because of Hashem's will to bestow goodness, one man becomes sick, and another man, healthy. This is the *ra'ava* behind all the *ra'avin*.

The *kedushah* of Friday night is not *ra'ava dera'avin*. It's not all-encompassing—it's just one aspect. Similarly, the *kedushah* of Shabbos morning is a certain *ra'ava*. It's more beautiful than that of Shabbos night, but it's still just one aspect. When we come to *seudah shelishis*, the great *ra'ava dera'avin* reveals itself: It is Hashem's one underlying will that unifies and encompasses all other wills.

At this time we work on our own fundamental will, which is responsible for all the various states in our lives. This is the time to change everything, to straighten out our *middos*, correct our shortcomings, and solve all our other problems.

On Shabbos morning we don't say *Attah Echad*. We say *Yismach Moshe*, because it is the time of the *simchah* of the wedding celebration. But every wedding, no matter how wonderful, eventually comes to an end. On Shabbos afternoon we say *Attah Echad*, which expresses the absolute Oneness of Hashem. This Oneness exists at every time and in every situation, and it never, ever ends. For if it would, it wouldn't be Oneness. The concept of Oneness is that even tomorrow, and even a week from now, it will be the same.

This comes to the fore at the time of Minchah and *seudah shelishis*. This is the time to work on keeping Shabbos with us all week; the Oneness of Hashem which we recognized on Shabbos should accompany us during the weekdays. This means living with the underlying truth of Hashem's Oneness: *Hashem Echad u'Shemo Echad*.

״וקראת לשבת עונג״

13

Oneg Shabbos—Eating at Hashem's Table

Eating and Drinking—the Beauty of Shabbos

THE MITZVAH OF *Oneg Shabbos* is unique; *Chazal* say amazing things about it:

> Whoever delights in Shabbos is granted a heritage without limits. For it says (*Yeshayahu* 58:14), "*Then you shall delight in Hashem... and I will grant you the heritage of your father Yaakov....*"[1]
>
> Whoever delights in Shabbos is granted the wishes of his heart. For it says, "*Take delight in Hashem, and He will grant you the wishes of your heart*" (*Tehillim* 37:4). But we don't yet know what delight this is. When it says, "*You shall call Shabbos a delight*" (*Yeshayahu* 58:13), we know that it is the delight of Shabbos.[2]

We see that the mitzvah of *oneg Shabbos* is very great. How do we fulfill this mitzvah?

Fortunately for us, *Chazal* also tell us how:

> How does one delight in Shabbos? Said R' Yehudah son of Shmuel bar Sheilas, in the name of Rav: with cooked beets,

1. *Shabbos* 118a.
2. Ibid., 118b.

large fish, and garlic heads.[3]

This means that when Shabbos comes we eat delicacies. We serve delicious food: fish, meat, kugel, and other dishes. I remember that on the Baba Sali's Shabbos table were thirty-six different salads. (Perhaps this number was the *gematria* of a certain Name of Hashem.)

Let us try to understand what this mitzvah is all about. At first glance it seems to actually go against our general approach in *avodas Hashem*. For it is said, "Building the body destroys the soul." This refers to indulging the body in physical pleasures. The more we indulge ourselves in physicality, the more we distance ourselves from spirituality. A tzaddik eats enough to sustain himself but doesn't indulge in delicacies.

Let's say a person passes a restaurant after having eaten lunch, and he's not hungry, but he just wants to enjoy something good. Or he sees an advertisement about a new kind of ice cream and feels he must taste it. Pursuit of pleasure for pleasure's sake is destructive to the *neshamah*.

But all this applies on weekdays. On Shabbos, it's a mitzvah! Hashem commands each Jew, "You shall call Shabbos a delight." On Shabbos we are told to enjoy food, and, *baruch Hashem*, the women constantly work on making it as tasty as possible.

Why do we have such a mitzvah? What do we gain spiritually by sitting down to enjoy a tasty meal? Let us push the question a little further. Yom Kippur is also Shabbos. It's called *Shabbos shabbason*. But on this day we eat nothing at all; we fast. It's a day that's completely spiritual. If so, why indulge in delicacies on Shabbos? It would seem more appropriate to recite Kiddush over a *Sefer Tehillim* and set the table with books of Gemara and Mishnah. Instead, we use meat, fish, cake, and ice cream to express the beauty of Shabbos. Why?

3. Ibid.

Guests in Hashem's House

Let us explain the difference between Shabbos and Yom Kippur.

Yom Kippur is a day for us. It's the day we can achieve the highest level of *kedushah*. And when we generate *kedushah* we give up everything for Hashem, out of love for Him. That's why Yom Kippur is called *Shabbos shabbason*: Not only do we refrain from working, we even abstain from eating, drinking, etc. It is a day of pure *ruchniyus*.

If Shabbos were a day for us as Yom Kippur is, we would fast and forgo physical pleasures. And we would surely gain more by doing so. But in truth, Shabbos is something else altogether.

Imagine a Jew receives the honor and privilege of being hosted by the Chasam Sofer, a monumental Torah figure. The Chasam Sofer is very fond of this Jew and happy to see him. "*Shalom aleichem,* Reb Yaakov!" he says with a beaming smile. "Welcome! I'm so happy you came. I want you to eat supper with me."

The Chasam Sofer himself goes into the kitchen and says to his Rebbetzin, "Did you hear? Reb Yankel from Boro Park is here. Please prepare a special meal for him." The Chasam Sofer emphasizes that a really nice meal should be served for his beloved guest. Soon the Chasam Sofer emerges from the kitchen with a plate of chicken and side dishes. He places it before the astonished guest and urges him to eat.

"I'm sorry, Rabbi," the guest says, "but I'm really trying to cut down on my intake of tasty food. You know, I'm working on the *middah* of *perishus*. Maybe you have a dry piece of bread and a cup of plain water? That's fine for me."

This surely is not the way to behave. When a person is in his own home and wants to work on being more spiritual, indulging himself in rich food is not the way to do it. The less he eats, the better off he is. But when in the Chasam Sofer's home, he should put his personal preferences aside. A great tzaddik has invited him to dine with him, and his own desires pale in comparison to the tzaddik's. The guest should stop thinking about what he wants and focus on what the tzaddik wants. That is the proper reaction.

When the Chasam Sofer asks you to enjoy a meal he has prepared for you, the relevant halachah is: "One should not refuse a great person."[4] Your *avodah* at that moment is to put aside what you want and do what he wants.

I travel a lot, and the state of *kashrus* varies from place to place. So I made an ironclad rule not to eat meat outside my own home. I simply don't touch anything *fleishig*. But once I broke my rule. I was in the home of a great Rosh Yeshivah at suppertime, and he insisted that I join him for the meal. We were served chicken, and I ate out of respect for this great man.

When Yom Kippur comes, we focus on our own *avodas Hashem*. That calls for fasting. But when Shabbos comes, we're not in the center of the picture, because we're in Hashem's house. We are guests at His table, and He says to us, "I want you to enjoy My delicious food!" And the halachah is, "One should not refuse a great person." We put aside what we want and do what Hashem wants.

This explains the mitzvah of *oneg Shabbos*.

"Serving Food Is a Great Matter"

Eating and drinking together is no small thing. *Chazal* say, "Serving food is a great matter, for it...draws close those who are distant."[5] Sharing a meal brings people closer. We see this from when Yitzchak gave the *berachos* to Yaakov and Esav. Yitzchak requested that food be brought to him: *"Make me delicacies such as I love, and bring them to me, so I may eat, in order*

4. *Bava Metzia* 87a.
5. *Sanhedrin* 103b.

that my soul will bless you."[6]

This is actually a deep matter. But on a simple level we may understand it as follows: Food keeps body and soul together. In other words, it's a connector. If a person doesn't eat for twenty-four hours, he feels weak. His *neshamah* starts fluttering in his heart. If another day or two go by without food, his *neshamah* already rises to his nose on its way out…but if he then eats, his *neshamah* goes back down to his heart and reconnects with his body.

Food may be understood as something that creates a connection. Therefore, when two people eat together, they begin to identify with one another. Eating connects a person to his body as well as to anyone eating with him. The nature of food is to draw close and connect.

That's why *Chazal* banned *pas akum,* the bread of non-Jews. It is explained in the Gemara[7] that eating their bread leads to drinking their wine, which in turn leads to marriage with their daughters. If a Jew drinks wine with a non-Jew, his children will marry the non-Jew's children. For food and drink draws people close to one another.

Among the most beautiful things Hashem has given us are the laws of *kashrus.* I often fly to many different places. I sit on the plane and see the non-Jew eating his airplane meal, while I take out my sandwich. (I ordered my *kosher l'mehadrin* meal, but of course no one knows why it's not on the plane…) So I'm sitting there eating my dry bread while he eats his *treif* meat. This distances me from him, and builds an invisible wall between us. Indeed, as the above-quoted *Chazal*[8] goes on to say, failure to serve food distances those who are close.

6. *Bereishis* 27:4.
7. *Shabbos* 17b.
8. *Sanhedrin* 103b.

On *Shabbos Kodesh* we dine with Hashem, so to speak. *Da hi seudasa d'Atika Kaddisha.* "Serving food is a great matter, for it draws close those who are distant"! It is as if we sit down to eat and drink together with Hashem, and this creates tremendous closeness with Him.

Wearing Nice Clothes—For Hashem's Sake

Now let's discuss Shabbos clothing. Imagine you're in a hotel on the other side of the world, spending Shabbos by yourself. You've packed everything you need. Will you put on your Shabbos clothes, or will you wear old, faded clothing? There is no question that all of us would wear the same special clothes we wear every Shabbos. Why? For whom are we dressing up?

And we wouldn't stop there. We'd put a white tablecloth on the table, and even flowers, if possible. For whom are we doing all this?

The answer is obvious: On Shabbos, we meet Hashem. When we meet someone, we want to look respectable. That's how we develop positive relationships. So wherever we may be, we put on Shabbos clothes for Hashem. We're saying, "Hashem, I'm dressing up in Your honor!"

We take out our best clothing and make ourselves look nice in order to make a good impression on Hashem, so to speak. We want to express how much we love and venerate Him, so we dress up when He comes!

השבת - יומו של הקב"ה

14

The World Turns to Nothingness in Hashem's Presence

Only Shabbos Expresses "Religion"

THE RAMBAM WRITES ON the subject of *das,* "religion":

> A non-Jew who involves himself in Torah study is liable for death. He may involve himself only in the study of [the non-Jews'] seven mitzvos. Similarly, a non-Jew who keeps Shabbos is liable for death. This applies even if he does so on a weekday, if he makes that day like Shabbos for himself. This is surely true if he makes a festival for himself.
>
> The rule is that non-Jews are not allowed to create a religion and make up their own mitzvos. Either [a non-Jew] should become a sincere convert to Judaism and accept all the mitzvos, or he should keep to his own "Torah" [of seven mitzvos] without adding or subtracting.... If he involved himself in Torah study or kept Shabbos...he is not actually put to death.[1]

The Rambam says that "non-Jews are not allowed to create a religion and make up their own mitzvos." He means that a

1. *Mishneh Torah, Hilchos Melachim* 10:9.

non-Jew who observes a day of rest is creating a religion for himself. This he may not do. The Rambam continues on to add in the next halachah that if a non-Jew wants to observe one of the other mitzvos in order to receive reward, he may.

We can accept a *korban* from a non-Jew; we can accept *tzedakah* from him. A non-Jew may put on tefillin. He may join us at the Seder table and fulfill the mitzvos of matzah, *maror* and *arba kosos*. He may put a mezuzah on his doorpost and walk around wearing tzitzis if he wants to! Why? Because he hasn't done anything yet defined as a *das*, a "religion." Only when a non-Jew keeps a Shabbos is he considered to have created a religion for himself, and this he may not do.

The Rambam tells us a fundamental point: The true meaning of "religion" is expressed through keeping Shabbos. Ceasing from work is religion. This explains why *Chazal* say that a Jew who publicly desecrates Shabbos is called a *mumar*, an apostate.[2] He is considered as if he is a non-Jew. For ceasing from work on Shabbos embodies the concept of religion, and a Jew who works on Shabbos loses his "religion."

Why does Shabbos, as opposed to other mitzvos, constitute religion?

No Nation Like This

The key is to understand how we relate to God.

"Walk modestly with your God."[3] This verse describes our relationship with Hashem as one of *tzeniyus*, "modesty." This means that we relate to Hashem from within the privacy of our own selves. And *Shabbos Kodesh* is the way to achieve this. As we shall explain, Torah and mitzvos without *Shabbos Kodesh* can easily miss the point.

Hashem declares, through the prophet Yirmeyahu, *"The*

2. *Eruvin* 69a.
3. *Michah* 6:8.

sages of the Torah did not know Me."[4] How can this be? *Nefesh HaChayim* explains at length how learning Torah is the greatest *deveikus* with Hashem, and how the Torah and Hashem are one. Indeed, this is all surely true beyond the shadow of a doubt. Yet the prophet Yirmeyahu cries out that it's possible to learn a lot of Torah without knowing Hashem! This is because a person could learn Torah all his life yet actually meet Hashem quite infrequently.

An example of this is illustrated by the following halachah:

> A person should pray in a manner of pleading and entreating, like a pauper at the door gently making his request. The prayer should not appear as if it is a burden on him, which he would like to be rid of.[5]

The *Mishnah Berurah* comments that merely saying the words in the manner described above is insufficient. A person must think to himself that he truly needs something and is coming to request it from the King. The *Mishnah Berurah* rules that it is incorrect to pray just because there is an obligation to do so, and one should be very careful about this point. The *Bei'ur Halachah* adds that it's extremely important to be careful about this because a number of *poskim* hold that praying merely out of obligation is halachically invalid and that the *Shemoneh Esreh* must be repeated in such a case.

According to these *poskim,* a man who davens Shacharis because that's what it says in the *Shulchan Aruch,* and goes to the seven o'clock minyan and utters every word with great *kavanah,* has not even been *yotzei.* Why? Because he did it as his fixed practice, not because he felt the necessity to ask Hashem for everything he needs.

4. *Yirmeyahu* 2:8.
5. *Shulchan Aruch, Orach Chayim* 98:3.

A Jew should pray because he gets up in the morning and knows that, *baruch Hashem,* he has a family, and they need bread and milk. His children also need to go to *cheder* or school and on their way will be crossing a busy street. It's impossible to manage without *siyata di'Shemaya*!

Our approach to prayer should be just like that of a person who gets up in the morning and goes to the store to buy bread and milk. He doesn't do it out of habit. He does it because he needs the bread and milk.

I once heard about a great tzaddik who went to the store every day in order to buy milk for his mother and fulfill the mitzvah of *kibbud eim*. This is a wonderful story. Personally, though, I don't go to the store every morning at nine o'clock as part of my daily routine. I go to the store because I need to buy something. If I don't need anything, I don't go!

The halachah we are discussing is based on a teaching of *Chazal*: "Do not make your prayer fixed, but rather [an act of] entreating for mercy."[6] The *Mishnah Berurah* understands this teaching on its simple level. It means a person should go to shul and daven Shacharis because he needs Hashem. He should simply go and beg for mercy! If he lacks this *kavanah* and instead davens out of routine, some *poskim* say he isn't *yotzei*. Nevertheless, the *Mishnah Berurah* rules that *bedi'eved,* one shouldn't repeat the *Shemoneh Esreh*.

Getting back to our point: Praying with the awareness that we truly need Hashem is an important part of having a true, personal relationship with Him. It is written, "*Which is such a great nation that has God close to it, as is Hashem, our God, whenever we call to Him?*"[7] Here the Torah emphasizes that God is close to us. We have a special relationship with Him.

6. *Pirkei Avos* 2:3.
7. *Devarim* 4:7.

Above, we mentioned the verse, *"Walk modestly with your God,"* which *Chazal* say is one of the three essential principles of the Torah.[8] It conveys the idea that "walking with God" is wholly a matter of "modesty." This means it's private, inside the person. No one in the world knows why the next man does what he does. We don't know his intention. No one can say for sure that he's right in this and wrong in that. We can't know, because what really counts is a private matter, revealed to none. Only the person himself knows what his *kavanah* is. *"Walk modestly with your God"* is a matter that's completely internal.

It seems to me that the greatness of the previous generations lies mainly in this point. Hashem used to be a living reality for a Jew—a real, live personality, so to speak. *Chazal* expressed this idea by saying, "May the fear of Heaven be upon you as is the fear of flesh and blood."[9]

This is a crucial point for a *ben Torah* to work on. Our spiritual greatness depends on it, and *Shabbos Kodesh* is the way to attain it.

The Most Basic Difference

Every holiday has its own special theme. Pesach is *cheirus*, Shavuos is *matan Torah*, Sukkos is *deveikus*. Shabbos is the day Hashem teaches us to recognize Him, so to speak. What is the special theme of Shabbos?

As mentioned, Rambam teaches us that Shabbos expresses religion. A person can do all the mitzvos, but these activities are not religion. Only Shabbos is religion! This is because *das*, "religion," means relating directly to the immediate presence of Hashem, and Shabbos itself is a Name of Hashem. This is the special theme of the day.

8. *Makkos* 24a.

9. *Berachos* 28b.

To grasp this point, let us consider the most basic difference between the Jewish people and the nations of the world. The nations of the world say, "There is a God in Heaven Who created everything—and not only that, He influences everything that happens in the world!" Indeed, the ancient Gentiles knew *parnasah* came through the stars, and the influence of the stars emanated from the angels, and the angels were Hashem's emissaries. What was their mistake? They thought Hashem granted the stars a certain amount of authority, and therefore one could pray to them without having to go straight to Hashem, the ultimate Source of all.[10]

Everyone used to know that all the plenty and goodness of this world comes down from Heaven. If you asked a non-Jew, "Where is Hashem?" he would answer, "In Heaven." This is the approach of the non-Jew.

And what does the Jew say? Hashem is not just in Heaven. He is also on earth! "*The whole earth is full of His glory.*"[11] This is the foundation of Judaism. Our goal is to reveal Hashem here on earth.

In truth, this is not just the foundation of Judaism. It's the foundation of religion as a whole. Being in the presence of God means everything else loses its importance and self-existence. We prostrate ourselves before God, because prostration—lying face down, stretched out on the ground—expresses negation of one's importance and existence. We are nothing in the presence of God.

If God is only in Heaven, it doesn't "disturb" our lives too greatly. We don't have to submit ourselves totally to God, since He is up in Heaven, while we're all the way down here on earth. A person can continue to be "himself." True, God has a certain

10. See Rambam, *Mishneh Torah, Hilchos Avodas Kochavim* 1:1.

11. *Yeshayahu* 6:3.

influence over man. He can bestow goodness upon him, or He can punish him. Thus, a person needs to "negotiate" with God and stay on good terms. How? He takes tefillin, tzitzis, mezuzah, matzah, and through them causes his faith in Hashem to permeate his heart and mind. By keeping mitzvos, he can stay on good terms with God in Heaven.

But if God is on earth, it's a completely different story. Then, there is nothing else in the world. Everything loses its self-existence in the overwhelming presence of God. We cannot even take a single step if it is against Hashem's will, because there is no reality other than Hashem's will. This is the meaning of "religion." In other words, religion means relating to God's presence in the world and realizing everything turns to nothing in His presence.

And the only way physical beings can express religion is by ceasing from work. Let us explain:

Somebody's walking down the street and notices his neighbor relaxing on the porch with a glass of lemonade and a book.

"Yankel!" he calls to him, "Now you're resting? Just look what's happening in your garden. All the effort you've put into your vegetables and plants is about to go down the drain. It's a scorching heat wave today, and you must water the plants immediately, before they all dry up and you have nothing left. All the time and money you've invested is going to be wasted!"

Yankel the Jew answers him, "Ivan, I don't know how to explain this to you, but today there is no garden and no vegetables. There are no banks and no loans. There isn't even a world. There's only God! If He wants to give me *parnasah,* He will. And if He doesn't, nothing will help anyway."

This is Shabbos. It is a day of cessation from work, when the whole world ceases to exist due to Hashem's all-pervasive presence. Even a non-Jew, if he wants to invent a religion — be it Christianity, Islam, or any other — needs a day of cessation from work. For this is the only thing a human being can do that expresses religion.

That is why the Christians, for example, make Sunday their day of rest. When Sunday comes, a Christian doesn't go to work, because this is what expresses his religion.

The Torah says a non-Jew who keeps a Shabbos is liable for death, although this punishment isn't meted out by Sanhedrin. A non-Jew has no real connection to the reality of God's presence filling our world to the point of all else ceasing to exist. So when a non-Jew keeps Shabbos, he is negating the very nature of his world. He is flying in the face of his reality.

Chiddush Ha'Olam

Let us explain further. Shabbos doesn't signify Hashem's creation of the world. If we wanted to mark the act of Creation, we wouldn't stop working! On the contrary, we would perform various types of *melachah* to commemorate Hashem's work of Creation.

Shabbos signifies *chiddush ha-olam,* the fact that the world is an entity which came into existence. That is how it is explained in Torah sources. The world wasn't just "there"; it didn't always exist. Furthermore, *chiddush ha-olam* means the world is constantly coming into existence anew every moment. Hashem is constantly creating it out of utter nothingness. What does this mean? The world has no true existence. The world is based on utter nothingness, and at every moment it must be re-created out of the utter nothingness that is its essential reality. This is the basic meaning of Shabbos.

Even non-Jews (at least the smarter ones) understand that God created the world. It simply cannot be otherwise. Anyone who fails to grasp this point is stupid. It is written, *"From my flesh I will see God."*[12] Can someone who sees through his eyes entertain the possibility that his eyes just came into being by

12. *Iyov* 19:26.

themselves? This is like someone saying: "When I buy a car, it makes no difference to me whether it has an engine. What do I care about the engine and all that mechanical stuff? As far as I'm concerned, the main thing is that it has gas, brakes, and a steering wheel."

Someone like this surely will not recognize God due to the wonders of his eyes. But someone who knows that a car moves because of its engine also knows that the eye sees because it's connected to the brain. And the astounding genius that created such a system is beyond human comprehension.

I remember grasping this point with special clarity when I was in a car accident and suffered some broken bones. I was sitting there in the car, unable to move. Someone came to me and said, "Get out of the car!"

"I can't," I answered him.

He again signaled to me and said, "Get out of the car!"

And I told him, "I don't know what happened to my legs. I can't move them."

"What's the problem?" he said. "You have legs..."

Then I realized that a person can have legs, but if something is disconnected from the "engine," it doesn't work!

There is no question that God created the world. Even the non-Jews believe this to be true. The point they fail to understand is that the underlying nature of the world is utter nothingness. It is constantly being re-created out of nothing. Non-Jews don't view the creation of the world that way. They see it as one long, unbroken process, as a constant that goes on forever. They consider God's existence and the world's existence indivisible. The world always was, is, and will be. So in their view, the world is a solidly based reality. It is the opposite of nothingness.

But how can they think the world always was if they believe God created it? The *Chasam Sofer* explains that it's like a man and his shadow. True, the shadow came to be because of the man. On the other hand, the shadow was there as long as the man was. The two are indivisible.

There is a principle that if something always was, then it always will be. If the world's creation always was — as the non-Jews claim — then it will never cease, for it is a fundamental reality. But this is not so!

How do we know? Simple: because Hashem completed the act of Creation. *"The heavens and the earth were completed...."*[13] This means Hashem stopped creating; he ceased the work of making the world. This shows that the whole process was something with a beginning and an end.[14]

Shabbos is when we commemorate Hashem's *cessation* from work. It signifies the concept of *chiddush ha-olam*.

When we say the world is constantly re-created out of utter nothingness, what point are we trying to make? That the world doesn't exist in its own right. For an entity's basic reality and existence stem from its source, and where did the world come from? Utter nothingness!

If so, why is there a world at all? Why does the floor feel so hard if it doesn't really exist? The answer is very simple. The world's true reality is Hashem's will. Hashem wills it to exist, so it does. It is nothing more than an expression of Hashem's will, and there is no reality other than Hashem's will. Hashem wants the floor to feel hard, so it does. That's all.

A non-Jew has no connection to all this. The idea that the world is based on nothingness contradicts his basic nature, because he lives in a world that's real and solid. Thus, a non-Jew is disconnected from the reality Shabbos expresses. To negate the world and say everything is God's will, a non-Jew would have to negate the entire reality he lives in. And he is not

13. *Bereishis* 2:1.

14. This matter is explained more fully in Rav Pincus's *Shabbos Malkesa*, part 2, chap. 1.

allowed to do so, since he has no true comprehension of the reality of a Jew, in which God's presence in the world makes all else as nothing.

A Country within a Country

Hashem is the true King of the Jewish people, and wherever Jews are, His Kingship is felt. This is true even in *galus,* for every nation expresses the kingship of its king. In olden times when Jews lived in their own country, His Kingship was felt even more strongly there. And one place was like a country within that country, where His Kingship was most strongly felt: the Beis HaMikdash.

We cannot imagine what it was like. Hashem's presence was tangible. It was seen through the beauty and grandeur of the Beis HaMikdash, through the specially dressed *Kohanim* who served there in holiness and purity, through the exceptionally stringent laws governing the various levels of impurity. This was Kingship on a whole different level. The Beis HaMikdash was special not just because it was a place with special halachos. It represented a whole different way of life, a different reality. A *Kohen* would come to the Beis HaMikdash, put on *bigdei kehunah,* and eat the meat of the *korbanos;* all the aspects of his life would change completely. He was living in Hashem's presence. He was standing before his King and serving Him!

This is exactly the reality of *Shabbos Kodesh.* A Jew's life is always special and different, but when Shabbos comes, it is *HaMavdil bein kodesh l'chol.* It's like a country within a country, like the Beis HaMikdash within Eretz Yisrael. When *Shabbos Kodesh* comes, everything changes. Now a Jew is in the King's presence.

If you enter the Jewish street in Amsterdam, London, Paris or anywhere else, even on a weekday, you feel the influence of Hashem's Kingdom. The language is different, the dress is different, the aspirations are different. But if you enter the Jewish street on Shabbos, it's like entering a different country and seeing a different people. This is a noble people who dress in special clothing, eat fine food, speak differently — as *Chazal* say, "Your speech on Shabbos should not be like your speech during the week."[15]

Jews always bear the character of Hashem's Kingship, but Shabbos transforms it into the Kingship of a country within a country. It rises to a level where we stand in the immediate presence of our King.

Not Moving a Hand or Foot

On Shabbos we're in the King's house, so to speak, and this calls for completely different behavior than during the week.

Once on Shabbos I visited one of my *rebbeim*, R' Yosef Liss, *zt"l*. I was standing and talking to him next to a fence around a yard. I fiddled around with the gate as we spoke, unconsciously pushing it open and closed.

Suddenly he asked me, "What are you doing?"

"Nothing," I answered, not quite getting the point.

He asked again, "What are you doing? You're doing something!"

Again I answered, "Nothing."

After the third time he asked what I was doing, I suddenly noticed my hands opening and closing the gate...

Then he said to me, "You know, something like that would never happen to me. My hands would not move on Shabbos without my knowledge of exactly what they're doing. You know why? Because I had a grandfather who was a *Kotzker chassid*. He was a great man. I remember that every *erev Shabbos* at noontime, his hands started trembling, and they wouldn't stop until Shabbos was over.

15. *Shabbos* 113a.

"When we visited him on Shabbos, he would look at our hands the whole time. 'Where are your hands, where are your hands…?' He trained us in the important behavior that on Shabbos a person should always be conscious of what his hands are doing!"

An amazing story cited in *Seder HaDoros*[16] teaches us the significance of what a person does with his hands. There was once a great man named R' Bustanai, who was a descendant of David HaMelech. While still a lad, he became renowned for his wisdom and Torah knowledge. The king was interested in seeing this "wonder child" and summoned him to the royal court. The king and his advisers were impressed with the lad, who stood there before them until nightfall without turning his head even slightly or lifting his foot.

After a while, a fly began buzzing around and settled on the lad's forehead. He didn't bat an eyelash. The fly started to bite him and draw blood. He didn't raise his hand to brush it away. The king found it rather strange: "Why don't you brush away the fly?" he asked.

The lad answered, "We have a hallowed tradition in our family that when in the presence of the king, one doesn't lift a hand or foot without the king's permission."

The king was pleased by the lad's answer. He accorded him great honor and made the "fly" that family's insignia.

That is what *Shabbos Kodesh* is like. Someone who has learned *hilchos Shabbos* well, especially the laws of *muktzeh*, knows that on Shabbos it is almost impossible to lift a hand or foot without the "permission" of our great King. If a person picked up his hand and is not aware of what he is doing, he is likely to desecrate Shabbos. Why? Because he's in the presence of the King!

16. *Seder Yemos Olam* 4420.

Kiddush Hashem

Being careful about what we do on Shabbos actually affords us a tremendous opportunity to sanctify Hashem's Name.

Rambam states that one way to fulfill the mitzvah of *kiddush Hashem* is by doing a mitzvah or refraining from a sin for the sole reason that Hashem said so.[17] If a person does a mitzvah *l'shem Shamayim,* not because of any personal considerations, he has actually fulfilled two mitzvos: the immediate mitzvah he has done plus the great mitzvah of *kiddush Hashem.*

Let's say on Shabbos morning the husband is in shul davening, and the children are playing in the yard. The wife is in the kitchen, and some sauce suddenly spills on the floor. She quickly looks around for something to wipe up the spill and spots a roll of paper towels—but on Shabbos it's forbidden to tear a piece off the roll! But no one is watching her...

If she would start searching for an old towel to soak up the spill, by the time she'd get back the sauce would have spread all over the kitchen...but she knows and remembers that Hashem is watching. And Hashem says, "*Remember the Shabbos day to sanctify it.*"[18] So she stays away from the paper towels.

This woman, besides keeping the mitzvah of Shabbos, has fulfilled another tremendously important mitzvah: *kiddush Hashem*!

It Boils Down to Emunah

It is fitting for *b'nei Torah* to work on this kind of *emunah.* This is the *emunah* of "*A tzaddik lives his faith.*"[19] It is the *emunah* of "*Walk modestly with your God.*"[20] It means bringing Hashem into the pri-

17. See *Mishneh Torah, Hilchos Yesodei HaTorah* 5.
18. *Shemos* 20:7.
19. *Chavakuk* 2:4.
20. *Michah* 6:8.

vacy of our own selves, so to speak—to live with Hashem. It means to say *"Baruch Attah..."* and feel we are actually talking to Someone! It means to walk down the street, see something, and pray, praise, thank, sing...simply to live with Hashem.

The special time for developing this kind of *emunah* is Shabbos. Shabbos is a Name of Hashem. This is the time when we are most capable of understanding the true nature of the world, of perceiving the reality of *"The whole earth is full of His glory."*[21]

This affects the way we prepare for Shabbos, too. When a *ben Torah* is standing in the kitchen getting something ready for Shabbos, he should understand why, and in Whose honor, he's doing it. Who is the "Guest" coming to his home tonight?

It is recounted that when R' Baruch Ber Leibowitz, *zt"l*, the Birkas Shmuel, bought himself a hat, he asked those around him, "Does the hat look right on me? Could I wear it to meet R' Chaim Ozer?" In other words, his whole reason for buying the hat and wearing it was so he could meet R' Chaim Ozer Grodzinsky, the *gadol hador*.

When a *ben Torah* puts on his hat, or helps clean the house for Shabbos, in whose honor is he doing it? In honor of the Creator of the Universe!

If the Chofetz Chaim or the Chazon Ish came to us for Shabbos, wouldn't we want to make sure everything was tip-top and as beautiful as possible? Would we leave cleaning the candlesticks for next Shabbos?

Our Shabbos guest is the *Ribbono shel Olam* Himself. This is what Shabbos is all about.

21. *Yeshayahu* 6:3.

האדם – "מן הארץ עד לרקיע"

15

On Shabbos, Hashem Raises Man to the Heights

Reaching around the World

UNLIKE PREVIOUS GENERATIONS, ours is characterized by the amazing development of science and technology. The modern world we live in has capabilities no one even dreamed of a hundred years ago: means of transportation, electronic communication, etc. People are very pleased and proud of all of this. We Jews also benefit from the cars, the ability to fly anywhere in the world, and the other wonders of science and technology.

One thing science has accomplished is that nowadays a person can circle the world without even leaving his chair! A person can sit in his office in New York and receive information that three seconds ago someone in China bought a few kilograms of gold. Nowadays, while sitting in front of their computers, people can change the world. Any one of us can phone a relative who lives on the other side of the world. Undeniably, this is an amazing achievement.

But I have a question: If these capabilities are so wonderful, why didn't they exist one hundred or two hundred years ago? If they're so important for human life, why don't they date back to the creation of the world? Why is it that until a few decades ago, someone who wanted to travel to a faraway place had to spend arduous months en route?

Man in His Original Form

Here is one approach to this matter:

There is a basic principle in physics, and in *Chazal*, that to comprehend the true nature of something, we must ascertain its original state. Let's take Formica, for instance. It is a synthetic wood, actually produced from petroleum, whose form may be transformed and molded in various ways. But it retains its true nature even after its form changes. It may *look* like wood, but it will never really be wood.

Accordingly, if we want to know what man really is, what his true nature is, we must find out what he was like in his original state. Many changes have taken place in man's form over the generations, but if we want to grasp man's true nature, we must go back to the beginning and find out what the first man, Adam HaRishon, was like. Then we will understand the true nature of ourselves as well.

The Gemara recounts as follows:

> Said R' Elazar: "Adam HaRishon reached from the earth to the heavens.... When he sinned, Hashem placed His hands on him and shrank him...." Said R' Yehudah, said Rav: "Adam HaRishon reached from one end of the world to the other.... When he sinned, Hashem placed His hand on him and shrank him...."[1]

We see that Adam HaRishon was created a giant. According to some Torah sources he was as tall as the heavens, and according to others he was as broad as the earth. After he sinned, Hashem shrank him down to one hundred *amos* (180 feet) tall. With each ensuing generation he grew smaller, until he reached his present size.

What are *Chazal* telling us here? That man's true nature, his

1. *Chagigah* 12a.

original nature, is to be tall as the heavens or broad as the earth. Although we don't see ourselves that way, that is our real nature. And this remains true in all generations.

Man by Nature Breaks Boundaries

Man has a very interesting characteristic: He hates to be imprisoned. We might wonder what's so terrible about being in prison. Nowadays the prisons are almost like hotels... Why is it such a terrible punishment? The answer is that being imprisoned is the opposite of man's nature.

We see this from the story of Shim'i ben Gera, who cursed King David. Cursing the king of Israel is indeed a grave sin, but as long as David was alive he didn't wish to punish him. When David's death approached, he commanded his son Shlomo to use his great wisdom and find a way to kill Shim'i, head of the Sanhedrin.

What did Shlomo do after becoming king? He ordered Shim'i to remain in Yerushalayim and not leave the city. If he left, he would be liable for death. Inside Yerushalayim, Shim'i could do as he pleased, but if he left the city he would incur the death penalty for two acts of rebellion: one against King David and the other against King Shlomo.

After three years, Shim'i traveled by donkey to the city of Gat to reclaim two slaves of his who had fled there. He returned with his slaves, and Shlomo put him to death.[2]

R' Chaim Shmuelevitz, *zt"l*, asks an illuminating question about this story. Shlomo was commanded by his father, King David, to use his wisdom and find a way to kill Shim'i. How did Shlomo know that ordering Shim'i to stay in Yerushalayim would lead to his death? Perhaps Shim'i would stay in the city as ordered, and Shlomo's plan would come to naught. If so,

2. See *I Melachim*, chap. 2.

why did this plan express Shlomo's great wisdom?

R' Shmuelevitz answers with an insight into human nature: As long as a person isn't limited by others, as long as he has the freedom to come and go as he wishes, he might very well decide to stay where he is. (In fact, in previous generations certain Jews were proud of having never left Yerushalayim.) But Shlomo's wisdom told him that as soon as limits are imposed on a person, he'll need to defy them. Being forever forbidden to leave one's place goes against man's nature. Thus, Shlomo knew that once he ordered Shim'i not to leave Yerushalayim, Shim'i would feel compelled to break out of his boundaries and not remain in the city forever.

Man's nature is to want to break out of his boundaries. He cannot be limited! A chicken sits happily in its coop day after day, but a person cannot stay in one place. He wants to see the world. Why?

It is because man originally spanned from one end of the world to the other. His true nature is to encompass the entire world, therefore he feels a need to conquer it. Imagine taking a man 25,000 miles tall and putting him in a chicken coop. He would suffer indescribably. A person feels a need to expand to his natural dimensions.

Our Generation as Opposed to Past Generations

As mentioned, *Chazal* describe man's dimensions in two different ways: vertically and horizontally. Man reaches either from earth to Heaven or from one end of the world to the other. This was the nature of Adam HaRishon, and so it is with every person throughout the generations.

A hundred fifty years ago, every person had his feet on the ground and his head in Heaven, so to speak. He lived with *kedushah* and *ruchniyus*. He lived with HaKadosh Baruch Hu. So it was for Jews. And the non-Jews lived in a world full of witchcraft, spirits, demons and supernatural forces. In this way, every person reached Heaven by his very nature.

In those days, if someone from a small village was asked, "Wouldn't you like to see the big world?" he wouldn't understand this question. After all, what was he missing? He was immersed in spiritual worlds. He saw the stars and appreciated the tremendous wisdom expressed in their movements and patterns. He didn't feel limited and constrained.

Years went by, and man fell from this *madreigah*. His feet used to be on the ground, and his head in Heaven. No longer. But his nature didn't change. So what did Hashem do? He gave man the telephone and radio, cars and planes, enabling him to reach from one end of the world to the other. For this is man's nature. If a person cannot reach the heavens, nor can he span the world, he feels as if cramped in a tiny prison cell.

Our grandparents didn't have the tremendous breadth that the modern world affords. Yet we are basically the same as they. The only difference is that our grandparents reached great distances in *ruchniyus* and in living with Hashem, while we do not. But man's nature hasn't changed a bit.

When Shabbos Comes

Some people feel that Shabbos is the worst prison possible. Why do they feel this way? Because on Shabbos, a person capable of circling the world is restricted to the narrow confines of his immediate environment.

One of the worst punishments you can give someone who drives every day is to take away his driver's license. His natural field of action stretches from north to south, giving him a feeling of control. Then Shabbos comes, and he feels imprisoned.

But in truth, Shabbos is tremendously expansive. On Shabbos, Hashem expands us vertically. Instead of reaching from here to China, man expands upward until his head reaches the heavens.

In our generation, people from New York are excited by the

ability to call Israel. By contrast, a Jew who lived a hundred years ago would "call" Hashem. Back then, saying, "*Baruch Attah, Hashem*," was the excitement. Their "long-distance line" was longer and more exciting than ours. But as far as we are concerned, this "long-distance line" is all but disconnected, because our consciousness deals only with this world.

We are proud of knowing what's happening throughout the world. Yet compared to our predecessors, we have little to be proud of, because we're like someone lying on the ground who cannot lift himself up even an inch. But when Shabbos comes, instead of lying on the ground, Hashem stands us up tall. And *ruchniyus* is no less interesting than worldly knowledge. It's simply a different dimension.

It is recounted in the Gemara[3] that when *talmidei chachamim* parted from one another, they would offer each other a blessing: "*Olamcha tir'eh b'chayecha* — May you see your world within your life." What does this mean?

A person cannot live without holding the world in the palm of his hand. That's how he was created. The only question is: Which world does he hold? *Talmidei chachamim* would bless each other to live in the world of *ruchniyus*. They would say, "May you find *your* world — the world you inherited from Avraham, Yitzchak, and Yaakov — within your life here in this world."

It is not uncommon for Torah Jews to be termed "narrow" and "limited." Is there any truth to this claim? The Torah indeed imposes limits. Moreover, *Chazal* say three types of people are like "prisoners," and one of them is the *talmid chacham*! A yeshivah is the most restrictive environment you can find. But this "prison" is a world unto itself, full of beauty and color. It is the deepest and most interesting world there is. It is the

3. *Berachos* 17a.

blessing of *olamcha tir'eh b'chayecha*. You don't have to wait until you leave the world; enjoy the world you're living in!

This idea explains why many people find it hard to sit and learn with their family. When I was engaged to be married and would get together with my wife-to-be, I would tell her over long *derashos*. I wrote her letters full of *divrei Torah*. But after we got married...

What's the difference? Before marriage, we want to fill our time with interesting content. And to *b'nei Torah,* nothing is more interesting than a good *d'var Torah*. But after marriage, we start living our actual life. Here is where we are likely to make a mistake: Do we see Torah and *Yiddishkeit* as our actual life? Do we live in the world of Torah?

Every night in Ma'ariv, before we recite the Shema, we say about Torah and mitzvos, "For they are our life and the length of our days and upon them we will meditate day and night." The only way to achieve "upon them we will meditate day and night" is through "for they are our *life* and the length of our days." When Torah and mitzvos are not our very lifeblood, it's impossible to focus upon them "day and night."

The general rule in spiritual matters is first *"sur me'ra"* and then *"aseh tov."*[4] First we turn away from the bad, and then we engage in the good. This is because a person cannot live in two worlds. Since Torah is a world unto itself, someone who wants to live in it must first give up the craving to keep abreast of current events. When he turns away from that, he'll discover what makes him unique as a person, and he'll find Torah.

The only way to close the newspaper and rid oneself of the modern-day obsession of knowing what's happening in the world is to find an appropriate substitute for it.

4. *Tehillim* 34:15.

Chazal say:

> There are three crowns: the crown of kingship, the crown of priesthood, and the crown of Torah.... Why does it say for the others, *"You shall make for it a crown,"* but for the *aron hakodesh* [which represents Torah] it says, *"They shall make on it a crown"*? To teach us that the crown of Torah is the highest of all. If a person acquires Torah, it is as if he has acquired all of them.[5]

The "crown" is the highest part of a person—it is above his head. A *talmid chacham* who lives in the world of Torah is above the common folk. To be a *ben Torah,* one cannot be like everyone else. He must lift himself higher. He must stand up tall rather than lay on the ground.

Instead of reaching from one end of the world to the other, let us reach from the earth to the heavens. This is the only way we can acquire the wonderful crown of Torah, which is called *"Your wisdom and understanding in the eyes of the nations."*[6]

5. *Shemos Rabbah* 34:2.
6. *Devarim* 4:6.

"וימלוך תחתיו הדר"

16

Shabbos Kodesh Brings Out Our True Beauty

Where Is the Beauty of Shabbos?

EVERY *EREV SHABBOS*, THE sanctity and beauty of Shabbos begin entering our world. Let us devote a little thought to how we can better appreciate Shabbos, utilize what it has to offer, and absorb as much *kedushah* from it as possible.

If we want to utilize something, we first have to know what it is. The reason many people don't take advantage of Shabbos and gain the greatness and beauty it has to offer, is because they don't know what Shabbos is. They don't understand what Shabbos can give them.

I was recently approached by a fine *ba'al teshuvah* who was learning in *kollel*. He shared with me his concern: "When I was thinking about becoming Torah-observant, I heard many lectures about how wonderful it is to learn Torah and keep mitzvos, especially Shabbos. Everyone excitedly described the Shabbos table, the light of Shabbos, etc.

"I decided to become *frum*, and I'm happy I did. I enjoy my learning, and I have a fine family and my own Shabbos table. But I haven't yet found the special beauty and light that I was told Shabbos has. What am I doing wrong?"

I'm afraid this man isn't alone. We all know Shabbos is very holy and spiritual. And surprisingly enough, what are we involved with during most of this holy day? *Gashmiyus*! We eat and drink, fulfilling the mitzvah of *oneg Shabbos* by having three special meals. How does this express the great *kedushah* of Shabbos?

Chazal tell us that Hashem gives us a *neshamah yeseirah* on *erev Shabbos* and takes it away on *motza'ei Shabbos*.[1] If somebody asked us what the *neshamah yeseirah* is, we probably would answer that it is something very exalted and lofty. But Rashi says otherwise:

> The *neshamah yeseirah* is an expansiveness of the heart regarding rest and joy, and [the quality of] being open wide, such that a person may eat and drink without repulsion.[2]

If a person would sit down during the week and eat as he does on Shabbos, he would be disgusted. But on Shabbos we eat and drink again and again without becoming nauseated. Rashi's explanation is very puzzling: Is that all there is to the *neshamah yeseirah*: the ability to eat large amounts of food without feeling sick?

It seems that we're unaware of the beauty and inner content of *Shabbos Kodesh*. We don't really understand why Shabbos is structured as it is, and how this is supposed to infuse us with *kedushah*. Let us explore this crucial topic.

Today's Lifestyle

First let us understand why Hashem gave us Shabbos.

Ever since the Torah was given, *Shabbos kodesh* has been the crown of the Jewish people. But today it's more important than ever to emphasize Shabbos and try to fathom its meaning.

1. *Beitzah* 16a.
2. Rashi, ad loc.

I will describe what I see as the problem of *Yiddishkeit* as practiced today. There is a concept called *yeridas ha-doros*. We all believe we lack the greatness and depth of understanding that our predecessors had. *Chazal* described this phenomenon even in their days and pinpointed how they differed from their predecessors. For instance, in the Gemara we find Mar Ukba calling himself "vinegar, the son of wine," because he didn't maintain his father's holy practices.[3]

With this approach, let us try to understand what our generation is lacking, which a century or two ago most Jews had. Of course we cannot know exactly what it was like then, as we weren't there. But we do have a significant amount of information.

Nowadays, *baruch Hashem,* we learn Torah and keep mitzvos in a very *mehudar* way. Even the girls learn *hilchos Shabbos* and *hilchos berachos* in the Bais Yaakov schools. People learn a lot of Torah and are meticulous in their mitzvah observance. But there is one point we're missing: The way we do things is a little bit like *Yiddishkeit* without HaKadosh Baruch Hu. We tend to "leave Hashem out," so to speak. Let me explain.

I wish to emphasize that I am not speaking about our level of mitzvah performance. *Baruch Hashem,* the way we keep halachah is good and getting better all the time. For example, it seems to me that the matzos we eat are better and more *mehudar* every Pesach. This is a great blessing from Heaven. Our tefillin and mezuzos are also becoming more and more *mehudar* as time goes on. We are building more *yeshivos* and more Bais Yaakovs. This is not our problem.

So what is the problem? Let's take a look at our lifestyle. If we compare the way we live our lives to how previous generations lived theirs, we'll see a tremendous difference.

3. *Chullin* 105a.

Every country has its own way of life. There are certain things that its people consider beautiful and proper, and certain things they don't like at all. So it is everywhere. For instance, we all know that the way people dress today has changed a lot. It wasn't like this at all one hundred or two hundred years ago. The *Alter* of Kelm recounts that when he first came to the town of Kelm, men and women walked on opposite sides of the street. In this Lithuanian shtetl, just walking on the same side of the street was unacceptable. So it was a hundred and fifty years ago.

Nowadays, it wouldn't occur to us that there's a problem with men and women walking on the same side of the street. It could be that in fact there is something wrong with it, but we don't sense it at all. Why? Because of the spirit of the country we live in — we've gotten used to living this way. I am not pinpointing *tzeniyus* as the main problem of our generation either. This is just an example of how attitudes change.

We should be aware that the spirit of our life today is influenced by the non-Jews. Our lifestyle as a whole, including what we see as beautiful and proper, is affected by the society that surrounds us. Our basic attitudes toward things have changed, and this has taken us away from our former lifestyle: living with Hashem.

But we can do something about it. We are capable of changing the attitudes we have picked up from the modern way of life. We can return to truly living with Hashem, as in past generations!

"Moshe Knew about the Heartbeat"

There is an amazing point connected to this topic. At the end of *parashas Vayishlach*, a brief passage speaks of seven Gentile kings who ruled, and then died:

> And these are the kings who ruled in the land of Edom... and Bela died, and in his place ruled Yovav ben Zerach of

Basrah... and Baal Chanan ben Achbor died, and in his place ruled Hadar.[4]

These verses contain great secrets of the Torah. Much of the Ari *z"l*'s writings are built on this passage. This seems strange: Why were these exceedingly holy matters communicated to us through verses recounting the history of Gentile kings?

Ramchal explains with an allegory. If a person needs to send an expensive diamond somewhere, what does he do? If he puts it in a fancy, attractive envelope, it's likely to be stolen. So he wraps it in an old rag, so no one will suspect there are valuables inside. This passage, says Ramchal, is one of the most important in the Torah. That's why it was hidden in the names of the kings of Edom. And what is the important teaching in this passage?

We cannot go into detail, but all the exiles are alluded to here. At the very end of the passage quoted above it says, "*And in his place ruled Hadar,*" which alludes to the *Melech HaMashiach,* who is called *hadar. Mashiach* has both "taste" and "scent," as does the *esrog* — which is called *hadar*. And *Mashiach* will rule in the end of days.

The commentators ask a strong question: How can Hadar be *Mashiach*? In *Divrei HaYamim* it says, "*Hadar died.*"[5] If Hadar is the savior of Yisrael, the *Melech HaMashiach,* how can it be that he died?

Mahari Saruk, one of the Ari *z"l*'s disciples, answers as follows: "Moshe knew about the heartbeat; Ezra didn't know about the heartbeat." In other words, Moshe Rabbeinu, who wrote, "*And in his place ruled Hadar,*" heard the heart beating. But Ezra HaSofer, who wrote, "*Hadar died,*" didn't hear the heart beating. We will explain with an allegory.

4. *Bereishis* 36:31–39.

5. *I Divrei HaYamim* 1:51.

Once there was a king who had a beloved only son. This son was more precious to the king than anything in the world. It happened that the son fell ill and the king sent for the leading doctors. They came, examined him thoroughly, and pronounced sadly, "Your Majesty, the child is dead."

The king heard the devastating news, and he prepared to call the *chevrah kaddisha*. But one doctor there, a great expert, said to him, "Before Your Majesty summons the *chevrah kaddisha*, I would like to examine the boy again."

This doctor had exceptionally fine senses. He put his ear to the boy's heart, listened for a few moments, and then exclaimed, "Your Majesty, I hear the heart beating. Your son is alive!"

The boy had fainted and was in such a deep coma that everyone thought he was dead. But this doctor had very fine senses and was able to find a heartbeat.

"Ezra didn't know about the heartbeat." He held that *Klal Yisrael* would one day be in such a deep coma that "*Hadar died*"—everyone would think the Jews were lost. Indeed, if we look around, we see that a large portion of the Jewish people is so far gone that it has never even heard the verse "*Shema Yisrael*." This resembles a state of death: "*Hadar died*." But "Moshe knew about the heartbeat." He listened carefully and said, "No, the heart is still beating. The *hadar* is not dead!"

What is this *hadar*? *Hadar* means "beauty." Judaism has beauty, as it is written, "*His palate is sweet, and He is all delight*."[6] I remember when I was nine or ten years old, when my father was a rabbi in Williamsburg, Brooklyn, that on Simchas Torah I davened in the Satmar *beis midrash*. I pushed in along with the others to catch a glimpse of the Satmar Rebbe, *zt"l*. I was very moved by the sight of him—such *kedushah*, such beauty. And Judaism has a certain glorious beauty, known as *hadar*.

6. *Shir HaShirim* 5:16.

Nowadays as well, we Jews learn and daven, but not as our predecessors did. And the grace and *tzeniyus* of the Jewish mother of old is no more. Jews continue to exist, but the *hadar* has disappeared — "*Hadar died.*"

Yet Moshe Rabbeinu discovered that the *hadar* is still alive. We can still bring back the simple beauty of *Yiddishkeit*.

The Missing Hadar of Our Generation

Let's talk about what makes our generation different. My father, *zt"l*, was a true Jew and a great tzaddik. When I was three, he wrapped me in a tallis and brought me to the *Talmud Torah*. He raised us in a spirit of Torah and *yir'as Shamayim*. Nevertheless, we spoke English at home.

Throughout the generations there never was such a thing — that a five-year-old Jewish child should know Polish or Russian. Such a thing simply did not exist. Once I asked my father-in-law, who was from Poland, if he knew Polish. He said to me, "No, of course not! Why should a Jewish child know Polish?"

This is just one small detail, but it points to a greater phenomenon. We are much more connected to non-Jewish society than ever before. There are fine *kollel* men who speak several languages. There are many Jewish homes where various kinds of magazines, etc., can be found. I wish to emphasize that I am not speaking of mitzvos and *aveiros*. I'm speaking of the *hadar*, the beauty of the Jewish people.

There is another difference between us and our predecessors: One of the outstanding characteristics of the Jew throughout the ages was *simchah*. I once heard in the name of a certain linguist, a non-Jew, that no language in the world has as many expressions of joy as Hebrew has. In English there are only two or three words for "joy." But Hebrew has very many terms, among them: *simchah, gilah, rinah, ditzah, chedvah*.

Why? Because each group of people emphasizes the things

that are essential to their lives. For instance, in the Eskimo language there are six or seven synonyms for "snow." In English there is only one word for "snow," and so too in Hebrew. But the Eskimos have a lot of words for snow, because they live in snow. Thus they distinguish between dry snow, wet snow, cold snow, etc. But snow is not an essential part of our lives, so we don't need a lot of words for it.

Jews throughout the generations lived in happiness and joy—it was an essential part of their lives. That is why Judaism has many words to express *simchah*. Why don't we feel this way? Because today we live in sadness. Our lives revolve around troubles, difficulties, and sadness. In our generation we try to create a false feeling of happiness by buying a new car, a new home, etc. We look for happiness but generally live in an atmosphere of sadness.

Just take a look at the young street people laughing raucously at the top of their lungs. What's that all about? It didn't used to be that way. Why do these young people laugh so boisterously these days?

My child once asked me the same question. I went downtown with him to buy shoes, and there were some people hanging around there doing nothing, laughing very loudly. "Daddy, why do they laugh so much?" he asked me.

I said to him, "Because they're so sad." Inside they're sad, so they need to laugh. All day long they look for something to make them happy, but they don't find it.

A person's soul, by nature, thirsts for something. When it doesn't get what it needs, it becomes hungry, and this feeling of lack makes a person sad. We should examine ourselves to see how much true *simchah* we really have. How much do we enjoy *Yiddishkeit,* Torah and mitzvos, and developing a relationship with Hashem?

"Your Friend"

Today, people don't derive the same joy and satisfaction from *avodas Hashem* as they used to. This can be seen from how people react to various subjects.

As we know, the Torah's mitzvos are divided into two categories: those between man and his fellow, and those between man and Hashem. Simply speaking, the mitzvos between man and his fellow require us to be kind to others, show consideration for them, and fulfill the great rule of *"V'ahavta l'rei'acha kamocha."* The mitzvos between man and Hashem require us to learn Torah, daven, etc.

As a public speaker, I notice that when I speak about interpersonal mitzvos — such as *shalom bayis,* showing sensitivity for others, greeting people with a smile, etc. — I get a certain reaction: The more I elaborate on the subject and go into detail, the happier and more satisfied the audience looks. Everyone looks pleased and wants to hear more, whether he or she is Torah-observant or not. It never happened to me after delivering a talk on interpersonal mitzvos that someone came up to me and said, "Rabbi, I think you're being a little extreme. What do you expect from people? No one can live that way!"

But when it comes to matters between man and Hashem, people react quite differently. Even if I'm speaking before a *frum* audience, I have to make sure I don't go too far. And when I speak before an audience that's not Torah-observant, I have to be extremely careful not to be too strict, because people will tell me, "Rabbi, I'm sorry, but this just is not for us. Do you think we grew up in Meah She'arim?"

Everyone, including those who aren't Torah-observant, understands the need to be a mensch and treat people nicely. Here, *chumros* are welcome. But when it comes to matters between man and Hashem, i.e., being *"frummer,"* we react to it as something that doesn't apply to us and our *madreigah.*

There's a misconception underlying these reactions. Most people know the teaching, *"V'ahavta l'rei'acha kamocha — zeh klal gadol baTorah.*"[7] But not as many know what Rashi says in Gemara *Shabbos*.[8] There it is recounted how a non-Jew came to the great Hillel and asked to be taught the whole Torah while standing on one foot. Hillel said to him, "Don't do to your friend what you dislike. This is the whole Torah. The rest is commentary; go learn it." How does Rashi explain this?

> "Don't do to *your friend* what you dislike," refers to, "*He Who is your Friend and your father's Friend, do not abandon*" (*Mishlei* 27:10). This means Hashem. Do not go against what He says, for you dislike it when your friend goes against what you say.

We see that "your Friend" is Hashem!

Our relationship with Hashem is also somewhat "interpersonal." God is not a philosophical or theological concept — He's a real personality. He relates to us, and we need to relate to Him, too. He hears everything we say. He is happy or pained, so to speak. When a person does a mitzvah, it "compliments" Him. If a person makes a *berachah*, it's like saying "thank you" to Him. And it's the opposite if a person does an *aveirah*. We should treat Hashem with due care and respect: "*You shall love your Friend as yourself.*"

Understanding this point is the heart and soul of Judaism. As Hillel said, "This is the whole Torah. The rest is commentary; go learn it."

"You Saw What I Did to Egypt"

The first time we met Hashem, what message did He give us? When the Israelites left Egypt and came to Mount Sinai, the first thing Hashem said to Moshe was as follows:

7. *Bereishis Rabbah* 24:7.

8. 31a.

> So shall you say to the House of Yaakov, and tell the Children of Israel: *"You saw what I did to Egypt. And I carried you on eagles' wings and brought you to Me."*[9]

What message does *"You saw what I did to Egypt"* convey? Hashem was saying to us: "In Egypt you saw harsh plagues that never happened to anyone in the history of the world. All the water turned to blood, frogs took over and were absolutely everywhere; all kinds of wild beasts roamed the streets and houses; there were locusts, hail, etc.

"Why did all this happen? Why did I smite Egypt so fiercely? Because we were about to make a marriage covenant between us."

The most important thing a wife needs to know about her prospective husband is that he thinks of her and cares about what happens to her. Without this element, the whole relationship falls apart.

Accordingly, Hashem was saying to us: "You saw what I did to Egypt — when the Egyptians afflicted you, it agitated Me greatly. I couldn't bear it, and I brought ferocious plagues upon them! I subjected them to punishments that had never been seen before."

What is the message here? That Hashem did not merely sign a legal contract with us: You do mitzvos, and I give you health; you keep Shabbos, and I give you good children. Hashem is not like an ATM machine, where you punch in the right code and get what you want. On the contrary, Hashem is saying to us, "This is not an automated service. We have a real, live relationship of love!"

9. *Shemos* 19:1–4.

Shabbos and Hashem Go Together

This real, live relationship of love is what Shabbos is all about.

Shabbos is the key mitzvah whose purpose is to grant us a relationship with Hashem. *Shabbos Kodesh* creates a situation in which we can find Hashem and be with Him in a real, live way. Hashem gave us Shabbos so we could find Him.

Just as nowadays we tend to forget about Hashem, we tend to forget about Shabbos, too, for they're really the same thing. As R' Shlomo Wolbe, *zt"l,* once said: "We still see *yeshivah bachurim* who have a good *Shemoneh Esreh*. But where can we see a *yeshivah bachur* who has a good Shabbos?"

I heard the following comment in the name of R' Chaim Brim, *zt"l,* on the words from the Shabbos davening, "והנחילנו ה' אלוקינו...שבת קדשך — Hashem, our God, give as our inheritance... Your holy Shabbos." He said, "Hashem, You gave me gefilte fish, You gave me meat, You gave me soda, You gave me a beautiful table. Give me a little Shabbos, too!"

Why don't we have a little "Shabbos" in addition to all the other nice things? Because we don't have Hashem! These two are one and the same. To the extent that we bring Hashem back into our lives, our Shabbos will be different as well. Shabbos is like a long *Shemoneh Esreh* when a Jew stands before Hashem.

Shabbos Expresses the Deep Feelings of the Heart

Someone who eats *treif* becomes closed off to matters of *kedushah* — as the verse says, *"ve'nitmeisem bam,"*[10] which our Sages interpret to mean "and you will become closed through them"[11] — but he still keeps his status as a full-fledged Jew. Whereas someone who doesn't keep Shabbos

10. *Vayikra* 11:43.

11. *Yoma* 39a.

is considered for many halachos as if he were a non-Jew. Why?

This may be compared to a husband and wife. They sometimes fight or disagree, but this is not yet a reason for them to separate. Whereas if we could look inside their hearts and discover that there is no real connection between them, and in fact they hate each other, then there is no reason for them to stay together. Each goes his or her own way.

Shabbos Kodesh is that connection deep down in the heart. Here is where we can tell whether they love each other; whether they have a real, live relationship.

This is the special importance of Shabbos. If a person keeps Shabbos, it means the basis of his marriage to Hashem is still intact. He yells, she yells, but they're still a married couple. But someone who desecrates Shabbos severs this connection. The basic love is lost, and the whole relationship is gone. This is where all of *Yiddishkeit* begins and ends.

In our generation we are very susceptible to ups and downs in our *ruchniyus*, and from time to time we need to be inspired anew, to bring Hashem back into our lives and our davening. As a certain tzaddik once said, "Every so often it's worthwhile to think Hashem exists. It won't hurt." And the very best way to do this is with *Shabbos Kodesh*!

Take Notice of Shabbos

A person could go into the Beis HaMikdash, spend a long time there, and see absolutely nothing special. This is because matters of *kedushah* require preparation. Before the *Kohen Gadol* went into the *Kodesh HaKodashim* he would prepare himself beforehand for an entire week. He would involve himself solely in acquiring the greatness and sanctity that was called for. And then, in fear and trepidation, shaking from head to toe, he would enter the Holy of Holies and feel the *kedushah* with every fiber of his being. But when the Gentile conquerors entered the Beis HaMikdash, they didn't see anything special at all.

Once a non-Jew entered the *beis midrash* of a large yeshivah and saw hundreds of people there immersed in their learning, many of them arguing excitedly in loud voices. He was surprised by the sight. He noticed another non-Jew calmly going about his business, and he walked up to him and asked, "What is going on here? What's the big argument all about?"

"I don't know, sir," he answered. "I've been working here thirty years, and every day they yell and argue and carry on like this. But I've never seen them hitting each other…"

If this non-Jew entered the Beis HaMikdash, what would he see? Nothing but a big slaughterhouse with marble walls. But a Jew who entered the Beis HaMikdash would see *kedushah* so strong you could touch it.

So it is with Shabbos. Many people have already been through hundreds of *Shabbosos,* living in the same house with HaKadosh Baruch Hu without even realizing He was there. They were unaware that they were sharing that wonderful oneness and unity called *Shabbos Kodesh.* It never occurred to them what an embrace of *kedushah* they were receiving. That's why they didn't take advantage of Shabbos, acquiring for themselves the greatness and beauty it has to offer. They were in the Beis HaMikdash and didn't even know it!

Since a person can keep Shabbos week after week without knowing what it actually is, our holy Torah tells us, "*See that Hashem gave you the Shabbos.*"[12]

Hashem is saying to us, so to speak, "When I give you the mitzvah of shofar, you will find out what a shofar is. And when you eat matzah, you'll sense the greatness contained within it. But Shabbos is not like that. A Jew can keep one Shabbos after another and never know its beauty.

"*See that Hashem gave you the Shabbos.* I am informing you

12. *Shemos* 16:29.

specially: You should know all about Shabbos and realize that on Shabbos you can reach a love and closeness to Me that is unattainable any other time, because this day is blessed and sanctified above all times."

Joy, Not Self-Sacrifice

That is why on Shabbos, a Jew must detach himself from everything going on around him and live with Hashem alone, like a *chasan* and *kallah* together in the *yichud* room.

This is not a matter of *mesirus nefesh,* of dedicatedly fulfilling Hashem's command without actually enjoying it. Rather, the goal is to live with Hashem in a spirit of gladness and enjoyment — to bring back the *hadar* of *Yiddishkeit.*

To understand this point, let us compare self-sacrifice with joy.

One of the three kinds of people over whom Hashem cries is, "He who cannot engage in Torah learning but engages in it."[13] What does this mean? Why does Hashem cry over such a person? Simply speaking, it means as follows: This person cannot learn Torah, because he's so busy. But with *mesirus nefesh,* in a spirit of self-sacrifice, he puts aside what's important to him and learns Torah nonetheless. And Hashem cries over him because — why does he need *mesirus nefesh*? Why in the first place did he get so involved with other things that he needs *mesirus nefesh* in order to learn Torah? On the contrary, Torah should have been his main interest!

This may be compared to a father who says to his son, "Please bring me a glass of water." The son sighs and says, "Daddy, I will have *mesirus nefesh* for you." He then rises heavily from his chair and goes to the kitchen to bring his father water. His father calls out, "It's okay; forget the *mesirus nefesh* — I don't

13. *Chagigah* 5b.

need any favors. But why is it so hard for you?"

Hashem says to the person who's too "busy" to learn Torah, "How did you get into such a state? Why do you consider learning Torah such a personal sacrifice?"

Let's say a man leaves the *beis midrash* at 11 P.M. and goes home. Before reciting *Kerias Shema she'al ha-mitah,* he opens a book again and doesn't notice the passing of time until suddenly he looks at his watch and discovers that it's already 3 A.M.!

He sounds like a great *masmid*. How does he do it?

Let's see what book he picked up: It wasn't a Gemara, a *Chumash,* or a *Mishnah Berurah* either. It was an action-packed novel.

Now we're not so impressed. It's no great feat to read a novel into the wee hours of the night. Why? Because it's enjoyable. But what about the Torah? Don't we enjoy Torah learning?

This is what Hashem is saying to the person who's too "busy" to learn Torah: Why is it that you can't learn Torah, but you can read a novel without even noticing the time going by?

This is the meaning of *"Hadar died."* That beauty was, but is no more. Once upon a time, Torah and *Yiddishkeit* were something enjoyable and sweet for Jews. Nowadays we do everything with *mesirus nefesh*. We're a generation that shows great self-sacrifice for Torah learning and mitzvos.

Where is the sweetness and enjoyment of *Yiddishkeit* that existed throughout the generations? When a Jew davened Ma'ariv every evening and said, *"Ki heim chayeinu v'orech yameinu* — for these are our lives and the length of our days," he felt the Torah was his life. Just as every person loves life, so he loved the Torah.

What does "love of life" mean? Let's imagine a person who goes to the doctor suspecting he has a terrible, malignant disease. He prepares himself for the worst. But after the examination the doctor smiles and says, "Reb Yankel, there is absolutely nothing wrong with you. Your health is fine!" There's no describing this person's joy. He feels as if he were just given life itself as a gift.

For every Jew, the Torah was always life itself—*Ki heim chayeinu v'orech yameinu*. There is no greater joy than being given life.

Let us bring back this *hadar*. When *Shabbos Kodesh* arrives, let us feel true Jewish *simchah* when we pick up a *sefer*. Let us learn Torah with desire and enjoyment. The same applies when we go to shul and have the wonderful opportunity to daven to Hashem. Let us restore the beauty of *Yiddishkeit*. And at the same time, let us reject all that belongs to the low, pitiful culture that surrounds us. We should feel disgust toward that which comes from the outside, understanding that it's not what Hashem intended for us. It's for them—not for us.

On Shabbos we enjoy three special meals. We eat more than during the week, and this is connected to the *neshamah yeseirah*, as we mentioned above. What is this all about? It comes to express our feeling of sweetness and enjoyment from *Yiddishkeit*! On Shabbos we don't talk about *mesirus nefesh*. On the contrary, we derive immense pleasure from being Jews and having a real, live relationship with HaKadosh Baruch Hu.

Hashem has blessed our generation with unprecedented material abundance, but we still lack happiness. If *Shabbos Kodesh* doesn't give us happiness, we go looking for it in other places. Happiness used to be inside—the Jewish home was full of happiness, a Jewish child was full of happiness. People didn't have to go out looking for happiness.

We lack *simchah* because we look for it "out there." That's why it seems that "*Hadar died*," and the wonderful *hadar* we used to have has disappeared.

But Moshe Rabbeinu taught us that the *hadar* isn't dead. It lives on! And we can bring back the true Jewish *simchah* that comes with a real, live relationship with Hashem, for "*His palate is sweet, and He is all delight.*"

השבת – "מקור הברכה"

17

The Key to It All Is Shabbos

Shabbos Is the Source

WE GREET SHABBOS BY calling it the source of all blessing: *"Likras Shabbos lechu v'nelcha, ki hi mekor ha-berachah."* Shabbos is also called *ma'ayn ha-berachos,* the "fountain of blessings."

In the *sefer Reishis Chochmah* there's a section called *Sha'ar HaKedushah.* It deals with various subjects connected with *kedushah,* such as the sanctity of one's eyes and thoughts, modesty in the home, etc. The author begins by stating that first, before everything else, comes the root and source of all the forms of *kedushah — Shabbos Kodesh.* The following parable from the Midrash expresses this point.

> Once there was a king who had a dear friend. He told his friend, "Ask for a precious gift, and I will grant it to you." The friend was very clever. He said to himself, "If I ask him to make me a governor or a duke, that's all I'll have. Rather, I will ask for the thing that everything else comes along with." He said to the king, "My master, since you've granted me this opportunity to ask something special of you, I ask you to give me your daughter in marriage, and I will be your son-in-law." The king replied, "By your life, so will I do."[1]

1. *Yalkut Shimoni, I Melachim* 17:3.

The clever man in the above parable asks to become the king's son-in-law, because as soon as he becomes part of the family, he has everything!

Shabbos is called a *bris*, a covenant: *"And the Children of Israel will keep Shabbos, making Shabbos an eternal covenant for their generations."*[2] This *bris* of *Shabbos kodesh* is what connects us to Hashem. Someone who knows how to use the power of Shabbos can acquire for himself all areas of the Torah, because Shabbos is the fountain and root of all blessings.

Appreciating What Shabbos Can Do for Us

Shabbos is the seventh day of the week, and Tishrei is the seventh month of the year. The month of Tishrei begins with accepting Hashem's *Malchus* on Rosh Hashanah and ends with the tremendous blessings and *siyata di'Shemaya* of Shemini Atzeres. And so it is on Shabbos. When we accept Shabbos upon ourselves on Friday afternoon, we're really accepting Hashem's *Malchus*. For Shabbos is not just an individual mitzvah in a person's life—it is a *kabbalas ol Malchus Shamayim* and leads a person to the tremendous outpouring of blessing described as, "Whoever delights in Shabbos is granted a heritage without limits."[3]

One of our shortcomings in our times is that we don't properly appreciate the tremendous power of Shabbos. We attach great importance to Rosh Hashanah and Yom Kippur, to Pesach and Shavuos, but we don't give Shabbos the esteem it deserves. Yet it is the true source and root of all blessings! The fountain of all greatness and *siyata di'Shemaya* is open on Shabbos.

Everyone is looking for *siyata di'Shemaya*. People want to increase their *hasmadah*, to improve their *kavanah* in prayer, to

2. *Shemos* 31:16
3. *Shabbos* 118a.

develop *middos tovos*, etc. Once a week, we have access to the fountain from which we can draw all these blessings. We stand right in front of it. Do we take advantage of this wonderful opportunity to obtain what we're seeking all week long?

Imagine we're in shul on Rosh Hashanah or Yom Kippur at one of the exciting and dramatic points, such as the blowing of the shofar. We notice standing at the back a handful of non-observant Jews who came today because "that's what you're supposed to do on Rosh Hashanah." It is clear from their tired, bored faces that they're missing all the beauty and grandeur of this awesome moment. Don't we feel sorry for them? It's such a shame: here they took the trouble to come to shul, the shofar is being blown, and they're missing out on all the greatness and holiness.

When it comes to *Shabbos Kodesh*, we're not so different. We're standing right at the fountain of salvation, at the gates of blessing and happiness. We're standing right at the source of all goodness and plenty! Yet we don't take advantage of this amazing day called Shabbos.

Stocking Up on Blessings

In the Shabbos evening section of the siddur, there's a passage from the Zohar:

> *"Remember the Shabbos day to sanctify it"* (*Shemos* 20:7). R' Yitzchak began by saying: It is written (*Bereishis* 2:3), *"God blessed the seventh day."* And it is written about the manna (*Shemos* 16:26), *"Six days shall you gather it, and on the seventh day, which is Shabbos, there will be none."* If there is no sustenance on Shabbos, what blessing does it have?

We should know that when the gates of blessing are open, they bestow both spiritual and material blessings. Thus R' Yitzchak asks, "If Hashem blessed Shabbos, why is there no manna — material blessing — on that day?"

> We were taught as follows: All the blessings of above and below depend on the seventh day. And we were taught: Why is there no manna on the seventh day? Because this is the day from which all six days are blessed. Each day has its sustenance due to the blessing it receives on the seventh day.

We may compare this to someone who comes to the grocery store and to his surprise finds it closed. "What happened?" he asks. "Why is the store closed? Is there no food?"

"No," answers the storekeeper, "it's because a massive delivery just arrived with all the Pesach products. We're very busy right now bringing in all the goods and putting them on the shelves."

In other words, a store doesn't close only because there are no goods. It can be closed for the opposite reason: an overwhelming abundance of goods arriving right then. Tomorrow we can come and benefit from the great supply.

On a simple level, this is what the Zohar is teaching us. There is no manna on Shabbos because there is so much blessing then. The blessings for the whole week are filled up on Shabbos. While the "store" is being stocked with truckloads full of goods, it is closed to customers. We need to come back later to avail ourselves of the abundance. It's due to Shabbos that a person has sustenance on Sunday, Monday, Tuesday, and the rest of the week. But right now, on Shabbos, "the shelves are being stocked."

The Zohar continues:

> Since this is so [that Shabbos is the source of blessing], someone who is on the level of *emunah* should set the table and prepare a meal on Shabbos night in order that his table be blessed all six days. For at this time the blessing is available for all six days, and a blessing doesn't come to rest on an empty table. Therefore, he should set his table on Shabbos night with bread and food.

The question is: Why is it at mealtime that we receive the Heavenly flow of plenty on Shabbos?

Eating Adds Life

There is something amazing about eating. When we eat, we feel connected to Hashem in an almost unparalleled way. First let us remind ourselves why we eat.

We eat because the food we ate before has already been digested, and our energy level is starting drop. Simply put, we're starting to feel a little weak. Weakness indicates a lack of vitality. We're missing a little life and liveliness, and when we eat, we feel re-energized immediately. Our vitality and life have been replenished without any further ado.

Let's say a person recites a chapter of Tehillim and asks Hashem for *parnasah*. He doesn't see directly how the Tehillim brings him *parnasah;* in contrast, when he eats he feels directly how it brings him life. Eating is a golden opportunity to feel a direct connection with Hashem.

The end of *Mesillas Yesharim* speaks about the highest rung on the ladder of *middos*: "*Kedushah* leads to *techiyas hameisim.*" There it is written:

> Someone who has total *deveikus* with Hashem can draw from Him even the continuation of life itself, which belongs to Hashem more than anything.[4]

On a simple level, *Mesillas Yesharim* is saying that Hashem is called *Elokim Chayim,* meaning that life itself comes from Hashem. We can store up everything needed to sustain life. We can even store up air and oxygen. But we cannot store up life itself for even a moment. We can get a handle on everything in the world except life itself, which is in the hands of

4. *Mesillas Yesharim,* chap. 26.

Hashem every moment. No one can grab hold of it. The moment Hashem stops giving life, the person is dead. We need to receive life anew every moment.

So when we receive the gift of life, we feel Hashem more than we do through anything else. And the best way to actually feel how we absorb life straight from Hashem is by eating. For this reason, eating can be a unique time to feel a great *deveikus* with Hashem.

Two Sides to Eating

As we know, there are two sides to every coin. The rule is: "כל המקודש מחבירו חרב מחבירו — The holier something is, the more destruction there is." In other words, the more potentially beneficial something is, the more detrimental it can be as well.

And so it is with eating: Nothing in the world can give us a greater feeling of connection to Hashem, and nothing can push us farther away from Him. It is written, *"Yeshurun became fat, and he kicked,"*[5] i.e., he rejected Hashem.

On a simple level, we can understand this as human nature. Let's say a person receives a large gift but doesn't want to feel a debt of gratitude. What does he do? Instead of saying thank you, he kicks. It's the same thing with eating — because the gratitude we should feel for receiving food from Hashem is truly immense. That's why some people react by kicking. They want to escape the overwhelming feeling of gratitude and indebtedness.

And there is another reason. We generally tend to forget to properly thank Hashem for the food we eat. And nowadays we have an additional problem: We hardly even notice we're eating. Food is so abundant today that people take it for granted, having never experienced a food shortage or gone without food

5. *Devarim* 32:15.

for an extended period of time.

But in truth, eating is the best way to allow our natural feelings to draw us close to Hashem.

Eating and the Blessings of Shabbos

The Zohar we quoted above teaches us that someone who has *emunah* should be aware of Hashem when He is bestowing His plenty. And this is on *Shabbos Kodesh,* when Hashem grants the blessings for the whole week.

We all understand that money doesn't come from the bank or from work. It comes from Hashem. Similarly, we should understand that our *parnasah* comes to us only through the plenty bestowed on *Shabbos Kodesh*!

We should grab hold of Hashem, so to speak, at the moment He's bestowing all the blessings. When is this? At the Shabbos meal. This is when we have the golden opportunity to receive everything good from the Source of all blessings.

"יאר ה' פניו אליך"

18

On Shabbos, Hashem Shows Us a Different Face

The Seasoning Called "Shabbos"

Chazal tell us that *Shabbos Kodesh* has a special flavor. The Midrash[1] recounts that Rebbi once invited his friend Antoninus, the Roman ruler, for a Shabbos meal. It was Shabbos afternoon, and the food was cold. The delicacies should have been less tasty, but Antoninus ate from them and found them tasty. All the food was especially delicious.

The next day, Sunday, Rebbi invited him for another meal in which he brought before him simmering dishes, not cold food as on Shabbos. Antoninus said to him, "I found those to be tastier than these." He liked the Shabbos food better. Rebbi told him why: "These are missing a certain seasoning." Antoninus was surprised: Were the storehouses of Rebbi—who was fabulously rich and influential—lacking?! Rebbi explained, "They are missing Shabbos. Do you have some Shabbos?" He was saying that we have a seasoning called "Shabbos," and only on Shabbos do we partake of it.

So we see that Shabbos has a certain flavor.

Taste is actually something secret and inexplicable. It relates

1. *Bereishis Rabbah* 11:4.

to something hidden deep within a person's soul. Why one person loves a certain cake while his friend cannot even bear a nibble is something we cannot explain. Similarly, it is impossible to explain the taste of chocolate or ice cream to someone who has never tasted them before, as taste cannot be adequately expressed in words.

We all taste Shabbos every week. We love Shabbos and are attached to it, and we're even prepared to demonstrate *mesirus nefesh* for it. Therefore, even if we don't know how to explain exactly what Shabbos is, it doesn't matter. Nonetheless, it would be beneficial if we could reveal the secret and explain a little bit of what Shabbos is. This would enable us to see greater beauty and depth in *Shabbos Kodesh*.

What's in a 'Face'?

It is written, *"You didn't see any image on the day Hashem spoke to you at Chorev from the fire."*[2] We are commanded not to express God by means of an image. Let us understand what underlies this command. An image, by nature, can express only a momentary state — it cannot reflect change. We are commanded not to ascribe an image — a static state — to Hashem.

Now let us compare the face with the rest of the body. Nothing in the rest of the body changes intrinsically from one moment to the next. Everything stays more or less the same. A person may modify his posture or reposition his arms and legs, but the body parts remain essentially the same — only the pose is different. One's face, however, is unique in that it constantly changes in a profound way. There is no way to describe exactly how a certain person's face looks, because it changes from moment to moment. Thus, the concept of "face" denotes something that constantly changes.

2. *Devarim* 4:15.

It is written, *"You shall not have other gods to My face."*[3] This verse communicates one difference between Hashem and idols. Idols are referred to as "אלהים אחרים," from the word "אחור, backside," whereas Hashem is described as having a "face," as it says, *"to My face."*

There is a *middah* called "face." We will describe it with an illustration from everyday life. Let's say a father comes home and discovers that little Yanky, his two-year-old, has pulled out his drawer of important documents and dumped them on the floor. What's more, Yanky is hard at work scribbling on them. The father is furious and his face turns red with anger. Yanky sees that his father is angry and doesn't know what to do. In the end, he takes his father's hat and puts it on his head. At that moment, the father simply bursts out laughing.

From here we see that a face can change in an instant; it's not a static thing. But the back is static — it always looks the same.

Idolatry, and in fact everything in the world — with the exception of man, who bears the Divine image — has fixed characteristics. Let's say a man goes down to the showroom to buy a new car. The salesman praises the latest model in glowing terms, "This car is absolutely brilliant!" The man thinks to himself: "Oh, come on. What's it going to do, sing a song?"

The man knows very well that the car won't surprise him with anything original. It may be the fanciest and most advanced vehicle in the world, but it's totally incapable of anything beyond its fixed characteristics. It can never sing a song that it wasn't programmed to sing. But a person can always surprise us with something new. A person can go beyond his present state, for he has a "face." And a face expresses infinity, eternity, and depth. All of a person's emotions are expressed through his face.

3. *Shemos* 20:2.

Idols are אלהים אחרים, the back, because they don't have a face. They're static and unresponsive. But Hashem has a "face," and if we keep asking Him for something, we can elicit a different response, sometimes an unexpected one. When it comes to the *middah* called "face," the possibilities are endless. As Hashem is described as having a "face," we can never predict what trait He will express, since a face is unlimited in its capacity for change.

The following is an example of the *middah* called "face." As we know, about seventy years ago, Hashem became angry with the Jewish people. Jewish blood was spilled like water throughout Europe as the *middas ha-din* revealed itself fiercely. Yet, as we also know, the Mir Yeshivah was miraculously saved. The entire yeshivah traveled from Mir to Vilna and eventually to Shanghai. One of my rebbeim recounted that they traveled from Vilna with tourist visas. They arrived in Communist Moscow en route as "tourists," whereupon they were brought to the finest hotel in the city and served bread, sardines, and even oranges—an exotic fruit which most of the yeshivah boys had never seen. Later, walking in the street, they saw lines of hundreds of people waiting for a piece of bread!

This is an amazing scene: The world is going up in flames, the Poland they've left behind is decimated, and even in Moscow there is a great famine. And in the midst of this Gehinnom, 350 *yeshivah bachurim* are sitting in a luxury hotel in Moscow, peacefully eating bread and oranges!

This is the *middah* called "face." There is no way to predict whether Hashem will do this or that. A person cannot say, "That's it. Hashem is angry at me, and that's the way it is." This is both nonsense and *apikorsus*. For the moment we cry before Hashem, He greets us with a smile. The whole world can be going up in flames, and in the middle of it all, Hashem is showing great love and care. A person can be living in Gan Eden while Gehinnom is all around him.

Hashem's Smile

When we had the Beis HaMikdash, the love between Hashem and the Jewish people was "face to face." When we went into exile, Hashem turned His face away from us, so to speak.

Shabbos Kodesh is like the Beis HaMikdash. During the week, a person lives with sadness, worries, and troubles. He knows very well how lacking he is in Torah, *yir'as Shamayim,* and mitzvos. Then Shabbos comes, and *"May Hashem shine His face upon you"*[4] — Hashem shows His smiling face to him, so to speak.

It's very important to know that when Shabbos comes, the wonderful elevation we experience is not due to us. Every Jew, regardless of his good deeds or his *yir'as Shamayim,* receives a kiss from Hashem, so to speak. There is a sudden change in the way Hashem relates to us. This change is even drastic. It is as if we were looking at someone's back, thinking he was angry, and suddenly he turns around, and we see he's smiling. Everything changes in an instant!

That is why *Chazal* taught us that one of the most important things on Shabbos is to feel that "all your work is done."[5] Shabbos means everything that was going on until now stops! It's a big mistake to take all the feelings of the weekdays into Shabbos. It's silly not to leave behind all the sadness, cares, and thoughts about our spiritual deficiencies, for they go against the whole idea of Shabbos.

This is because Shabbos is a time when Hashem's "face" is revealed, and He is "smiling." It is not the time to cry and plead before Hashem over mundane matters. On Shabbos the approach is, "All your work is done!"

The Brisker Rav, *zt"l,* was known to be extremely careful not

4. *Bemidbar* 6:25.
5. See *Mechilta, parashas Yisro* 7.

to embarrass people who came to see him. He never removed anyone from his home, no matter how big of a *rasha* the person was.

When *Shabbos Kodesh* comes, we enter Hashem's home. We wear priestly garments, light the "Menorah," sit at the Shabbos table, and eat the food Hashem prepared for us and even paid for. We are His guests. At that moment, every Jew receives a smile from Hashem. *"May Hashem shine His face upon you."* And Hashem doesn't remove any Jew from His home, regardless of lack of merits.

All we ask is: "Bless us, our Father…with Your shining countenance." If You just show us a smile, then we'll have everything. "For by the light of Your countenance You have given us…the Torah of life and the love of kindness and righteousness, blessing and compassion, life and peace."[6] That's what Shabbos is all about. A day when Hashem smiles at every Jew.

During the week there's a lot going on, and everyday life is not easy. On Shabbos everything ceases. There's only Hashem, and we are His guests. At this moment He shows us a shining face. Perhaps that's why the *minhag* arose that when Shabbos arrives one recites *Shir HaShirim,* in which it's written, *"Let Him kiss me with the kisses of His mouth."*[7] For when *Shabbos Kodesh* comes, Hashem gives every Jew a kiss, so to speak.

The Beis HaMikdash Exists on Shabbos

To this day we are crying over the destruction of the Beis HaMikdash. This is because we lost the most wonderful thing imaginable: Hashem's house.

Let's say we had a father who was wealthy, wise, and powerful and an excellent doctor to boot. Our father could solve

6. End of *Shemoneh Esrei.*

7. 1:2.

any problem. All we had to do was go to his house and ask him. So it was with the Beis HaMikdash. Whatever problem a Jew — or even a non-Jew — had, there was a clear address where he could turn to find Hashem. A Jew would go to the Beis HaMikdash, daven there to Hashem, and receive whatever he needed.

Nowadays we dwell in darkness.

What would happen if someone walked in and said, "You'll never believe this — *Mashiach* has come, and the Beis HaMikdash has been rebuilt!" If we had any sense, we would rush out, get on a plane or hail a taxi, and get to Yerushalayim as fast as possible. Such a wonderful thing — Hashem rebuilt His house and is living in our midst once again!

But we do have a Beis HaMikdash. It's here! Hashem is with us every Shabbos. Of course He is always with us, but on Shabbos He is with us in the same special way as in the Beis HaMikdash.

What should we do on Shabbos? Just one thing: *"Remember the Shabbos day to sanctify it."*[8] Know that today is Shabbos. Understand that for the duration of this day you are living with Hashem. If a person doesn't know he has a wealthy father, he is liable to live seventy years without utilizing the wealth that could be his. So it is with Shabbos.

You don't have to go and get Shabbos — it comes to you. Shabbos doesn't depend on us — it comes from Hashem. If we understand that today is Shabbos, if we observe its laws and protect its sanctity as we should, as time goes on we will develop a wonderful feeling for *Shabbos Kodesh* which is Hashem's special gift to every Jew.

When we bathe for Shabbos, we should believe that everything that has happened until now is being washed away. We

8. *Shemos* 20:7.

enter the home of Hashem and are greeted with a smile. Not because we deserve it, but because this is Hashem's house, and this is the smile of *Shabbos Kodesh*. If we learn how to take advantage of this smile, and pray as we should, all our problems will be solved, as in the time of the Beis HaMikdash. All we need to do is open our eyes and understand how wonderful it is to be with Hashem.

Shabbos Is a Deep Healing

After hearing about how wonderful and exalted Shabbos is, many people will surely ask, "I've been keeping Shabbos for many years. Why don't I have this experience?"

The answer may be understood through the following allegory: Someone goes to the doctor because of skin sores, and the doctor discovers that the underlying cause is a blood infection. The doctor treats the source of the infection, and the blood clears up. Now the person is completely healthy — the cause of his illness is gone. Superficially he looks the same as before, as it will take a little while for the sores to go away, but inside he is already healed of his illness.

When this person looks at himself, he doesn't believe he's healthy. His skin is full of sores! So he ignores the doctor's orders to avoid certain foods that will cause the illness to return. He sees himself as still ill; therefore he doesn't understand what he has to lose by eating these foods that he is accustomed to and enjoys. So he continues consuming the harmful foods, and his illness indeed returns.

Shabbos is the summit of all the holy days. But after Shabbos a person goes back to life as usual, because he sees only what's on the outside. And superficially, nothing has changed; he feels he is the same person and doesn't see why he shouldn't continue doing the same things. Why should they now be harmful to him? But if he could see inside, he would know a tremendous change has taken place.

The underlying cause of all a person's troubles — his sins — was completely healed on Shabbos. *Chazal* say that on Shabbos evening, two ministering angels come and place their hands on a person's head and say to him, "Your iniquity is gone, and your sin is atoned for." But it takes time until the healing reaches the outer levels. If a person believes he is now healthy, he would surely try to keep a safe distance from the cause of the illness: his sins.

We could explain it another way: On Shabbos, a person receives a check. This check is full of *kedushah* and *taharah*. But everyone knows that a check must be cashed or deposited. If you don't do anything with it, a check is worthless. A person who understands the value of the "check" he received on Shabbos will cash in on it and apply its value to his practical deeds and everyday life. A wise person will utilize its inner light in all that he does.

Let us hurry to cash our check, before it's too late to use it! May Hashem help us hold onto the tremendous spiritual assets we gain through *Shabbos Kodesh*.

השבת – יחוד עם השי"ת

19

The Love Relationship of Shabbos Requires Privacy

The Basis of a Successful Relationship

SHLOMO HAMELECH DESCRIBES THE great love between Hashem and His people:

> Great waters cannot extinguish the love, and rivers cannot wash it away. If a person would give all the wealth of his home for love, he would be despised.[1]

When we're together with Hashem, it sparks a powerful love. We become inseparably bound up with Him.

Judaism is like a marital relationship. The giving of the Torah was like the marriage ceremony between us and Hashem. That's why on Shavuos the Sefardim recite a *piyut* called *Ketubah*. It resembles reading the *kesubah* contract between Hashem and the Jewish people. All this being so, let us consider for a moment the basis of the relationship between husband and wife, which will also shed light on the love relationship between us and Hashem.

We say in the Shema twice a day: "ואהבת את ה' אלקיך – *You shall love the Eternal, your God,*" which is the mitzvah to love

1. *Shir HaShirim* 8:7.

Hashem. However, this is actually the second message of the Shema. The first message is: "שמע ישראל... ה' אחד — *Listen, Yisrael!... Hashem is the One and Only!*"

The basis of a viable relationship is that each looks at the other as his one and only. There is no one else. When they relate to one another like this, and all others are excluded, love will develop.

When a *chasan* marries his *kallah,* he says to her: "הרי את מקודשת לי כדת משה וישראל — You are betrothed (מקודשת) to me, according to the law of Moshe and Yisrael." The word "betrothed" is not an accurate translation; מקודשת really expresses a "prohibition" or "limitation." It means the *kallah* is now forbidden to all other men and belongs exclusively to her *chasan.*

If she is his alone, then their relationship is properly founded, and they will attain love as time goes on. The problems begin when one of the spouses starts glancing to the side. That is the beginning of the end.

The same applies to our relationship with Hashem. Even though we might be "ugly," if we are alone with Hashem, we will have a "happy marriage," so to speak. But the moment we bring other interests and points of view into our lives, our relationship is at risk.

Let's pose a question: What can we do to make sure Hashem will hold onto us no matter what and never cast us away? How much Torah must we learn, how many tears must we shed over our siddur, in order to know that we're firmly connected to Hashem?

The truth is that such a question is missing the point. If Hashem came to our home and saw only a Gemara and a siddur, it wouldn't matter so much whether they were open or closed. The main thing would be that these were the only books there, without books of another nature lying around. This way we'd show Hashem that we haven't partitioned our lives into "Hashem's area" and "other areas." We haven't divided our interest and involvement. This is the only guarantee of a lasting relationship!

If we want to establish our relationship with Hashem, a wonderful way to do so is to disconnect ourselves from the newspapers, magazines, and other forms of media. True, simply disconnecting ourselves will not automatically turn us into *gedolim*. A person cannot attain *gadlus* just by turning off the radio, ignoring the newspaper, and not looking at magazines. But doing so does make a person devoted to Hashem. He becomes *mekudash* to Hashem — and in turn, Hashem will shower upon him *gadlus* and intimacy with Him.

If we just say the word אחד, we'll be filled with love of Hashem — ואהבת את ה' אלקיך.

Wedding Customs

This idea is reflected in a certain wedding custom. There are all sorts of interesting Jewish wedding customs, some of which are not practiced today. Once it was customary on the wedding day to lead the bride throughout the town in a carriage. At first glance, this seems to be against *tzeniyus*, but in fact it was the *minhag* of very righteous people. What was the idea behind this *minhag*?

Tomorrow, this woman will be within the confines of her home. As befitting a proper Jewish wife, she will not show herself outside anymore as she did before. But if she married in secrecy, then tomorrow, if a fight broke out between the newly married couple, she could go out and walk around outside just as before, without any concern. No one would know she'd gotten married! But now that everyone saw her riding in the carriage as a bride, if she left her husband, she would be too embarrassed to show her face in public.

This is why people hold large, festive weddings. Under the *chuppah*, the bride obligates herself to belong exclusively to the groom. And we wish to publicize this, as this is what safeguards the *kedushah* of the Jewish people.

This applies to our relationship with Hashem as well. If we set up a situation that preserves our love of Hashem — for instance, we say, "*Ribbono shel Olam,* for the next thirty days I will not allow any newspapers or magazines into my home. I will belong to You alone" — Hashem will bring an unbelievable amount of *kedushah* into our hearts.

If we live a life of *echad,* we will attain the state of "*Like a suckling child at his mother's side.*"[2] The main thing is not to save even a little corner of our heart for something other than HaKadosh Baruch Hu.

Eretz Yisrael– A Yichud Room

Among the Torah's 613 mitzvos is the prohibition of allowing a Gentile idolater to dwell in our land. Rambam writes:

> When the Jewish people have sovereignty, we mustn't allow Gentile idolaters to be among us. Even if he is a temporary resident, or traveling for business purposes, [a Gentile idolater] may not pass through our land, unless he accepts upon himself the seven Noahide laws. As it says (*Shemos* 23:33), "*They shall not dwell in your land.*" This includes dwelling even temporarily.[3]

Let's imagine the following scene: In the time of Shlomo HaMelech, a Gentile from Italy arrives at Jaffa Port. The guards ask him, "What are you doing here?" He pulls out his Italian passport and says, "I'm a tourist. I want to go through Israel and get to Babylon."

Rambam rules that if they let him in, they transgress a negative Torah mitzvah. Why such ethnocentrism? Why should he need a special "visa" just to pass through the country?

The following allegory provides the answer. A just-married

2. *Tehillim* 131:2.
3. *Mishneh Torah, Hilchos Akum* 10:6.

chasan and *kallah* step down from the *chuppah,* enter the *yichud* room, and sit together at the table. Suddenly they hear a knock on the door. They open it a little and ask the fellow standing there, "What do you need?"

"I just want to pass through the room in order to get to the balcony," he says.

"No," they say firmly. "You have to go around."

Eretz Yisrael is like the *yichud* room for Hashem and His people. *Klal Yisrael* dwelled in Eretz Yisrael, the location of the Beis HaMikdash, and they lived there with Hashem, with His *kedushah.* It was an indescribable personal relationship with God. That's why a Gentile idolater was not allowed to pass through even for a moment.

But as time went on, what did the Israelites do? They "modernized." Why live just with Hashem? They brought all sorts of Gentile things into the "*yichud* room" and thereby destroyed their relationship with Hashem. As they brought other things into the room, they themselves were eventually thrown out, into a bitter exile.

Even nowadays, after two thousand years of exile, we must know and remember what Judaism was like in its original form: living in a *yichud* room with HaKadosh Baruch Hu.

Shabbos Needs Privacy

The above-mentioned halachah about not allowing a Gentile idolater to walk through our "*yichud* room" applies even more when it comes to Shabbos. As we mentioned above, in the name of the Rambam, a non-Jew is allowed to observe most of the mitzvos and will even receive a certain amount of spiritual reward for doing so.

But he may not keep Shabbos. It says that a non-Jew who keeps Shabbos is liable for the death penalty (although, as Rambam says, this punishment was not meted out by

Sanhedrin).[4] Why is Shabbos off limits for non-Jews? The Midrash[5] explains that Shabbos is compared to a king and queen who are sitting down together. Whoever passes between them and disturbs them is deserving of punishment. On Shabbos, Hashem wishes to spend time alone with His beloved people Yisrael. He doesn't want the privacy to be disturbed.

The greatness of Shabbos requires privacy. A non-Jew may not enter Shabbos! Thus we say in the Shabbos morning prayers: "ולא נתתו ה' אלוקינו לגויי הארצות, ולא הנחלתו מלכנו לעובדי פסילים, וגם במנוחתו לא ישכנו ערלים, כי לישראל עמך נתתו באהבה — You did not give it, Hashem our God, to the nations of the world, nor did You, our King, give it as an inheritance to the idol worshippers; it is not the uncircumcised that dwell in its rest, but it is Yisrael, Your people, that You gave it in love." Shabbos is not for them. It's only for us — with love.

Shabbos is love. Shabbos is a kiss. Shabbos is the relationship between a Jew and Hashem. And this type of "face to face" relationship requires privacy, for love cannot be expressed in the outside world.

That is why as soon as Hashem brought us out of Egypt and took us to be His people, he announced to us: "*I will bring you up... to a land flowing with milk and honey.*"[6] It's like a *chasan* and *kallah*: Even before standing under the *chuppah*, they discuss where they'll live afterward.

Why do they need their own place to live? There are plenty of parks with benches where they can sit together and talk to their hearts' content! The answer is that the *chasan* and *kallah* need privacy, so before the *chuppah* they have to choose a place to live.

4. *Sanhedrin* 58b.
5. *Yalkut Shimoni, Ki Sisa* 391.
6. *Shemos* 3:17.

Similarly, Hashem said to us: "After the *chuppah* of Mount Sinai, I will bring you to Eretz Yisrael, to the Beis HaMikdash, and there we will live together. There, I will shower My love upon you."

Sometimes people who are ignorant of Torah and mitzvos look at Shabbos as if it were a "prison." By the same token, the *Shemoneh Esreh* is also a prison. It's like wearing a ball and chain: You can't even move your feet! You're "locked in" with Hashem.

If Shabbos is a prison, then it's a prison like the *yichud* room. The *kallah*, too, cannot escape from the *yichud* room. Of course, she can open the door and walk out if she wants. But if she wants to stay—if she wants it to be *yichud*—then she is as if locked in. That is the nature of *yichud*: the door is locked, and no one goes in or out.

Shabbos is a *yichud* room—it is just us and Hashem. We even ask the angels to leave the room, saying to them: *"Tzeis'chem l'shalom, malachei ha-shalom."* This is because *Shabbos Kodesh* requires privacy with Hashem.

"All Your Work Is Done"

This privacy we enjoy with Hashem on Shabbos calls for a different approach to our practical matters: "Keep Shabbos as if all your work were done."[7] On Shabbos, we don't think about business.

Imagine a *chasan* entering the *yichud* room, and as soon as he sits down, he lets out a sigh and says, "Oy, who will pay for this wedding?"

The *kallah* says, "Not now. When the time comes, we'll worry about it, but not now."

This is what Shabbos is: a time of privacy. On *Shabbos Kodesh*

7. *Yalkut Shimoni, Yisro* 296.

we sit down together with Hashem. We eat at the same table and enjoy His meal. We speak *divrei Torah,* because *divrei Torah* means speaking with Hashem.

And what else do we do? Nothing. We just remember that this is Hashem's day. On Shabbos we hardly have the opportunity to do any mitzvos. Even tefillin, such a beautiful mitzvah — where we "bind ourselves" to *Shema Yisrael,* which is written inside — cannot be fulfilled on Shabbos. Neither may we tie tzitzis to our garment or write a mezuzah for our doorpost.

To engage in mitzvos as usual would be like a *chasan* and *kallah* who are sitting together in the *yichud* room, and the *kallah* picks up a broom and starts sweeping. The *chasan* says, "That's very nice of you, but this is not the right place and time. Now, let's just sit together."

On Shabbos there are no mitzvos. We just dine with Hashem, dress nicely in His honor, and understand that our relationship with Him is real and live.

A Miniature Mikdash

Hashem says, *"I will be for them a miniature Mikdash in the lands to which they have come."*[8] Just as there was once a great Beis HaMikdash in Eretz Yisrael, Hashem says He will make a "mini-*Mikdash*" for us in *galus*. It will be like the Beis HaMikdash, only smaller.

The great Beis HaMikdash really refers to the entirety of Eretz Yisrael, in which *Klal Yisrael* lived in seclusion with Hashem, thanks to the *kedushah* brought down by the Mikdash. The "mini-*Mikdash*" refers to the *batei knesses* and *batei midrash.* In shul and in the *beis midrash* as well, we are meant to live in privacy with Hashem.

Let's say we ask a Jew: "Tell me, are you a newspaper reader?" He answers, "No." We ask further: "But do you get the

8. *Yechezkel* 11:16.

newspaper at home?" He says, "Well, yes." Then we ask: "Why do you get the newspaper, if you're not really a newspaper reader?" He replies, "Just to know the news, that's all."

Then we ask him: "Tell me, do you go to the *beis midrash*?" He answers, "Yes, of course." We ask: "Is there a newspaper there?" He says, "No, there isn't." We respond: "Why don't they have a newspaper there just so people would know the news?"

The answer is simple: The *beis midrash* is a Beis HaMikdash. It's a *yichud* room. In the *yichud* room, there's just Hashem and the Jew. No one else may walk in, even if he has a reason.

Today we are in *galus*. Although we live in a Jewish society, it's not Judaism in its true form. That's why we are given moments when we can return to our former state: We enter the shul, or *Shabbos Kodesh* arrives. These are times when we don't go to work or do anything else; we just live with Hashem.

The Ramifications of Privacy

After their wedding, the *chasan* and *kallah* do not begin routine life. For instance, the husband doesn't leave the next day for *kollel* or work. They have a full week of *sheva berachos*, during which they're together the whole time.

On Shabbos as well, we need to create this intimacy.

That's why we have a halachah on Shabbos not to speak as we do during the week. We don't sit around and talk about nonsense, since we're with Hashem all the time. We eat with Him, drink with Him, and sleep with Him. We're in Hashem's house! This is the simple reality of *Shabbos Kodesh*.

The first step in feeling the *kedushah* of Shabbos is to remove all the extraneous elements, all those things that aren't really forbidden, only "pareve." My grandfather, *zt"l*, used to say, "Pareve is *treif*!" He was referring to something else, but the expression is appropriate to our topic as well. Sitting on the couch, reading about meaningless things such as what happened in India—is *treif*. It introduces another element in the home besides Hashem, and as a result we won't have the "kiss" of Shabbos.

Shabbos is a matter of being alone. Hashem comes to our home in order to enjoy being with us. Sometimes this isn't easy — for instance, on a long, summer afternoon, when there's nothing to do. But if a person gives Hashem this "kiss" and puts aside his ordinary approach to life during these hours, he will immediately receive a kiss in return. He will feel the *kedushah* of Shabbos, the *mei'ein Olam HaBa* of Shabbos.

Someone once asked me: "What's so terrible about reading a newspaper on Shabbos? For me, it's *oneg Shabbos*!"

I said to him: "Imagine you have guests for Shabbos, such as your parents or brothers. Everyone is sitting around the table, and you pull out a newspaper and read..."

One of the most moving moments of the year is on Yom Kippur when the *chazan* recites the *avodas Kohen Gadol* and recounts how in the Beis HaMikdash the *Kohanim* used to utter Hashem's ineffable Name and bless the people: "And the *Kohanim* and the people...when they heard the Name...would bend their knees, bow, avow, and cast themselves down...." At this point, everyone prostrates himself on the ground. It used to be customary in many shuls to hand out old newspapers to spread on the floor for the prostrations. Once I was davening in a certain shul and I noticed, while everyone was caught up in the prayer's great fervor, how someone was bending down and reading the newspaper lying on the floor!

If I had asked him, "What are you doing?" he surely would have answered, "What did I do wrong? The article had nothing forbidden in it!"

True. But now, on Yom Kippur? Is this the time?

So it is on *Shabbos Kodesh*. This is not the right time to read newspapers! On Shabbos the whole world ceases to exist, and we are in the Beis HaMikdash, sitting in the company of Hashem, at His table: זה השולחן אשר לפני ה'.

״הקב״ה, אין רשות אחרת עמו״

20

What Is a Melachah?

Beginning at the End

MASECHES SHABBOS SEEMS TO start backward. The first Mishnah discusses the *melachah* of *hotza'ah,* "carrying." This *melachah* entails transferring an object from one domain to another.

Why does it start with this? As Tosafos point out, the tractate dealing with Shabbos should really follow the order of Shabbos itself. It should begin with the halachos of *erev Shabbos,* proceed to the halachos of the onset of Shabbos, and then discuss the thirty-nine *melachos* — the very *last* of which is *hotza'ah.*

Tosafos offer several answers to this question, and the following Midrash points to an additional approach.

> The wicked Turnus Rufus challenged R' Akiva: "If Hashem honors Shabbos as you say, He shouldn't make the wind blow on Shabbos, nor should He make it rain or make plants grow."
>
> R' Akiva answered him: "I will explain it by way of a parable. If the homes of two people share a courtyard, and one of them fails to participate in the *eruv,* neither may carry in the courtyard. But if only one person's home opens to the courtyard, he is permitted to carry throughout the courtyard.
>
> "And so it is with Hashem. For Him there is no other domain,

since the whole world is His! Thus, He is 'permitted' throughout the world."[1]

What was the debate all about? Turnus Rufus asked R' Akiva how Hashem can do *melachah* on Shabbos. Hashem moves things from place to place by means of the wind, He brings down the rain, and He makes the plants grow.

R' Akiva answered that for Hashem, the entire world is one private domain, since everything is His. Hashem may move things around freely, as a man would do within his own courtyard.

Does this answer the question? Apparently not. It indeed explains why Hashem moves things from place to place by means of the wind, but Turnus Rufus asked a more general question, involving additional *melachos*. For instance, he asked about making plants grow — this is the *melachah* of *zore'a*. What did R' Akiva answer him about that?

He answered him that the *melachah* of *hotza'ah* expresses the nature of all thirty-nine *melachos*, as we shall explain.

Refraining from *melachah* means desisting from a certain type of act. On the seventh day of Creation, Hashem desisted from any act connected to this world, and instead He seated Himself on His Heavenly Throne of Glory, as we say in Shabbos morning prayers: "ביום השביעי התעלה וישב על כסא כבודו — Who on the seventh day ascended to sit upon the Throne of His Glory." Similarly, our refraining from *melachah* on Shabbos means that we desist from any act connected to this world.

But what type of *melachah* is actually forbidden on Shabbos? Only *meleches machsheves* — a creative *melachah*. The Torah did not forbid us to work. By Torah law, one may carry heavy burdens around his yard on Shabbos. Only creative acts are forbidden. Why?

1. *Bereishis Rabbah* 11:5.

When a person creates something, he ventures out of his limited framework. He goes beyond his boundaries and builds something new. This is the nature of the thirty-nine *melachos* forbidden on Shabbos.

And this was R' Akiva's answer to Turnus Rufus: When a person carries an object within his own domain, he's not creating anything. Only when the object has been transferred in a significant way has something new taken place. So it is with the entire world, as far as Hashem is concerned: The things Hashem does in His already created world are not creative acts. They're not *meleches machsheves,* so they don't contradict the halachos of Shabbos. They're like carrying within a private courtyard.

Thus, the *melachah* of *hotza'ah* reveals the nature of all the *melachos*. That's why *Maseches Shabbos* begins with it.

"Torah Scholars Have No Rest"

The entire world—with its rain, dew, and wealth, etc.—is Hashem's private courtyard. Nevertheless, there is a concept of separate domains even for Hashem:

> Said R' Chiya bar Ashi, said Rav: "*Talmidei chachamim* have no rest either in this world or in the World to Come, as it says (*Tehillim* 84:8), '*They will go from strength to strength…*'"[2]

What is *menuchah,* rest? We find this concept mentioned in connection with Shabbos as well. There, as explained, it means staying within one's domain, creating nothing new.

But it says that *talmidei chachamim* have no *menuchah*—rather than staying within their limits, they change domain. They go from one reality to another, both in this world and in the next. As Rashi comments on the Gemara cited above: "They have no

2. *Berachos* 64a.

menuchah; rather, they go from yeshivah to yeshivah and from Midrash to Midrash."

What does it mean to "go from yeshivah to yeshivah"? It doesn't mean they gain more understanding in Torah, or more joy. It means they go "from strength to strength." This conveys a totally different awareness, a whole new outlook and comprehension, an entry into a new domain.

We can understand this idea by means of the Vilna Gaon's comment on the well-known verse, "*Az yimalei sechok pinu — Then will our mouth be filled with laughter*."[3] The Gaon explains the difference between *sechok* (laughter) and *simchah* (joy): *Sechok* connotes the outburst of joy a person feels when something good happens to him, whereas *simchah* connotes the stable happiness he experiences afterward. For instance, let's say a person wins ten million dollars in a lottery. First he experiences *sechok* over the new thing that has taken place. Later, living as a wealthy man, he has only *simchah*.

Says the Gaon: "*Az yimalei sechok pinu*" teaches us that in the future, we will experience constant *sechok* due to the never-ending changes that will constantly be occuring.

This is the meaning of "*Talmidei chachamim* have no rest": The entire physical world, with all its riches, is but one courtyard of Hashem. By contrast, a Jew who learns Torah can ascend from domain to domain. And even in the World to Come, there is another domain and yet another. How many domains are there?

The above Gemara continues:

> Said R' Elazar, in the name of R' Chanina: "*Talmidei chachamim* increase *peace* in the world, as it says, 'All your children are learned of Hashem, and the *peace* of your children is great' (*Yeshayahu* 54:13). Read it not as בניך ("your children")

3. *Tehillim* 126:2.

but as בּוֹנָיִךְ ("your builders"). 'Great *peace* to those who love Your Torah; they shall not stumble' (*Tehillim* 119:165). 'May there be *peace* in your vicinity and *tranquility* in your palace. For the sake of my brothers and friends, I will now speak *peace* regarding you. For the sake of the House of Hashem, our God, I will seek good for you' (*Tehillim* 122:7–8). 'May Hashem give strength to His people; may Hashem bless His people with *peace*' (*Tehillim* 29:11)."

The Gaon points out that the word "peace" (and its synonym "tranquility") is mentioned seven times, corresponding to the seven *reki'im,* the seven levels of Heaven. "*Talmidei chachamim* have no rest either in this world or in the World to Come," for they ascend from Heavenly level to Heavenly level, from perfection to perfection, until reaching Hashem's Throne of Glory.

On Shabbos, it is forbidden to transfer an object from one domain to another. But one may himself ascend from one domain to the next. In fact, "Shabbos and Yom Tov were given only in order to be spent engaged in Torah study,"[4] to ascend from level to level by means of Torah and prayer on this holy day.

4. *Yerushalmi, Shabbos* 15:3.

"וביום השביעי שבת וינפש"

21

How Shabbos Revolutionizes Our Lives

What It Means to Stop

It once happened that everything simply stopped:

> When Hashem gave the Torah, no bird squawked. No winged creature flew. No cow mooed. The *ofanim* didn't soar. The *seraphim* didn't say, *"Kadosh kadosh...."* The sea didn't sway. People didn't speak. Rather, the world was completely silent, and a voice rang out: *"I am Hashem, your God...."*[1]

It sounds like the Midrash is saying that when Hashem gave the Torah everything had to be quiet in order that He could say, "I am Hashem, your God...." It seems as if silence was required so Hashem's voice could be heard.

But the truth is the exact opposite. Hashem's message is always loud and clear. His presence fills and dominates the world. But we're so preoccupied that we don't even notice what's in front of our eyes. This is why we don't see Hashem!

This may be compared to a great and wonderful king who invites one of his subjects to meet with him in the royal palace.

1. *Shemos Rabbah* 29:9.

The subject has never been there before. There are many other people in the palace as well, all serving the king. There are musicians, sages, advisers, etc.

The subject arrives and enters the palace. The first thing he hears is beautiful music playing on one side of the hall. He stops there to listen for a moment. He hardly manages to pull himself away from the enchanting music when he sees a great sage on the other side of the hall, expounding amazing words of wisdom. He is riveted by the lecture. And then he notices the magnificent works of art hanging on the walls...

The subject gets so involved with what's going on all around him that he doesn't even notice the king, who's sitting there in the middle of the hall, waiting for him. The visitor could spend hours taking in all the beauty of the palace and never even gaze upon the glorious countenance of the king himself. But the king is fond of this man and wants to converse with him. What does the king do? He announces, "Silence, everyone! Stop what you're doing and go home." Suddenly everything is quiet, and the overwhelming beauty and glory of the king fill the palace.

"The whole earth is full of His glory"[2] — Hashem's overwhelming beauty always fills the earth, from one end to the other. But the world is such a fascinating place. People go to and fro and instead of noticing Hashem's greatness, they're drawn in by the beauty of all the things they see, by physical pleasures, etc.

Hashem's world deters us from noticing Him. If a person walks into a flower shop, before he recognizes Hashem through the greatness and beauty of His works, he gets so involved with the beauty of the flowers themselves that he forgets about Hashem. We live in a wonderful world of skies, oceans, great mountains and forests. Hashem's magnificent world was created so we would point to it and say, "This is absolutely

2. *Yeshayahu* 6:3.

astounding. Who created all this?"

It is like the king in the above allegory. His orchestra played beautiful music for him, all in his honor, but visitors to his palace became so enthralled by the music, they forgot the king was even there.

For this reason, when Hashem wanted to talk to us and give us the Torah, He brought the whole world to a halt. Everything was silent. Then the great Voice issued forth: *"I am Hashem, your God!"*

This is *Shabbos Kodesh* — a day of absolute cessation. All the bustle and confusion of the world stops. While on weekdays a person runs around attending to his physical needs, on Shabbos everything stops and is silent.

When everything ceases, when "everyone goes home," what's left? Hashem. This is Shabbos: the day when the Jewish people are alone with Hashem — there is nothing besides Him.

That's why we were given Shabbos: so we would have a day on which to find HaKadosh Baruch Hu.

Shabbos Is Like a Seminar

"On the seventh day, He rested and was refreshed."[3] The experience of cessation on Shabbos is like going away to a special retreat, a "seminar," which revolutionizes a person's life. First let us take a look at what a seminar is all about.

Our generation has been blessed with an amazing thing. In previous times it took a spiritual giant the likes of R' Aharon Karliner or R' Levi Yitzchak of Berditchev to turn a wayward Jew into a *ba'al teshuvah*. Very few became *ba'alei teshuvah* in those days.

In our generation, as we all know, there are a lot of *ba'alei teshuvah*. Jews have come back to Torah Judaism from the farthest

3. *Shemos* 31:17.

places imaginable. I remember that when this phenomenon began certain people simply didn't believe it was for real. They didn't think these fresh returnees to *Yiddishkeit* would stick with it. But the returnees now have children and grandchildren following the Torah path, learning in *yeshivos* along with the others. It is now evident to all that even someone who is deeply sunken in the impurity of secular society can turn around and become a good, *frum* Jew.

Since many people have never actually attended a *kiruv* seminar, I will describe it briefly. The organizers take completely non-religious people, who lead a solidly secular lifestyle, and put them up in a hotel for a few days. They bring in talented speakers who speak on topics of interest. As the days go by, the people attending the seminar begin to change. You see tears in their eyes. They start donning yarmulkes and covering their hair, and they go on to become complete *ba'alei teshuvah*. They don't make do with just laying tefillin once a day or ceremoniously lighting Shabbos candles — they start observing even the most demanding aspects of halachah.

The *teshuvah* revolution came about largely by means of these "seminars." Then some wise people realized the "seminar" technique also suited a different type of audience: full-fledged Torah Jews and men learning in yeshivah or kollel. Great numbers of such Jews from many countries have since participated in such seminars, returning home changed people.

Let us consider how this technique worked in its original form.

A totally non-religious Jew walks in. He doesn't know what Shabbos is, what tefillin are, or anything. Where do you even start? The task of turning him into a *ba'al teshuvah* seems akin to climbing a towering mountain. And you can't sit down with him and explain all about Torah, because it won't work. Judaism is not acquired through careful explanations about how to daven, how to learn Torah, and how to observe the many different laws.

And a revolution doesn't happen by itself. You have to open his heart, and *Chazal* say only one thing can open the heart of a Jew: *"I created the yetzer ha-ra, and I created the Torah as its cure."*[4]

The nature of Torah is that when you take a Jew and learn Torah with him—*"'Behold, My words are like fire,' says Hashem, 'and like a hammer that shatters a rock.'"*[5] The words of Torah break through the *yetzer ha-ra* and reach the heart. But how do you take a Jew and sit him down to learn Torah? How do you get him to feel that he and Torah have something in common? If you offer to bring him to the *beis midrash,* he won't agree.

That's why seminars for the non-religious are composed of topics involving a special combination: they're relevant and fascinating, and they're connected to Torah and *Yiddishkeit*. This is the trick of how to get these non-religious Jews to absorb Torah over several days. And the nature of Torah is that it sparks a revolution in a Jew's heart.

In truth, this "technique" is already mentioned in the Torah: *"Three times a year, all your males shall appear before the Master, Hashem."*[6] In ancient times, all Jews would ascend to Yerushalayim for the *Shalosh Regalim,* the "pilgrimage festivals," and gather in the Beis HaMikdash, Hashem's house. There they saw the *Kohanim* performing the service, the *Leviyim* singing, and the *Yisraelim* standing by as representatives of the entire Jewish people.

The *regel* was a whole week of living in a spiritual world—a "seminar!" Indeed, this week revolutionized their lives. They went home transformed into completely different people.

This is one goal of *Shabbos Kodesh* as well. *Chazal* say:

4. *Kiddushin* 30b.
5. *Yirmeyahu* 23:29.
6. *Shemos* 34:23.

"Shabbos and Yom Tov were given to Yisrael so [its people] would engage in Torah study on them."[7] During the week, people are occupied with their business, with their various occupations, whatever they may be. On Shabbos, Hashem says to us, so to speak: "Today everything stops. Today we're having a 'seminar,' a day devoted to Torah!" This day is capable of revolutionizing our lives. It can make us into higher and more uplifted Jews on a totally different level.

7. *Yerushalmi, Shabbos* 15:3.

Nefesh Shimshon

Inspirational Essays

Rav Pincus originally wrote these articles (in 1989–1991) for *HaMa'ayan*, a magazine published by Be'er Yitzchak, a boys' elementary school in Be'er Sheva.

שנים מקרא ואחד תרגום

1

Shnayim Mikra V'Echad Targum

EVERY YEAR ON SIMCHAS TORAH we start reading again from the beginning of the Torah, from the very beginning of *Bereishis*. It's so exhilarating and exciting to start anew! When we read *"Bereishis bara Elokim,"* it feels as if the heavens and earth were just created. It's like the wonderful feeling of going out at sunrise: Everything is glowing and fresh, a delightful breeze is blowing, the birds are singing in full chorus, and your soul is singing along with them. It is surely an experience to begin the Torah anew from *"Bereishis bara."*

However, as we know, nothing of lasting value comes from momentary excitement alone. The key is:

> A person should always complete his *parashah* with the community, [reading] *mikra* twice and *targum* once.... Anyone who completes his *parashah* with the community will have his days and years lengthened.[1]

There is no better time than now to strengthen ourselves in reading *shnayim mikra v'echad targum* each week. The Ari *z"l* would finish the *parashah* on *erev Shabbos* and afterward immerse in a mikveh, because the combination of the two enables

1. *Berachos* 8a.

a person to fully receive *kedushas Shabbos*. At least one should try to finish before the Shabbos day meal.

And when you go through the *parashah*, it shouldn't be a mere recital. You should take a moment to understand the words. Imagine you've never seen these words before. You're now reading "*Bereishis bara Elokim*" for the very first time. It's awesome: The great heavens, with millions and billions of stars, each many times bigger than the whole world — Hashem created all of this!

The same applies to the stories of Adam HaRishon, Noach, and Avraham Avinu. When we relate to them as if the Torah were given just today, as the Shema tells us to do — "And these words which I command you *today* shall be upon your heart" — we find them sweet and inspiring.

The intense celebration that surrounds the starting of the Torah anew is akin to a wedding. Just as by a wedding, on Simchas Torah we sing and dance for hours. And just as a wedding celebration is the culmination of all the preparations, the Simchas Torah celebration is the culmination of all the preceding Yomim Nora'im.

But let us take the comparison a step further: The real purpose of a wedding celebration is that the bride and groom should live their lives together from now on. Similarly, the real purpose of the Simchas Torah celebration is that we should live our lives together with the Torah throughout the coming year. *Bereishis bara* is just the beginning...

"זכור ושמור" – ביראה ואהבה

2

Uniting Fear and Love of Hashem

We read the *Aseres Hadibros* in *parashas Yisro* and again in *parashas Va'eschanan*. There are a few differences between the two. Probably the most famous is that the first time, it says, "*Zachor es yom haShabbos*," whereas the second time, it says, "*Shamor es yom haShabbos*." As we know, Hashem performed a great miracle by speaking these two different words simultaneously.[1] But what message did Hashem teach us through this feat?

Here lies the proper approach not just to Shabbos but to all the mitzvos. *Zachor* includes all the positive mitzvos we must remember to keep. *Shamor* includes all the negative mitzvos we must guard ourselves from transgressing.

Usually, keeping positive mitzvos stems from love of Hashem. If a person loves Hashem and delights in fulfilling His will, then he will certainly put a lot of energy into positive mitzvos such as learning Torah, davening, Shabbos, etc. Keeping negative mitzvos, on the other hand, usually stems from fear of Hashem. If a person fears Hashem and the severe punishments for sin, then he exerts himself not to transgress negative mitzvos such as theft, unfair business practices,

1. *Rosh Hashanah* 27a.

Shabbos desecration, *lashon ha-ra,* etc.

Ordinarily, love and fear stand in complete contradiction to one another. I can't love someone if I'm afraid of him. And I can't fear someone I love. Fear makes me pull back and keep my distance, whereas love draws me close. These are polar opposites, going in reverse directions.

But *avodas Hashem* is different. When a person fears Hashem, this feeling itself is the greatest pleasure, causing him to love and draw close. Thus, fear of Hashem doesn't distance us — on the contrary, it brings us close. As R' Shlomo ibn Gevirol expressed it in his well-known *piyut* entitled *Keser Malchus*: "I will flee from You — to You." When a person flees out of terror of Hashem, to where does he escape? To Hashem! He draws close to Hashem and increases his love for Him.

The same is true when it comes to love of Hashem. The closer a person draws to Hashem and the more love he has, the more fear of Hashem this generates, until the love and fear unify. The negative mitzvos become beloved, and the positive mitzvos become awesome. Everything is one.

Some people think that fear of punishment and extreme concern about what's forbidden make a person nervous and unhappy. But the opposite is true, for exercising care and caution in Torah matters is actually the greatest pleasure. The more careful a person is about keeping the commandments and not violating the Torah, the more pleasure he has in life! This is tried and true. Sometimes even serious *b'nei Torah* are misguided in this area and are afraid to dedicate themselves too much to davening and Torah learning. But in truth, the closer a person draws to Hashem, the more beautiful and pleasant his life will be.

And that is why *Zachor* and *Shamor* were said simultaneously: In a Jew's heart, love and fear of Hashem should be completely unified!

זהירות מכעס

3

Harmony on Shabbos

It says about Shabbos: *"You shall not kindle a fire in all your dwelling places on the Shabbos day."*[1] *Chazal* tell us that "kindling a fire on Shabbos" also alludes to the fire of anger.[2] In other words, there is a special prohibition about getting angry on Shabbos.·

In truth, anger is forbidden at all times. *Chazal* spoke against it very strongly, comparing it to idolatry[3] and saying that someone prone to anger will suffer in the end from all types of Gehinnom.[4] Anger causes more damage than all the evils in the world. This is because when a person gets angry he loses his mental balance and self-control. He acts against his better judgment and is liable to do practically anything bad.

But occasionally a bit of anger is appropriate—for instance, when it's necessary to disapprove of wrongdoing and stand up for the truth. At home as well, it's sometimes necessary to gently arouse one's anger in order to steer family members in the right direction. But even in these situations, it is absolutely forbidden to let anger take hold. Rather, as our Rabbis teach:

1. *Shemos* 35:3.
2. *Tikkunei Zohar, Tikun* 48.
3. See Rambam, *Mishneh Torah, Hilchos Dei'os* 2:3.
4. *Nedarim* 22a.

"Anger should be on one's face and not in one's heart."

This may be compared to someone who lights a fire in order to warm his home. As long as it's under control and moderate, it's useful and positive and doesn't endanger the home.

So what does our verse teach us? That there is a place for anger—but not on Shabbos! On *Shabbos Kodesh*, it is altogether forbidden to kindle the fire of anger. Shabbos and Yom Tov are days of rest and joy, when we shouldn't arouse our anger.

A Jew whose occupation is Torah study resembles *Shabbos Kodesh*. Shabbos is the main fountain of *kedushah* in the world, and similarly, Torah learning is the source of life. It is the world's *neshamah*. So a person who dedicates his life to Torah study should minimize anger, avoiding it even when it seems permitted.

Sometimes an unfortunate incident brings something good in its wake. Often we can learn invaluable lessons from when things go wrong. Let us apply this idea to our topic: In life, there are many situations where a person loses control of himself and suddenly is overcome by anger, against his will. In such cases, this anger should serve as a warning to him, as *Chazal* say:

> Regarding a person who becomes angry, it is known that his sins are greater than his merits, as it says (*Mishlei* 29:22): *"The wrathful person has greater iniquity."*[5]

In other words, anger signals to a person that he's in a "danger zone," in a state of more sins than merits. This situation is dangerous, as Rambam writes:

> Each and every person has merits and sins. Whoever has more merits than sins is righteous, and whoever has more sins than merits is wicked.... If a person has more sins than

5. *Nedarim* 22b.

merits, he immediately dies in his wickedness....[6]

A person cannot determine his state based on his own self-knowledge. Even if he knows he does a lot of mitzvos, Rambam writes:

> The merits and sins are weighed against each other according to the judgment of the God of Knowledge. Only He knows how merits are balanced against sins.[7]

But when a person finds himself angry, he has a clear sign—given by the Torah—that he's in the "danger zone." He's in trouble, and he should do *teshuvah* quickly—not just for the sin of anger, but also for the inordinate number of sins he just discovered he has.

In this way he can save himself, turning the unfortunate incident around and utilizing it for his own good!

6. *Mishneh Torah, Hilchos Teshuvah* 3:1–2.

7. Ibid.

"זכור את יום השבת לקדשו"

4

Shabbos Brims with Kedushah

A JEW IS CAPABLE OF feeling wonderfully *Shabbosdik*. He also is capable of desecrating Shabbos and thereby chasing away its *kedushah*. Without the blessed influence of *kedushas Shabbos*, our Shabbos is emptied of its true content.

We should know that *chillul Shabbos* is not just doing *melachah*. It can also be talking about nonsense on Shabbos. It can be sitting and reading things other than *divrei Torah*. This too is *chillul Shabbos*.

What's wrong with these things if they aren't *melachah*? The problem is that they go against *Zachor es yom haShabbos*. If we forget it's the holy day of Shabbos and occupy ourselves with all sorts of innocuous but mundane matters, the *kedushah* of Shabbos flees from us. To feel *kedushas Shabbos* and attain its blessings, we have to remember Shabbos constantly and keep the mitzvos of the day. If we act in this manner, Shabbos, in turn, will watch over us. All the tremendous *kedushah* and *berachah* of Shabbos will subsequently rest upon us.

The mitzvah of Shabbos is unique in the great benefit we feel from it. *Chazal* say that the shine of a person's face is different on Shabbos than during the week, because on Shabbos a person's face naturally shines with the light of *kedushah*.[1]

1. *Bereishis Rabbah* 11:2.

And early Torah sources mention often that Shabbos is an overflowing *ma'ayan* (fountain) of every form of goodness we may seek.

To our dismay, Shabbos observance is weak nowadays. We go out into the street and see Jews driving cars without any awareness of *hilchos Shabbos*. We should know that just seeing Shabbos desecration harms our souls.

Chazal say a person is subjected to the sight of a sin only if he has sinned himself.[2] And he is rewarded with the sight of a mitzvah if he has merits. Torah sources explain that a person sees only those things to which he has some connection, directly or indirectly. If a person is absolutely unrelated to a certain matter, he won't even see it!

If we kept *Shabbos Kodesh* the way we should, one hundred percent, we wouldn't even see public desecration of Shabbos.

With so much to gain from *Shabbos Kodesh,* it is a pity so few people know how to tap into it. In fact, the way to do so is found in the *Aseres HaDibros*. There it says: *Zachor es yom haShabbos le-kadsho.* What is the message? Remember Shabbos! Keep your mind on it, don't forget about it, and subsequently you'll treat it as you should. This is the key.

Shabbos differs from all other forms of *kedushah,* for only Shabbos has had *kedushah* since the very beginning of Creation. As soon as Shabbos came into existence, "*God blessed the seventh day and sanctified it.*" From the time of Creation, Hashem Himself granted Shabbos its great *kedushah,* and so it remains to this very day.

Shabbos, in its very essence, is brimming with *kedushah* and *berachah.* Shabbos is holy even without our input and effort. To illuminate ourselves with its exalted *kedushah* and attain its blessings, we must remember that it's Shabbos and uphold its mitzvos!

2. Tosefta, *Shevuos* 3:3, quoted in *Ta'am V'Da'as.*

נר דלוק מערב שבת לערב שבת

5

Three Fundamentals in the Jewish Home

WHEN YITZCHAK MARRIED RIVKAH, he found her to resemble his mother, Sarah: "The Shabbos candles burned from one Shabbos to the next, the dough was blessed, and a cloud was positioned over their tent."[1] What is the meaning of all this?

On a simple level, it means that Rivkah was a great *tzadekes* and continued along the path of Sarah Imeinu, so she regularly enjoyed these same three miracles. But on a deeper level, these three things hint at the three foundations of the Jewish home. These things are not exclusively for Sarah and Rivkah—rather, every Jewish woman everywhere should make sure she has them in her home.

The first is the Shabbos candles, kindled for every Shabbos. *Chazal* explain that the reason for this mitzvah is *shalom bayis*. Without light in the home, people are prone to trip and bump, and this unpleasant situation can lead to irritability and friction. By obligating us to have light in the home, the halachah places special emphasis on having peace in the home on *Shabbos Kodesh*.

But in the homes of tzaddikim, the lights burn from one Shabbos to the next. There's *shalom bayis* not just on Shabbos

1. Rashi, *Bereishis* 24:76.

when the family happily gets together and forgets the mundane troubles of the world, but all week, despite the difficulties and challenges that can come up! In the homes of the tzaddikim, Shabbos's light of peace and harmony burns on, illuminating one day after another until the next Shabbos comes.

The second is that the dough was blessed. *Chazal* say[2] that aside from special expenditures such as for Shabbos, Yom Tov, and teaching children Torah, a person's yearly *parnasah* is fixed on Rosh Hashanah. Therefore, one needs a blessing that a small amount of "dough" will suffice for a long time. A person shouldn't spend his money on luxuries, lest debts pile up disturbing the peace of mind required for *avodas Hashem* and destroying the tranquility in the home. A person should limit his spending to what he really needs. This brings happiness to the home, and his "dough" will be blessed.

The third is that a cloud was positioned over the tent. This cloud of *kedushah* alludes to *tzeniyus*. It is as if a cloud were enveloping the home and covering it from sight. This applies in its simple sense, as it is written, *"All the dignity of the king's daughter is found within."*[3] This also includes not publicizing private matters. And a person should make a special effort that the voices in the home not be heard outside.

These three things bring with them great *siyata di'Shemaya*. The lights burning from one Shabbos to the next: May there always be peace and harmony in the home. The blessing of the dough: May there always be plenty of *parnasah*. And the cloud positioned over the tent: May there always be the holiness and purity of *tzeniyus*, and may the *Shechinah* fill the home.

2. *Beitzah* 16a.

3. *Tehillim* 45:14.

"וביום השבת שני כבשים בני שנה תמימים"

6

Double Portions on Shabbos

SHABBOS HAS THE MOST modest *musaf* offering of the Torah: no bulls, no rams, and only two lambs. Why? The Midrash[1] says that Shabbos complained about this to Hashem, and He answered that two lambs are in fact the most appropriate *korban,* since everything about Shabbos is double: Shabbos has a double expression of song: "*A hymn, a song for Shabbos;*"[2] a double expression of *oneg*: "*and you declare Shabbos as a time for delight, and the holy day of the Eternal as honored;*"[3] a double expression of punishment: "*Those who desecrate it must be put to death* (מות יומת)";[4] and a double portion of bread, לחם משנה.[5] Thus it is appropriate that its *korban* also be double — two lambs.

The Midrash then compares it to a king who asked his servants to prepare a meal for his son. They prepared certain foods. Then the king ordered that they prepare a meal for him. The servants asked, "What should we prepare for the king?" He responded, "And what did you prepare for my son?" They said, "Such and such." He replied to them, "Prepare the same

1. Quoted by *Da'as Zekeinim* on *Bemidbar* 28:9.
2. *Tehillim* 92:1.
3. *Yeshayahu* 58:13.
4. *Shemos* 31:14.
5. *Shemos* 16:22.

for me, no more than what you prepared for my son."

From this we learn that the two lambs of the Shabbos offering are actually one lamb for Hashem and one for us. What is the significance of this?

Shabbos is called a *bris olam,* an eternal covenant. This covenant is the relationship between Hashem and the Jewish people. The relationship is so close that Hashem does as we do, so to speak. The above allegory recounts how the king was so fond of his son that he passed up a grand repast so he could be together with him and eat the same food.

This is why everything about Shabbos comes in pairs: one for Hashem and one for us. *Shabbos Kodesh* is like the *Kodesh HaKodashim* of the Beis HaMikdash, where the *keruvim* embraced one another. One *keruv* represented Hashem, and the other, the Jewish people, demonstrating the great love that exists between Hashem and His people. Even nowadays, with the Beis HaMikdash destroyed, this love is seen in *Shabbos Kodesh.*

This is why we must be so careful about Shabbos — not to desecrate it through any forbidden act, not to take our minds off it, and not to occupy ourselves with mundane matters on this day. We are together with Hashem on *Shabbos kodesh,* and we should devote the entire day to matters of Torah and *kedushah.* In this way we will see doubled and redoubled blessings in everything we do!

השראת השכינה בבית

7

Bringing the Shechinah into the Home

THE ISRAELITES WORKED HARD in the *midbar* to build the Mishkan, and when they finished, Moshe Rabbeinu blessed them for their efforts. He said, "May the *Shechinah* rest in the work of your hands; may the pleasantness of Hashem, our God, be upon us...."[1]

Now, let's ask a question: Did the Israelites do Moshe Rabbeinu a great personal favor by building him such a nice Mishkan? Was it even a voluntary act? The Torah emphasizes that the work of building the Mishkan was an obligation: "*Moshe saw all the work, that they did it as Hashem commanded, so did they do it, and Moshe blessed them.*"[2] It is clear that had the Israelites been negligent in the building of the Mishkan, it would have been considered a grievous sin. Nevertheless, after they had done all the work properly, Moshe Rabbeinu smiled upon them. He blessed them fervently that Hashem's pleasantness should be upon them!

The message from this is clear. The wife works to prepare the home nicely. Sometimes this entails great effort—for instance, on *erev Shabbos*, when there's so much to cook and clean and prepare.

1. Rashi, *Shemos* 39:43.
2. *Shemos* 39:43.

Sometimes a husband feels: After all, isn't that her job? Isn't that a woman's role? And then he neglects to smile at her and bless her that the pleasantness of Hashem should rest upon the work of her hands. Let us learn from Moshe Rabbeinu, who blessed the Jewish people for fulfilling their obligations and gave them the greatest and most pleasant blessing of all: that the *Shechinah* should be with them.

When should the wife be blessed and thanked? This, too, we can learn from Moshe Rabbeinu. He blessed the people when they completed the work, as mentioned above, and he blessed them again when he and Aharon actually used the Mishkan and offered *korbanos* there.[3] Thus, a man should express his appreciation to his wife when everything is finished Friday afternoon. And he should thank and bless her again at night, after partaking of the meal.

Indeed, the Jewish home is a miniature Beis HaMikdash. This is surely so on *Shabbos Kodesh,* which is like the Beis HaMikdash in so many ways. It is only appropriate to bless the wife when she prepares the *avodah* of the home and again after we have actually performed the *avodas ha-kodesh* of the Shabbos meal.

This brings Divine protection to the home. *Chazal* say that Moshe Rabbeinu blessed the people as follows: "May it be Hashem's will that the enemy will never touch the work of your hands." [4] And in fact the Mishkan was never captured by the Gentiles — it was hidden in tunnels under the Beis HaMikdash.

Surely, a Jewish home in which the husband smiles abundantly upon his wife and blesses her — and the children, who each contribute in their own way — will merit Heavenly protection.

3. See *Vayikra* 9:23 and Rashi ad loc.

4. *Midrash Aggadah, Shemos* 39:43.

לימוד התורה בימי ששי ושבת

8

Torah Learning on Friday and Shabbos

The following is a letter that was written by Rav Pincus during a time when chillul Shabbos in Eretz Yisrael was becoming more widespread.

BS"D

My dear brethren and friends, members of the *kehillah* of Ofakim, I wish you much *shalom* and *berachah*!

Allow me to speak a few words about a current topic. We live in a topsy-turvy and turbulent generation; in truth we are in a constant state of emergency. Today we see with our own eyes what was always known with perfect emunah: Torah learning has a tremendous power. Only Torah learning can break down the bastioned walls of complacent secularism that has done so much damage to our people. Hashem has sent us to help the thousands of Jews whose lives are utterly lifeless…our Torah has the power to revive the dead, to awaken the slumbering, to quench the thirsty….

At a time like this [when shopping malls in Israel are starting to open their doors on Shabbos], we cannot behave in a cool and collected way, either as individuals or as a community, as we would in a time of peace. This is a time to act and take steps we would otherwise not consider.

The matter is as follows: Now that daylight savings time is here, several things have changed. One of them is that *erev Shabbos,* which is a holy time and has special potential for *kedushah* and Torah learning, has become very long. From the end of Friday morning *kollel* until sunset are more than seven hours, and "a gap in the fence calls out for a thief to come." Five months ago, candle lighting was at 4:00 P.M. *Erev Shabbos* was a full three hours less than it is now, yet we all managed to accept Shabbos on time.

If so, we should hold ourselves accountable for these three hours: where are they going? They are so precious, especially in these unstable times. Is there nothing we can do to save these hours? What are they being utilized for? The same applies to Shabbos afternoon. There are over nine hours from the end of Shacharis until sunset. These are special and wondrous hours when the *kedushah* of Shabbos is in full strength.

Let us note that daylight savings time has brought in its wake a terrible wave of *chillul Shabbos*. We live in a region plagued by war and terrorism. As we know, the nature of things is that every attack from one side draws a counterattack from the other side. If so, what will be our counterattack? Shall we allow the *yetzer ha-ra* to strike us down with complete impunity? Let us all respond by strengthening our Torah learning—specifically on Shabbos! This will illuminate all our surroundings with a great light, to drive out *chillul Shabbos* and bring *kedushah* in its place.

To you, the members of this holy *kehillah*, we can apply the verse from *Mishlei*,[1] "*Many women have done valiantly, but you have surpassed them all.*" You are always the first ones to strengthen matters of *Yiddishkeit*, whether it be *tzedakah*, Torah learning or mending any gap in the fence of *kedushah*. You have always shown tremendous dedication, and the sound of your Torah learning during this past *bein ha-zemanim* pierced the heavens to bring down abundant and great blessing. May its merit grant us the ability to go from

1. 31:29.

strength to strength, to undertake this difficult mission as well. Let us all join together to increase the *hasmadah* of our learning on Friday and Shabbos as befits the friends and colleagues that we are.

Our request is that from now on, anyone who is able should come to learn together on Friday afternoon from 3:30 P.M. until 5:30 P.M. at least, and on Shabbos afternoon from 3:00 P.M. until 5:00 P.M. at least. This is despite the fact that everyone is learning at home anyway. Let us all gather together, either in the *beis midrash* of the yeshivah or in the *Kivisi Hashem* shul. Each person who participates is strengthening others as well.

May we merit great blessing and pure *yir'as Shamayim, nachas* and happiness, and all of Hashem's goodness, forever.

Shimshon Dovid Pincus

NEFESH SHIMSHON

Shabbos with Rav Pincus

Foreword

THIS BOOK, WHICH SPEAKS of the sublime greatness of Shabbos, would not be complete without a description of how *Shabbos Kodesh* was actually lived by Rav Shimshon Dovid Pincus, *zt"l,* himself. Besides providing ample testimony that he lived according to his teachings, there is nothing like true-life stories to inspire us to change and show us how. After all, the purpose of this book is to put its ideas into practice!

The anecdotes and accounts mentioned here are not just to be read with reverence. They are to be emulated, each person according to his own level. They show that the lofty ideas contained in this book are not meant to remain abstract, but should be brought down to earth and become part of the tangible reality of our lives. This is the only way to gain the most from our Shabbos.

These anecdotes and accounts—reported by Rav Pincus's students, congregants, and acquaintances—create a composite picture of an extraordinarily uplifting Shabbos, a day on which a Jew attains great spiritual heights. Yet this modest sampling provides a mere glimmer of the true greatness of Rav Pincus and his ways. With Hashem's help, we plan to publish a more comprehensive biographical work containing much more extensive material.

May Hashem grant that our lives be illuminated by the great light he radiated, and may we merit to follow in his holy ways.

"וְהֵכִינוּ אֵת אֲשֶׁר יָבִיאוּ"

1

Erev Shabbos

Getting Ready

Shabbos preparations were a form of *avodas ha-kodesh* for the Rav. He invested great thought and energy in them and performed even the smallest act of Shabbos preparation with proper *kavanah*. R' Chanina would declare each *erev Shabbos*: "Come, let us go out to greet the Bride, the Queen!"[1] Shabbos preparations lead up to that magnificent moment, and every step of the way the Rav's deeds declared: *Bo'i Kallah, Bo'i Kallah, Shabbos Malkesa!*

Doing It Early

The *Shulchan Aruch*[2] tells us that Shabbos preparations should begin first thing Friday morning. However, the *poskim* explain that one should first daven Shacharis.

Since Shabbos preparations come second only in order (not in importance), the Rav made sure not to push them off any more than absolutely necessary. He wouldn't tolerate delays. True, Shacharis precedes Shabbos preparations—but nothing else should come before them!

Concerned with doing the mitzvah with proper *zerizus*, the

1. *Bava Kamma* 32b.
2. *Siman* 250.

Rav found it difficult to wait until he came home. He settled upon a characteristic solution: When he left the house Friday morning to go daven, he took along the wicks for the Shabbos lights, and right after Shacharis he would spend a few moments preparing them, *lichvod Shabbos Kodesh*. This way he was able to prepare for Shabbos immediately after davening, thereby doing the mitzvah as early as possible.

One of his students similarly recounted that he saw the Rav cleaning and brushing off his hat right after Shacharis, explaining that "I need to start Shabbos preparations right after davening!"

Preparing the wicks in honor of Shabbos was an *avodah* of considerable involvement for him. For it says[3] that whoever is careful about fulfilling the mitzvah of Shabbos lights will have children who are *talmidei chachamim*. And, as he was wont to emphasize, his opinion was that in all areas (including this one) a *segulah* alone is insufficient; it must be accompanied by a heartfelt prayer. He would say, "The *segulah* on its own is not enough, and *zechuyos* on their own are not enough. Without *tefillah*, you're missing the key that opens up Heaven's flow of blessing!"

So while he was preparing the wicks for the Shabbos lights, his lips would whisper a prayer that emanated from the depths of his heart: that he should merit having children who are *talmidei chachamim* and *ovdei Hashem*!

Polishing the Candlesticks

Not only did the Rav prepare the wicks and set up the lights, he even polished the silver candlesticks himself. Every Friday he put time and thought into this activity. He even came up with "*chiddushim*" in this area, as he did in every facet of his *avodas Hashem*.

3. *Shabbos* 23b.

The Rav tried various polishing methods. Whenever he heard of a new and more effective way of polishing the candlesticks, *lichvod Shabbos Kodesh*, joy was written all over his face. He would experiment with various techniques aimed at achieving the maximum gleam from the candlesticks, so they would shine with all their brilliance. For instance, when he heard that boiling water adds to the sheen, he dipped each candlestick in boiling water. On a different occasion, he tried polishing them with liquid soap and toothpaste. Once, when he returned from abroad, he brought back a special silver-polishing solution. Dipping the candlesticks into this solution was purported to produce a perfect gleam. And so forth.

When the children awoke Friday morning, they would see their father bent over the candlesticks, laboriously polishing their intricate designs.

The Rav would explain that in the Beis HaMikdash, besides the actual kindling of the Menorah, there was a special *avodah* of preparing its lights. And so it is with *Shabbos Kodesh*! For *Shabbos Kodesh* is like the Beis HaMikdash (see above, Chapter 7). Consequently, there are two separate tasks to be performed: Preparing the lights and polishing the candlesticks corresponds to the first *avodah* of preparing the Menorah of the Beis HaMikdash. This is the husband's job. Kindling of the lights corresponds to the *avodah* of kindling the Menorah in the Beis HaMikdash. This is the wife's job.

A great light of *gadlus* radiated from the Rav during those moments. He would often say: "A non-*Kohen* was fit to kindle the Menorah in the Beis HaMikdash, whereas only a *Kohen* was fit for the mitzvah of preparing the Menorah. This shows how important the mitzvah of preparing the lights is!"

Shopping Just as Torah learning requires proper preparation from the earliest stages,[4] so it is with Shabbos. If we want to be illuminated by the great light of Shabbos, if we want to truly feel the *mei'ein Olam HaBa* and draw ample amounts of spiritual elevation for the six weekdays to come, we need to prepare accordingly.

During the week, Rav Pincus, rav of Ofakim, had little contact with matters of this world; he barely ate a regular meal. He didn't think about the pleasures of this world, and was totally uninvolved with material pursuits. On Friday, he acted differently. He departed from his normal practice and went to the grocery store to shop for Shabbos. But these were no ordinary purchases. His shopping was a matter of *shleimus,* of *avodas Hashem,* and was imbued with a special atmosphere.

There was a period when he would bring along two young *kollel* men, because he wished to strengthen them in the ways of living with true *emunah*. This entailed teaching them the ways of *kedushas Shabbos,* which is the foundation of *emunah*. He sought to give them proper appreciation of Shabbos and show them the great importance of preparing for it: shopping for Shabbos isn't a material pursuit; it's a lofty, spiritual *avodah*!

One of these men described what it was like to be the Rav's 'shopping *chavrusa*': "We would go with the Rav to the grocery store, and as soon as he entered he would whisper to us excitedly, 'Remember, now the store is all yours! Everything is free; you can take generously, because everything goes on Hashem's bill. *Chazal* said: "All a person's sustenance is allotted to him from Rosh Hashanah to Rosh Hashanah, except for expenses of Shabbos and Yom Tov. For if he spent more, he is given more."[5]

4. See *Bava Metzia* 85b.

5. *Beitzah* 16a.

"'Now, if someone offered to let you shop in this store for free, wouldn't you jump at the opportunity to fill up a few shopping carts? In truth, you have a weekly opportunity to shop for Shabbos on HaKadosh Baruch Hu's bill.'

"You can imagine how we shopped after such an introduction. We bought generously (observing the limitations stated in *Shulchan Aruch, Orach Chayim* 242:1). Together with the fish, delicacies, and sweets for the children, we acquired for ourselves a whole new world: life with *emunah,* life with *bitachon,* life in *deveikus* with Hashem. Under the influence of the Rav's pure-hearted affection, we acquired a deep, internal feeling that we are in Hashem's hands."

The Rav's son once came along for the "*avodah*" of shopping and asked, "About the things we actually use on Shabbos, *Chazal* surely said, 'Except for expenses of Shabbos.' But what about all the leftover treats and fancy foods that end up getting eaten during the week? You don't buy just enough for Shabbos. You buy generously, knowing that a lot of the food is likely to be left over for the weekdays!"

The Rav was insistent: "It doesn't matter when we actually use the items. Since I buy them all in honor of *Shabbos HaMalkah,* they don't go on my bill. Even if in the end they get used during the week."

The Rav's approach—that purchases made *lichvod Shabbos* don't cost anything because they go on Hashem's bill—wasn't limited to himself. He made a point of conveying to his children the feeling that *Chazal*'s words are true on an actual, practical level. He occasionally let them go to the grocery store on Friday and buy whatever they wished. "They are now giving away treats for free at the store!" he would announce in his home. "You can all go and buy whatever treats you want, *lichvod Shabbos.* 'All of a person's sustenance is allotted to him except for expenses of Shabbos and Yom Tov.' Today it doesn't cost money!" The children rushed to the store and bought treats in honor of *Shabbos Kodesh*.

While on weekdays the Rav never communicated a feeling of scarceness or lack despite the family's humble circumstances, on Shabbos the abundance in the home was completely out of proportion to the other days of the week. The Torah states that a Jew may partake of great delights on Shabbos, all expenses paid by the King's treasury. Why not take advantage of this wonderful opportunity?

The Rebbetzin, *a"h,* always avoided using a *talmid chacham* for mundane matters. She did everything she could so her husband wouldn't have to take care of the home. But she knew that on *erev Shabbos,* the Rav would take for himself the *zechus* of participating in the Shabbos preparations. He would try to carry home the things he'd bought at the grocery store himself. The residents of Ofakim would marvel at the sight of the community's rabbi walking down the street carrying cartons of soda, treats, and other foods.

Even when the Pincus family spent Shabbos away from home—for instance, when the Rav was leading a weekend seminar—he would take along ample treats for his family. "Who knows what they'll serve us there?" he would say, ensuring that nothing would be lacking from *kevod* and *oneg Shabbos* even while away from home.

This was but one aspect of the *"avodah"* of shopping for *Shabbos Kodesh*.

The Best Fish in Town

In Ofakim of those days, most products were available with a good *hechsher,* but not all. Freshly ground fish with a *hechsher* satisfactory to the Rav, or even fresh fish suitable for grinding, was not sold in this relatively isolated Negev city. So many of Ofakim's residents used the ready-made gefilte fish sold in the stores.

But the Rav frowned upon this practice: "*Lichvod Shabbos,* if possible, one should prepare fish at home, in order to delight in preparing for Shabbos. The ready-made fish from the store is missing the ingredients of *kedushah* and *kevod Shabbos*."

His preference was clear, as was its urgency, but what could be done? The fish was simply not sold in Ofakim. The Rebbetzin found the perfect solution: She organized a weekly delivery of freshly ground fish, straight from Yerushalayim. This afforded her the opportunity to do a great *chesed* for the many other residents of Ofakim who wished to honor Shabbos in this way.

It became well known that whoever wanted fresh fish for Shabbos could order it at the Rav's home and rest assured that it would arrive on time. The Rebbetzin, and sometimes the Rav himself, would call up with the good news that "The fish *lichvod Shabbos* has arrived!" whereupon the recipient of the call could come and pick it up at the Pincus's home, which, for a few hours, turned into a regional distribution center.

It was common to see one of the Rav's children go up to the apartment of someone who had ordered fresh fish but was late in picking it up. The child would inform them that their order *lichvod Shabbos* had arrived, while the Rav waited downstairs before continuing on to the next building. In this and other ways, Shabbos and *chesed* became intertwined in the Rav's home. It was his way to enrich each deed with as many mitzvos and *middos* as possible: *chesed*, Shabbos, helping people, and serving God—outward, simple actions masking deep, inner *avodah*.

Likewise, when the Rav drove to the bakery on Friday to buy *challos* for Shabbos, he would take advantage of the opportunity to add an act of *chesed* and bring *oneg Shabbos* to other Jews. His daughter Miriam, *a"h*, would go to the neighbors and others who lived nearby and ask what they wanted from the bakery. Then the Rav would drive there himself and buy what was needed.

When he returned, the scene with the fresh fish described

above would repeat itself as the neighbors came to pick up their baked goods, *lichvod Shabbos Kodesh*.

In the Kitchen

On Friday, the Rav would help with the housework, including in the kitchen.

Certain regular household tasks were his, and he wouldn't let anyone else do them for him. He was very meticulous about what it says in the *Shulchan Aruch*: "Even if a person has many servants, he should exert himself to prepare something for Shabbos himself, in order to honor it. Rav Chisda would dice the vegetables, Rabbah and Rav Yosef would chop the wood.... Every person should learn from their example and not be concerned about his honor, for honoring Shabbos *is* a person's honor."[6]

One thing the Rav did himself was prepare the hot water urn. In his home, despite Ofakim's desert heat, hot water was available even on summer *Shabbosos*, just as it was during the winter months—even though in the summer, hardly anyone wanted a hot cup of tea. "We need to prepare hot water to honor Shabbos," he would explain, "even if no one actually uses it!"

Sometimes on *erev Shabbos*, you could find the Rav washing dishes. Needless to say, during the week you would never find him in the kitchen, as his devoted Rebbetzin was protective of his precious time and didn't allow him to help out at home. But on *erev Shabbos*, he would wash the dishes after the cooking was finished. This was something he was very particular about: He couldn't stand the sight of dirty dishes piled up in the kitchen when Shabbos commenced. Everything had to be clean and shining in honor of the arrival of *Shabbos Kodesh*!

When the Pincus family lived in Tifrach, a small town in the

6. *Orach Chayim* 150:1.

Negev, there was another task he was fond of on *erev Shabbos.* In those days, the floor of their house wasn't tiled (as used to be common in Israel) but consisted of simple cement. A cement floor by nature develops a lot of cracks, and it's not smooth and flat. Every Friday, in honor of Shabbos, the Rav spread sand over the floor to make it smooth and flat, so it would look respectable.

When the Pincus family moved to Ofakim, a *kollel* man bought their house in Tifrach. Among other renovations, he put down a proper floor. He recounted that the Rav once came to their home and, upon noticing the new floor, he blushed and then commented with his characteristic humor: "What did you do? Look at this — you ruined the house!"

For Rav Pincus, nothing was more perfect than a simple cement floor which conveys the message of modest living, of making do with little — and which enables its owner to honor Shabbos each week by spreading sand over it to make it look nice!

Mikveh on Erev Shabbos

When the chareidi community of Ofakim was first established, there was only one *mikveh* nearby, and it closed early in the afternoon. Many members of the community would run there on Friday at the last minute before it closed.

The Rav often drove people to a *mikveh* farther away, so they could immerse in honor of Shabbos. He would wait for them and then bring them back home. He would make this circuit several times in order to assist anyone who wanted to go to the *mikveh.*

After a while, he declared that they couldn't go on like this; Ofakim needed its own *mikveh,* where people could immerse *erev Shabbos* without such time limitations and pressure. It was decided that a *mikveh* would be built underneath the shul. This *mikveh* was designed by a member of the community, under the guidance of the Rav. When it came to connecting the cistern of rainwater to the *mikveh,* the Rav and a group of *kollel* men did the work with their own hands. (When the *mikveh* was completed, he requested that the water should not be heated too much, so people wouldn't stay in the water long. He said, "A person should enter the *mikveh* and then leave immediately.")

Whether at home or overseas, it was very important to the Rav to immerse in a *mikveh* before Shabbos, and he went to great lengths to do so. Once he performed the tremendous *chesed* of accompanying a member of the community abroad for urgent medical treatment. But a "problem" arose: they had to spend Shabbos in the town where the hospital was located, and there was no *mikveh* there.

What could be done? In the end, the solution was a distant seashore, and the Rav's immersion there almost cost him his life. He found out afterward that this seashore was founded on quicksand! Upon entering the water, he'd felt he was slowly sinking in the mud and could not get out! By sheer miracle, he succeeded in getting back to solid ground, thereby saving his life. When later asked what thoughts he'd entertained while sinking in the quicksand, he responded that he'd prayed in his heart that he should at least be found and given a proper Jewish burial.

During a certain period, he decided to complete his learning of the weekly *parashah* before going to the *mikveh* on *erev Shabbos.* This way he felt he reached a higher *madreigah* by preparing for Shabbos before going to the *mikveh.*

Fresh Ideas

The Rav devoted a lot of thought to how he could honor Shabbos more. He always came up with *chiddushim* on the subject of *kevod Shabbos.*

This *avodah* of fresh ideas for *kevod Shabbos* included remembering Shabbos during the week. Sometimes he came home with a new item for Shabbos: a goblet, a set of glasses, etc. He remembered Shabbos all week and was always thinking of new ways to honor it.

The Rebbetzin lit a Shabbos candle for each of their children, in addition to two silver candlesticks filled with pure olive oil, for extra *hiddur mitzvah*. To hold the oil, the Rav bought little cups of fancy crystal that were very hard to obtain in Israel. He purchased them abroad and would occasionally buy extra ones — regardless of the cost — lest they break, detracting from *kevod Shabbos*. Although they were expensive, they too were surely included in "expenses of Shabbos and Yom Tov."

The Rav would innovate regarding Shabbos clothing as well. Until approximately age fifty, he never wore a tie. Imagine everyone's surprise when he showed up in shul one Shabbos wearing one. Observing the looks of amazement, he explained: "It occurred to me that every day I wear identical clothing. On weekdays I wear a frock, and also on Shabbos! My Shabbos frock is newer and nicer, but it's essentially no different from my weekday clothes. So I decided to add a special garment *lichvod Shabbos*, something noticeable that emphasizes the difference between weekday clothing and Shabbos clothing. This better fulfills the halachah of 'What you wear on Shabbos should not be like what you wear during the week.'"[7]

The Rav also saw to it that his family members wore special clothing on Shabbos. For instance, one of his children recalls having a new garment that had been purchased for Pesach, which he wore the Shabbos right before, as that year e*rev Pesach* fell on Shabbos. At first his father was surprised and asked, "Why are you wearing it now instead of saving it for Pesach tonight?" But after a moment he reconsidered and said, "Actually, you're right. Shabbos is no less important than Pesach, so wear it now!"

7. *Shabbos* 113a.

No Shabbos Is an "Exception"

The Rav's special efforts and concern to honor *Shabbos Kodesh* applied every Shabbos of the year. Even on *Shabbosos* when most people cut corners, he would not diminish the honor of Shabbos in any way.

For instance, one of the Rav's neighbors recounts that on *erev Shabbos HaGadol,* which fell that year on 11 Nisan, his wife happened to meet Rebbetzin Pincus. Their conversation was naturally drawn to the topic of Pesach preparations. This woman asked the Rebbetzin if the Pincus's stove was already clean and kosher for Pesach. The answer she received caught her unexpectedly: "Is the stove kosher for Pesach?! How could it be kosher already on *erev Shabbos HaGadol*? We still need to bake cakes *lichvod Shabbos Kodesh*!" As the Rav would say, "Why should Shabbos suffer just because it's close to Pesach?"

For this reason he would not use paper plates on Shabbos, even on *Shabbos HaGadol*. "This Shabbos is no different from any other," he insisted. "We must honor Shabbos just as we do during the rest of the year. Disposable dishes aren't fitting for *kevod Shabbos*," he emphasized.

In their last years, to ease their Pesach preparations, the Rav and his family ate their *Shabbos HaGadol* meals in a small hall near their home. But even then, they never compromised the honor of *Shabbos Kodesh*. The Shabbos delicacies were plentiful and served on regular dishes, as on every Shabbos, since "Shabbos need not suffer just because it's close to Pesach."

Furthermore, in the Rav's home, Friday was completely dedicated to preparing for Shabbos. One family member tells of a certain Friday early in Nisan when Shabbos preparations were finished earlier than expected. The Rebbetzin decided to take advantage of the time and make some progress with the Pesach cleaning. She asked the girls to go through one of the cabinets and clean out any chametz.

The girls were happily working—until their father found

out. "On *erev Shabbos* we don't do anything that's not connected to preparing for Shabbos," he told them. "Not even *lichvod Pesach*. On *erev Shabbos*, we only prepare for Shabbos!"

Shabbos Abroad

Even when the Rav was abroad on one of his many trips devoted to disseminating Torah, he carefully observed every aspect of preparing for Shabbos.

A student who accompanied him on his visit to the *kollel* in Chile recounts that on weekdays, the *kollel* men would take turns preparing meals for themselves. But on Friday after Shacharis, the Rav heartily declared, "Everyone out of the kitchen. Today is my day!"

Another anecdote was offered by a *kollel* man from Johannesburg, who hosted the Rav for Shabbos. The Rav never ate meat outside his own home, due to kashrus considerations. But what about cholent on Shabbos? The Rav prepared a pareve cholent for himself. Yet without meat, what was special and *Shabbosdik* about such a cholent? For this purpose, the Rav added pareve Swiss chocolate to the cholent, giving it a special flavor!

Neither did he neglect the practice of eating garlic on Shabbos night while he was abroad. He would prepare a special dish of garlic for himself. The Rav never allowed a visit to a country far from home deter him from any mitzvah or *minhag* connected to *Shabbos Kodesh*.

Entering Shabbos Relaxed

Despite the Rav's exceptional concern for the honor of Shabbos, and his tremendous care that all the preparations should come out just right, he would welcome Shabbos into his home with a smile, in a calm and relaxed manner.

The Rav repeatedly explained to his family that the Gemara says the *yetzer ha-ra* "works overtime" on *erev Shabbos*, creating a tense, pressured atmosphere in order to prevent Jews from greeting *Shabbos Kodesh* with proper calm and ease. "The pressure isn't real; it's not proper or justified. It is merely the work of the Satan!" he would often repeat. The Rav emphasized: "We have to beat the *yetzer ha-ra*. We must overcome him at this time." After all the preparations were finished, the Rav would wait until the Rebbetzin lit the Shabbos candles. When he saw the home was peaceful and tranquil, only then would he leave for shul.

Every week the Rav would post a notice wishing his neighbors a good Shabbos. This notice featured a pretty, Shabbos-related illustration, such as a picture of Shabbos candles. These notes extended the special Shabbos feeling to those who lived nearby.

When speaking publicly, the Rav would often dwell on the importance of greeting Shabbos peacefully. He emphasized how important it was to relate calmly and respectfully to great and small alike even at pressured times such as late Friday afternoon. He once elaborated on this point in a characteristic vein: "Many people claim that matters such as these are too 'great' for them and they just can't do it. But a Jew should know there is no such thing. Nothing is 'too great.' If you really want it, if you keep trying and don't give up, in the end you will succeed!

"But the truth is," explained the Rav, "the problem with matters such as these is completely different: We feel they're too small! We minimize their importance and don't devote enough attention to them. That's why we're negligent, even though we're capable of them.

"Giving a drink of water to a thirsty child while one is in the middle of Shabbos preparations, and adding a little juice if necessary, is also a mitzvah! And if it's a mitzvah, why not do it? Yet we underestimate mitzvos like these. We feel they're minor, and this is the root of the problem. Even at the most pressure-prone time, we should not belittle even the slightest mitzvah, such as fulfilling the request of a child."

Teaching Children about Shabbos

Someone close to the Rav once lamented that his younger children had a hard time enjoying the long summer *Shabbosos* because of the abundant free time with so many "restrictions." For little children, it's unpleasant to spend a whole day unable to color or play with many of their toys. These children wait impatiently for Shabbos to end. "I don't know what to do," he complained to the Rav. "My kids simply hate Shabbos."

The Rav answered: "You need to educate them and guide them to love Shabbos. You think you can sit in the *beis midrash* on Shabbos afternoon in front of a Gemara, leave your children without direction, and expect them to love *Shabbos Kodesh* and know how to appreciate it on their own. It doesn't work that way. If you want your children to feel the spiritual *oneg* of Shabbos, if you want them to look forward to its coming and not to its leaving, you have to invest time and energy. Go for a walk with your children on Shabbos morning, when the streets are empty and the atmosphere is right. Give them a chance to spend time with their father. Learn with them in a calm and pleasant spirit. You'll see how the atmosphere will be transformed!"

Friday Nap

One of the Rav's regular Shabbos preparations was to nap at least half an hour on Friday. He would quote Rebbe Aharon of Karlin as saying that if someone doesn't sleep on *erev Shabbos*, his meal that night is not a Shabbos meal but a weekday meal! Even in the winter, when *erev Shabbos* was very short, the whole family knew the Rav wouldn't miss his nap *lichvod Shabbos*.

The Rosh Yeshivah of Ofakim, Rav Chaim Kamil, *zt"l*, also adopted this practice. Someone close to the Rosh Yeshivah recounted: "I once called the Rosh Yeshivah's home on Friday and was told he was sleeping. The Rosh Yeshivah later explained to me, upon observing my surprise: 'What — don't you know about the importance of sleeping on *erev Shabbos*? I heard from Rav Shimshon that if you sleep on Friday, the night's meal is considered a Shabbos meal. But if you don't sleep, the meal is just "supper"! Therefore, I must sleep on *erev Shabbos* in order to keep the mitzvos of Shabbos properly.'"

One of the Rav's practices, which he disguised so no one knew what he was really doing, was to drive out to the Ofakim turnoff on the highway late Friday afternoon and check if anyone was stuck there and trying to get to Ofakim. To spare hitchhikers any discomfort about imposing on him, he would drive past the intersection, turn around, and come in from the opposite direction, as if on his way home from another town. Of course, his true intention was to make sure no Jew should be left stranded as Shabbos commenced.

In summation, the Rav prepared for Shabbos all week. He took care of all sorts of seemingly "small" matters, attributing immense importance to any act that honored *Shabbos Kodesh*. Every such act became fertile ground for his *avodas Hashem*.

These preparations were the foundation on which his astounding Shabbos was built, a Shabbos which could be sensed by observing his ways and being in his presence, as will be described in the coming chapters, *b'ezras Hashem*.

"לא ניתנו שבתות...אלא לעסוק בהם בתורה"

2

Learning on Shabbos

Filling Shabbos with Content

SHABBOS WITH RAV SHIMSHON Dovid Pincus, *zt"l,* always overflowed with rich spiritual content. He would fully utilize the special opportunity afforded by Shabbos for growth and elevation in Torah.

Many Ofakim residents attended his Shabbos classes and talks, which transformed their Shabbos into an uplifting experience.

After *Kabbalas Shabbos,* he would deliver a *derashah* in shul. He didn't prepare the *derashah.* In shul, he simply approached the Rosh Yeshivah, R' Chaim Kamil, *zt"l,* who would share a thought on the *parashah.* Between these two great men, a fascinating discussion of Torah and *hashkafah* then developed.

The Rav would base his *derashah* on this discussion between him and the Rosh Yeshivah. His opening words would be, "I'll tell you what the Rosh Yeshivah said...," "I'll tell you what I saw...," or "I recently heard..." Then he would bring out several points on that topic, weaving them into a spellbinding sermon.

The Rav utilized Friday night, too, for learning. For instance, he would sleep a little after the meal, then hurry to shul before midnight. There he sat engrossed in his Gemara until morning. The Rav maintained this practice on both the short summer nights and the long winter ones. He would take special advantage of the powerful spiritual benefit afforded by the latter, on which there were so many uninterrupted, quality hours of *Shabbos Kodesh*.

When he lived in Bnei Brak, the Rav maintained a regular study session in his home with Rav Yisrael Eliyahu Weintraub, *shlita*. What they learned together remains a secret. They would start right after the Friday night meal and continue into the wee hours of the morning, after which the Rav would escort his honored guest home. Then the Rav would return to his own home and allow himself a little rest until morning.

The Ohr HaChayim HaKadosh

When the Rav lived in Ofakim, he had a special *avodah* after the Friday night meal. For many years he held a sort of *tish*. This gathering consisted primarily of a *shiur* on the *Ohr HaChayim* commentary on the *Chumash*, during which he gave over Torah *hashkafah* to dozens of regular listeners and many others who happened to be in Ofakim for Shabbos.

For instance, a *kollel* man who lived in Ofakim recounts that his father, who lived up north, would sometimes come to spend Shabbos with him. On these *Shabbosos* his father would unfailingly attend the *tish*, no matter how tired he was, saying that a *shiur* by Rav Pincus gave him strength that lasted from one Ofakim visit to the next. Many people spent Shabbos in Ofakim just to attend the Friday night *shiur*.

The *shiur*'s regular participants ranged from erudite *kollel* men to simple working men, some of whom did very little Torah learning during the week. It's hard to teach such a diverse audience, but the Rav expertly delivered his message to all. Unique was his ability to simplify deep Kabbalistic ideas such that every participant could grasp them. Even the most uneducated listener understood the deepest points. As is known, he was the greatest of his generation in this respect.

It was not uncommon for him to turn to a participant who looked surprised and confused and say, "Did you understand? Are you sure you understood? Perhaps I should go over it again?" Whenever the point hadn't been fully grasped, he would explain it repeatedly with unending patience, illustrating it with various allegories from daily life — a method he made great use of in his many talks.

The *shiur* would begin with a passage from the *Ohr HaChayim* or the Ramban on the *parashah* but quickly expanded to a variety of subjects, based on questions from the participants. The Rav related with utmost seriousness to each question, regardless of who asked it and what level he was on. He engaged in a special *avodah* of treating all Jews with respect and care, thus fulfilling *"Toras chesed* — the Torah of lovingkindness," while teaching the Torah itself.

He barely finished one paragraph in the *Ohr HaChayim* before launching into all sorts of topics, answering participants' questions one after another in a way that strung together pearls of wisdom. The only times the *shiur* would stick to its subject were when the Rosh Yeshivah, R' Chaim Kamil, *zt"l*, was present. In his honor, since he made the effort to attend the *shiur*, everyone focused only on the words of the *Ohr HaChayim HaKadosh*.

It was beautiful to see the Rav turn to the Rosh Yeshivah, who sat next to him, and ask with humble grace, *"Nu*, was it good?" whereupon the Rosh Yeshivah would affectionately nod.

Officially, the *shiur* lasted until midnight. When it ended, the custom for many years was to bring out hot kugel, so the participants could properly fulfill the mitzvah of *oneg Shabbos*. When everyone finished partaking of the food, the Rav would heartily declare, *"Gut Shabbos! Gut Shabbos!"* with his glowing smile. His face shone particularly on *Shabbos Kodesh*.

That was the sign that the *shiur* was officially over. But

even afterward, a long discussion would continue around him, touching on various issues of Torah outlook arising from the questions of those who couldn't bring themselves to leave. This discussion sometimes lasted a good hour.

After the *tish* was finally over, the Rav still had the *avodah* of finishing to prepare for his *shiur klali,* to be delivered the next day in the yeshivah of Ofakim.

Unity

The Shabbos night *tish* was indeed the focal point around which, for many and various people, the atmosphere of Shabbos revolved. But few know how this *shiur* began. This interesting story deserves attention because it brings out an additional aspect of the Rav's unique message to us.

There was a period when several fine *kollel* men and their families moved from Yerushalayim to Ofakim. Soon after their arrival, they decided to hold a sort of "*oneg Shabbos*" on Friday nights in one of their houses. To solidify their group, they wished to hold the *oneg* in Yiddish, a language inaccessible to many Ofakim residents.

The Rav was not so pleased by the idea, lest it divide Ofakim's *kollel* community, which then numbered only forty families. As is known, he was always a strong advocate of unity among various groups. If the community were split, he reasoned, it wouldn't contribute to the development of a vibrant Torah life in Ofakim. On the other hand, he didn't want to stop these *kollel* men from holding an *oneg Shabbos,* as their intentions were good, and their goal was to elevate themselves in Torah and *yir'as Shamayim.*

In the end he came up with an original solution: The next Shabbos, right after the *seudah,* he showed up at the gathering, whereupon he was immediately asked to say a few words. That Shabbos, the Rav indeed spoke in Yiddish. But little by little, after a few *Shabbosos,* he began using more and more Hebrew, until after a number of weeks the entire talk was in Hebrew, making it accessible to anyone who wished to participate.

Once the gathering began drawing a lot of participants, the Rav was concerned it would disturb the neighbors' sleep. He used this concern to further his goal of unifying the community: he implored the organizers to move the *oneg* to a nearby shul. After they agreed, the *shiur* turned into a mass event attended by many residents of Ofakim every week.

Maximizing Friday Night

Although the Friday night *tish* was close to the hearts of many, the Rav decided to discontinue it when he began traveling the world, disseminating Torah and *Yiddishkeit*. But since the Friday night learning of the *kollel* men of Ofakim was based on the *tish* and its *shiur*, he concluded that his trips overseas caused *bittul Torah*, and he couldn't make peace with that.

So the Rav restructured the Friday night "program." Instead of his regular *shiur*, he instituted *shiurim* in the central shul, to be delivered by local or visiting rabbis. Thus a *shiur* was guaranteed, as it didn't depend solely on him or anyone else. The Rav took his turn delivering the *shiur*, too, on the *Shabbosos* he was in town. With this new setup, Friday nights remained well utilized and full of spiritual content.

Learning on Shabbos Day

The Rav filled Shabbos day as well with spiritual content by delivering classes and talks. Whenever someone sponsored a "Kiddush" on some happy occasion, the Rav would be the honored speaker. The congregants looked forward to hearing him.

For a long time, the Rav delivered a *shiur klali* in the yeshivah of Ofakim before Minchah on Shabbos. The yeshivah students and *kollel* men actively participated in the *shiur*. Many members of the community also came to experience the excited and lively Torah debates that ensued.

On many *Shabbosos* the Rav also delivered a *mussar shmuess* in the yeshivah after *seudah shelishis.* The powerful words he spoke at this special time provided many yeshivah students with a proper Torah *hashkafah* which they utilized for every aspect of their lives.

"זהירים לשומרי"

3

Keeping Shabbos

Extreme Care with Halachah

RAV SHIMSHON DOVID PINCUS, *zt"l,* studied *hilchos Shabbos* intensively. He would emphasize to his family and students that unless a person learns this subject in earnest and in depth, it is difficult to avoid *chillul Shabbos.*

While still a *bachur,* the Rav began studying *hilchos Shabbos* in great detail. He learned all of *Maseches Shabbos* thoroughly, later commenting that this background gave him a special feel for and understanding of these halachos. "If you want to acquire a special sense of *hilchos Shabbos,*" he would recommend to *bachurim,* "learn *Maseches Shabbos* several times while still in yeshivah, when one's heart and mind are still wide open. This kind of learning will serve you well your whole life!"

The Rav was indeed blessed with a special sense of *hilchos Shabbos.* Coupled with his powerful *yir'as Shamayim,* this gift produced an exceptionally meticulous approach to halachah. Multitudes of stories are told about the Rav's carefulness in halachah. A few examples:

A neighbor recalls being summoned by the Rav one *Shabbos HaGadol.* The neighbor hurried to the home of the Rav, who got right to the point: "What size shoes do you wear?" Surprised, the fellow replied that he wore size forty-six. The Rav continued imperturbably: "Would you mind taking off your shoes for a moment, so I can try them on?" The neighbor responded, "I would be happy to," without the faintest idea why the rabbi of the community was interested in his footwear.

The Rav quickly tried them on and, when they fit, asked whether the neighbor had another pair. Upon hearing that the fellow did, the Rav asked to borrow the first pair for a few hours.

"What happened?" the neighbor asked.

The Rav answered, "This morning, on my way back from the yeshivah through the field, I suddenly noticed that one of the little metal rings reinforcing the shoelace holes in my shoes had gotten loose and was hanging in the air. This raised a serious question in my mind regarding carrying on Shabbos!

"I had no choice but to leave my shoes in the field and continue home without them. But then I had another problem: It's *Shabbos HaGadol,* and I need to deliver the *derashah*. It's improper for me to do so shoeless, so I'm asking if you could lend me your shoes for a little while."

The neighbor agreed, of course, and the Rav later thanked him, commenting that, "Your shoes spoke well today."

Similarly, after davening one Shabbos morning in the yeshivah, the Rav discovered a thread hanging from a button on his shirt. With his characteristic meticulousness in halachah, he thought the thread might present a problem of carrying on Shabbos. The Rav discussed the issue with the congregants, and then decided to act stringently: He took off his shirt and walked home in his frock.

The Rav was exceedingly concerned with other Shabbos prohibitions as well. A *kollel* student recounts: "I once told the Rav that the pieces of the Shabbos toilet paper in the lavatory were attached to one another in a way that might constitute a halachic problem. He jumped up in great alarm and ran to investigate the matter in order to prevent public *chillul Shabbos*. The way he jumped up made an indelible impression on me."

Another Shabbos, a neighbor developed severe abdominal pains. He seemed to be in danger. Anyone else would have simply called the emergency medical center and requested a doctor. But the Rav sought to minimize *chillul Shabbos*.

He grabbed one of his children's bicycles and, disregarding all personal and rabbinic honor, rode to the nearby center himself to get help. For riding a bike on Shabbos is at most a Rabbinic offense, whereas phoning violates a number of Torah prohibitions!

Yet the Rav then rode with the doctor in his car, lest the doctor send the sick neighbor to an inferior hospital.

Concern for the halachos of Shabbos permeated the Rav's very flesh and blood. All Shabbos he feared even the slightest transgression. And since even major Shabbos prohibitions can easily be transgressed if a person lacks proper awareness, his constant preoccupation with *hilchos Shabbos* was an important form of *avodah*.

For instance, the Rav would often warn about the *chillul Shabbos* involved in biting one's fingernails or pulling off little pieces of hanging skin. He knew many people did these things on Shabbos without thinking, so he frequently warned of the great danger of unwittingly desecrating Shabbos in these ways.

On Shabbos, if someone in shul was absentmindedly biting his nails, the Rav would hurry over to him and explain the grave *chillul Shabbos* the person was about to fall into. Even if the offender was standing in the back of the shul, the Rav would walk all the way from the front to prevent him from transgressing. *Chillul Shabbos* is no less serious than *pikuach nefesh,* and if someone's life were at stake, wouldn't he do anything he could to help him?

The Rav once advised a nail-biting friend, "It is a very good idea to quit this habit. Now it's a weekday, so biting your nails is permitted, but you could end up doing the same thing on Shabbos, *chas v'shalom*!" The Rav truly feared sin. He lived a life of caution regarding transgression and clearly envisioned the danger looming before his friend.

The Rav's habit of warning people about the *chillul Shabbos* of nail biting actually led to his being kissed in the street. Walking in Bnei Brak one Shabbos, he noticed someone biting his nails. The Rav immediately pointed the problem out to him. This man did not just stop what he was doing; he expressed his deep appreciation for being saved from *chillul Shabbos* by grabbing the Rav and giving him a kiss!

Helping Others Keep Shabbos

As these stories indicate, the Rav did not keep quiet regarding *chillul Shabbos*. If he saw children violating a Torah prohibition, he would gently ask them to stop. If he saw non-observant Jews desecrating Shabbos, and he thought it would help to say something, he did.

Back when Ofakim was surrounded by wilderness, people would hunt birds there on Shabbos. The Rav often deemed it best to say nothing to non-observant Jews about Shabbos desecration; since they won't listen anyway, better they not know the severity of what they're doing. But whenever the Rav thought it might help to say something, he dashed out the door on his holy mission, hurrying to the distant hunters and hoping his words would be effective.

Expanding the Eruv

Eventually a stadium was built on the edge of Ofakim. It hosted soccer games on Shabbos and drew large crowds of Jews who were woefully distant from *Yiddishkeit*.

The Rav couldn't stop the games from taking place or the spectators from attending, but he did everything in his power to minimize the enormous *chillul Shabbos* involved. To this end, he insisted that the city's *eruv* include the stadium.

Similarly, when roadwork produced a large mound of dirt

that threatened to invalidate the *eruv*, the Rav hired a tractor to level the mound, under his own supervision.

Checking the Eruv

The Rav was incredibly dedicated to maintaining the *eruv*. On *erev Shabbos* he would drive around the city borders to check if anything had happened to the *eruv* during the week. Even on rainy winter days, he drove through mud and puddles to keep up his vigil.

Whenever the *eruv* needed repair, the Rav saw to it with total dedication. A *kollel* student who was close to him recounts that after the funeral of R' Yitzchak Hutner, *zt"l*, which took place on a Friday, the Rav returned home close to Shabbos but then discovered something had happened to the *eruv*. "Come, we're going to fix the *eruv*!" he said to this *kollel* man, who could not help but join the mission even at this most inconvenient hour.

Another anecdote: A few minutes before commencing his first Shabbos as the rav of Ofakim, the Rav learned of a problem with the *eruv*. He hurried out in his Shabbos clothes, put a ladder on his shoulder, and raced by bike to the spot where the problem had arisen. He had to leave the bike there, since it was too late to come back home with it. But nothing would stop him from doing whatever was necessary to ensure that Jews would not carry on Shabbos, *chas v'shalom*.

The *eruv* was actually not the Rav's responsibility. Another Ofakim resident was appointed to maintain it. Thus, the Rav's involvement with the *eruv* stemmed purely from his heartfelt desire to prevent *chillul Shabbos* and honor Shabbos to the best of his ability.

For this reason, the Rav did not limit his concern to the *eruv* of Ofakim alone. When he heard about *eruv* problems in other towns, he did whatever he could to help. Once he corresponded with the rabbi of another Negev town about its *eruv*, which Rav Pincus considered invalid. We don't know whether his involvement improved the situation, but he clearly cared about *eruvin* in a special way, since a valid *eruv* prevents Shabbos desecration.

"No" to a Neighborhood Eruv

Although the Rav invested tremendous effort in maintaining the city *eruv*, he opposed the construction of a *mehadrin eruv* serving only the chareidi community. Initially he argued simply that such an *eruv* was impossible and put forward various claims to deflect the issue. Only under great pressure did he finally explain his position:

"You see, as long as there is no neighborhood *eruv*, and we have only the city *eruv*, the *b'nei Torah* do not rely on it. This stricture prevents them from strolling through the streets on Shabbos. And when people don't spend their time walking around, they usually busy themselves with more valuable activities, which are more fitting to the honor of Shabbos. But if we had a *mehadrin eruv* that even *b'nei Torah* could confidently rely on, everyone could easily stroll with his wife and children. Shabbos would then turn into a day of amusement and milling around. This I don't want! I don't want Ofakim to become like the big cities."

(Later, for various reasons, a neighborhood *eruv* was established.)

These anecdotes are but a small sampling of what there is to tell about Rav Shimshon Dovid Pincus, *zt"l*, on this subject. They offer a glimpse of the stature of a *gadol b'Yisrael*. They show us something of his astoundingly meticulous observance of halachah as well as his concern for all Jews. They portray someone who went out of his way to guard and protect *Shabbos Kodesh* from all directions. May we be privileged to follow in his holy footsteps, to keep Shabbos as it should be kept — and in this *zechus*, may we be speedily redeemed!

"מלחמה על כבוד שבת קדשנו"

4

His Fight for Shabbos

Standing Up for Shabbos Kodesh

RAV SHIMSHON DOVID PINCUS, *zt"l*, fought for the honor of Shabbos. When he held that protest was necessary and potentially productive, he put all personal considerations aside and fearlessly cried out against those who trampled upon *Shabbos Kodesh*.

The Rav once overheard two *kollel* men arguing about the demonstrations then taking place against *chillul Shabbos*. One of these men was against the whole idea. The Rav turned to him and said, "My dear friend, I apologize for intruding on your conversation, but I must comment that what you're saying is not right at all. You seem to hold that Shabbos is a mitzvah like all the other mitzvos, and therefore we should evaluate how important and worthwhile it is to struggle for our non-observant brethren to keep Shabbos a little better. But that is not the story.

"Shabbos is not just another mitzvah. It is a sort of a 'personality,' an entity in its own right. *Chazal* often quote what 'Shabbos said' to Hashem, and similar expressions.[1] This indicates that Shabbos is not just a mitzvah. It's a certain being that

1. See *Bereishis Rabbah* 11:8 for an example.

Hashem created. It may be a spiritual being, but it's a living thing nonetheless, with its own personality!

"Now, when we see the honor of Shabbos trampled upon, when we see Shabbos publicly degraded and humiliated, our struggle is not to save the Shabbos desecrator from sin. That surely would be an important goal on its own. And as regards that goal, it indeed would make sense to evaluate whether the struggle is worthwhile, for the reasons you just mentioned.

"Rather, when we go out to battle and raise an outcry, we do so because the non-observant are fighting a war against *Shabbos Kodesh* itself. We're defending the honor of Shabbos. We didn't initiate the conflict. On the contrary, we are standing on Shabbos's side and fighting back for her! It is Shabbos's war. And during war, different rules apply. We weigh the benefit it will provide to Shabbos, and if we think we can save her honor from being trampled underfoot, then we must come to her aid with every means at our disposal!"

"You Ran Over My Father"

On another occasion the Rav was riding with a non-observant taxi driver, who was telling his friend on the phone how he drives on Shabbos. He was cheerfully recounting that last Shabbos he took a trip here, and the Shabbos before he had a great time touring there, etc. Everything he recollected involved flagrant Shabbos desecration.

The Rav could not remain silent in face of such hurtful conversation. He turned to his fellow passenger and started telling him a story, so the driver would overhear:

"Listen to this story — I was driving in my car, and suddenly in my rearview mirror I saw my father standing behind the car. You know what I did? I immediately shifted into reverse and plowed backward at full speed, and I ran over my father! Yeah, it was really funny. Then I drove forward again and happily went on my way. It was so much fun!"

"You should be ashamed of yourself!" screamed the driver. "What's the matter with you—are you crazy or something?! If you had the nerve to do such a terrible thing to your own father who brought you into the world, why aren't you at least embarrassed to talk about it?!"

The Rav could now make his point: "And what about you? Didn't you run over your mother? Why aren't you embarrassed about running over Shabbos, your own mother, each week? Why doesn't it shake you up?"

The Rav's question went unanswered.

"We Love You!"

The Rav held that we are obligated to do whatever we can to prevent *chilul Shabbos,* regardless of what non-observant Jews may think and what practical benefit will result.

When a sports complex was built on the edge of Ofakim, which held public activities on Shabbos, the city's dismayed religious community debated how to react. In the end it was decided to hold a peaceful demonstration outside the facility, singing Shabbos songs without being drawn into violence of any sort.

The founders of the sports complex were not at all pleased with the demonstration. They would have preferred a stormy confrontation that would place the chareidim in a bad light. For this reason, one of the managers came out of the building, approached the demonstrators, and tried to stir up some violent conflict.

The Rav told him warmly and gently, "My fine fellow Jew, my dear brother, we did not come here to hurt you. On the contrary, we are here only because we love you! We have not even a trace of hatred in our hearts for you. Only because of our love for you did we come here to demonstrate, to try to dissuade you from the grave act you are committing, unaware of its terrible consequences."

The manager was astonished. He wasn't ready for that. Without a word, he turned around and went back inside. Although he most unfortunately did not change his ways, the experience surely left an indelible mark on him.

That story did not end with tangible success, but in many cases the Rav's reproof did. His heartfelt protests and other efforts prevented massive *chillul Shabbos,* saving many Jews from severe transgressions. The following is an example:

There was an old theater in Ofakim. When it first opened, it was very active, but in time business slowed down and eventually stopped altogether. The place was deserted. Then there was talk of renovating this cinema and opening it all week, including Shabbos.

The Rav was shocked by this prospect and the *chilul Shabbos* it would cause. "What?! A theater will operate here, bringing people to terrible sins and trampling the honor of *Shabbos Kodesh*? This is not going to happen!" he declared with great determination. When he found out that the owner lived up north, he and a close associate immediately traveled to the man's home.

Forcefully and emotionally, the Rav spoke to this elderly Jew about life after death, about reward and punishment: "What will you say after one hundred and twenty, when they show you the terrible damage caused by the place you owned, and they hold you responsible for opening it on Shabbos as well? You will have nothing to say in your own defense!" The Rav spoke with great agitation, yet his compassion and care for the man were unmistakable.

"You're right," the owner conceded. "It's wrong for me to go ahead with this plan. But what will I do with the place? It's a big building worth a lot of money. Maintaining this empty structure costs me a fortune, and I have to cover my losses one way or another!"

The Rav made him an offer on the spot: "If you don't know

what to do with the building, I have an idea for you. Rent it to us, and we'll set up a center for disseminating the values of Judaism. This way, instead of supporting sin every day, you'll share in multitudes of merits."

The man accepted the proposal.

According to market prices, the rental for such a building was around $10,000 a month. After speaking with the Rav, however, the owner agreed to rent the premises for only $4,000, and eventually he went down to a mere $2,000. And he didn't even ask for the money up front. He immediately put the building at the Rav's disposal, so that, while awaiting payment, he would be a partner in all the blessed activity that would take place there.

The theater closed for good, and a large Jewish center opened in its place. From this center, many people went on to participate in *teshuvah* seminars and eventually became fully observant Jews. Years later, even after the center closed, the theater did not reopen. All this was thanks to the Rav's urgent meeting with the owner years before.

Through care and dedication to the spiritual well-being of every Jew, great things can be accomplished. And there is no telling the eventual ramifications. Indeed, this owner's children returned to the Torah path, and some of his grandchildren even study in *kollel*!

Not Everyone, Not All the Time

Although the Rav himself was utterly dedicated to protesting when necessary, he did not instruct the public to do so regularly.

There was a time when the honor of Shabbos was threatened in the Negev town of Yerucham. Public transportation continued on Friday after Shabbos commenced and began Saturday night before Shabbos concluded. The yeshivah students wanted to do something about it. They wished to protest and even to block the buses with their own bodies.

The Rav cooled them down and prevented the volatile demonstration from taking place. In this case, he understood that such tactics would fail. The students were surprised that the Rav of all people opposed their struggle. He explained his position by way of parable, as he was wont to do:

"Imagine a soldier is leaving camp to go out to war. Alone, he finds an enemy soldier and fights him. Then he continues on his way, looks for another enemy soldier, and fights him too, and so forth. Well, what do you say? Is this a war? Obviously not!

"So it is in our case. It is very painful to see *chillul Shabbos* in the streets. It's heartbreaking to see the honor of Shabbos trampled upon. But a war has to be fought according to a clear battle plan. The kind of war you want to wage will never achieve its goals."

The Rav's view was accepted.

“טהורים ירשוה ויקדשוה”

5

More On Shabbos with Rav Pincus

IN CONCLUSION, WE HAVE collected a number of various practices of Rav Shimshon Dovid Pincus, *zt"l,* connected to *Shabbos Kodesh.*

Kabbalas Shabbos

The Rav's Shabbos *avodah* began with Minchah on *erev Shabbos*. He would daven Minchah right before Shabbos began. He often opined that this was the right way to go into Shabbos. But when invited to speak in a shul where they davened Minchah after sunset, he would go to an early afternoon minyan so as not to miss the proper time of this prayer.

In later years, during *Kabbalas Shabbos,* he would go outside to say, *"Bo'i kallah, bo'i kallah,"* greeting Shabbos's arrival and accepting its sanctity upon himself. He literally went out to greet the Shabbos Queen as she arrived, so to speak, a practice mentioned in Torah sources. But to remain inconspicuous, he would act as if approaching the bookshelf to take a book. Then he would step out for a moment on the little balcony of the shul, greet the Shabbos Queen, and return to his place.

When Rav Pincus was younger and lived in Jerusalem, he would daven *Kabbalas Shabbos* and Ma'ariv with the Karlin Chassidim, who wear a tallis for the Friday night davening. (Since the Rav would not carry on Shabbos [despite the existence of an *eruv*], a child would carry the tallis for him.) He later explained why he davened there: "It's very simple. I wanted to cry during the Friday night davening, so I preferred to go to the Karlin Chassidim, where I could cover my head with a tallis and cry as much as I wanted!"

When he came home Friday night after Ma'ariv, the Rav went straight to the table to begin the prayers leading up to Kiddush. There was a period in his younger years when he refrained from singing *Eishes Chayil*, because he lacked understanding of it. Only when he gained a deep understanding did he begin singing it.

In *Shalom Aleichem* the Rav omitted the stanza of "*Barchuni l'shalom*," since the *Rishonim* dispute whether one should recite it (because it seems to be asking the angels to bless us). When asked about it, he said, "This stanza has indeed been accepted by the Jewish people, but I just don't feel I can say it." When it came to making requests, he would make them only of Hashem!

The Rav once heard a melody from the Vizhnitz Chassidim for a line at the end of the *Ribbon HaOlamim* prayer (commonly recited before Kiddush): "I have set You, Hashem, before me, that You may show me added mercy in my exile, to redeem me, and arouse my heart to Your love." He sang these words with great longing, repeating the phrase "arouse my heart to Your love" dozens of times, to the great inspiration of those present.

Blessing the children on Shabbos night was not customary in Rav Pincus's father's home. But after becoming acquainted with this *minhag* in his father-in-law's home, the Rav began blessing his children as well, after receiving his father's approval. He would recite the blessing of the children with *deveikus*, saying each word slowly and carefully, and afterward he added a verse found in certain siddurim in connection to this blessing: "ונחה עליו רוח ה', רוח חכמה ובינה, רוח עצה וגבורה, רוח דעת ויראת ה'"—A spirit from the Eternal will rest upon him, a spirit of knowledge and understanding, a spirit of counsel and might, a spirit of inspiration and the fear of God."[1] When blessing his daughters, he would add: "בחיק ירא אלקים תנתני — May you merit marrying a God-fearing man."[2]

Shabbos Morning Davening

During *Musaf,* the Rav had a special *avodah* in the *kedushah,* when it came to the words, "The universe is filled with His glory; His servants ask one another: 'Where (איה) is the abode of His glory?'" When he said the word איה, his voice was heard throughout the shul. For when the *chazan* draws out the word איה during the prayers of the Yomim Nora'im, it's a special time to pray that one's children should be *talmidei chachamim.* So when he served as *chazan* during these days, he recited this word slowly, so the congregants would have time to pray for their children. Even on Shabbos, he recited the word with noticeable emotion and inspiration.

When the Rav moved to Ofakim, the main minyan on Shabbos morning was in a shul that davened *nusach Sefard.* After a while the central shul was built, where the *nusach* was *Ashkenaz,* so he began to daven there. But he longed for *Kedushas "Keser,"* the *Sefard* version of *Kedushah.* "We are missing the *keser*!" he would say to his family. Sometimes the Rav would go out for a moment after the Torah reading, and right then the nearby Sefardic shul would begin the *Kedushah* of *Musaf.* He would hurry to join in with them, and afterward he'd excitedly recount that that day he'd "gotten '*Keser*'"!

Shabbos Minchah

The Rav often served as *chazan* at Minchah in order to complete his hundred daily *berachos* (through

1. *Yeshayahu* 11:2.
2. Based on *Yevamos* 63b.

reciting the repetition of the Amidah). He followed a special custom, mentioned in Torah sources: Since Moshe Rabbeinu died on Shabbos afternoon, the *chazan* begins the repetition of this Amidah not with the regular Shabbos melody but with the weekday one. Only after *Kedushah,* in *"L'dor va-dor naggid gadlecha,"* does he switch to the Shabbos melody. Similarly, the Rav would recite the Kaddish before this Amidah with the weekday tune. He instructed his sons and others to do the same.

Unlike the other Shabbos meals, which were graced by *divrei Torah* as well as by *zemiros,* at *seudah shelishis* there would be only *zemiros*. The Rav sang with great *deveikus* and seemed to be in other worlds. He explained his special relationship to this meal as follows: According to Torah sources, this meal is known as *ra'ava d'ra'avin,* the peak of *Shabbos Kodesh*. It is comparable to the *Ne'ilah* prayer of Yom Kippur.

Neighbors said they would look forward to the Rav's *zemiros* at this time, which brimmed with love and longing for HaKadosh Baruch Hu.

At *seudah shelishis* the Rav would drink a *revi'is* of wine, thus fulfilling the halachic obligation according to the Rambam. He also made sure to eat fish before sunset. Even away from home, he would make an effort to have fish for *seudah shelishis*.

Shabbos Meals

Shabbos meals with the Rav were dedicated to *divrei Torah* and *zemiros*. No mundane conversation accompanied these meals, as they are an elevated form of *avodas Hashem*. During the meals he would tell his family what he'd said in his *derashah* earlier that day. Sometimes he would reveal the *chiddushim* he was to say later that day.

Since he insisted on no small talk at the Shabbos table, he tried not to make the meals too long. There was time only for *divrei Torah* and *zemiros*. He once explained: "At long meals it is hard not to get pulled into mundane conversation, and such talk is not befitting the honor of the Shabbos table."

The Rav held that *divrei Torah* should precede *zemiros*.[3] Thus, he began the meal with *divrei Torah*, then sang *zemiros*. As he writes,[4] *Chazal* in *Megillah* 12b point out that non-Jews begin their meals by speaking of meaningless matters, while Jews begin by speaking words of Torah and singing praises to Hashem. Here, *Chazal* mention "words of Torah" before "singing praises," so the Rav followed this order.

The Rav would recite Kiddush specifically over wine, even outside his home.

He would eat fish at every Shabbos meal. When eating in someone else's home, such as when he was away for Shabbos, if no fish was served for the day meal, he would ask for some left over from the night meal and eat it *lichvod Shabbos Kodesh*. This practice was sometimes awkward, as his request was not always so well understood, but he did not give up. Sometimes the Rebbetzin would go into the kitchen and ask, "Maybe there's a piece of fish left over from last night? Perhaps there are at least a few crumbs?"

All week long, the Rav had very little to do with food. His family recounts that he hardly ever sat down for a meal; he would just grab a little food here and there. But on Shabbos he tasted every dish on the table, thus fulfilling the mitzvah of *oneg Shabbos*.

After the meal, the Rav made sure everyone cleared the table right away and set the "Shabbos room" in order, rather than insult Shabbos by leaving a mess. But salt and challah would remain on the table all Shabbos, as mentioned in early Torah sources.

The Rav saw to it that wine, too, remained on the table from one meal to the next, yet he was very careful that this wine

3. See *Shabbos Malkesa*, p. 125, note.

4. Ibid.

stay closed. He was delighted to acquire a goblet with a lid, in which one could leave wine without worrying about its being exposed. (This expensive goblet resembled that of the Rebbe of Rozhin, *zt"l,* and bore various designs of deep significance.)

The Rav insisted that all family members wear Shabbos clothes at the meals — even the girls, and even at *seudah shel-ishis.* He would say, "*Lichvod Shabbos,* one should dress up and not just wear a robe."

The Rav had a special practice even regarding the table itself. One of his sons recounts that soon after his wedding, when he was shopping for a dining room table, his father told him that early Torah sources attach special significance to a Shabbos table with four legs: "I don't know if this matter is important to you now, but in time it might be. So buy a table with four legs."

Maximizing Kevod Shabbos

Rav Pincus was concerned over the well-known halachic question regarding lighting Shabbos candles in a room with electric light. Since the candles are overpowered by the electric light, adding no noticeable illumination, perhaps one does not fulfill the mitzvah this way?

The Rav devised a unique solution to this problem, thereby maximizing *kevod Shabbos.* According to the *Achiezer,* electric light is a form of fire. Consequently, one may use it to fulfill the mitzvah of kindling Shabbos lights. Thus, he simply placed a light bulb next to the Shabbos candles, so the Rebbetzin could turn it on *lichvod Shabbos* when she lit them. Then, even though the candlelight wasn't noticeable, the light of the special bulb was!

As mentioned above, there is a mitzvah to recite one hundred *berachos* every day, and on Shabbos (due to the shortened Amidah) a few are lacking. The Rav made up for them by eating snacks between meals, as recommended in the halachah. For a while, lest he forget to make up all these *berachos,* on *erev*

Shabbos he would prepare a cup filled with pieces of snack food equaling the number of those missing *berachos*. Every time he recited an extra *berachah* on Shabbos, he removed one piece of snack food and put it in another cup. And so he did until the original cup was empty — showing that he had reached his goal of one hundred *berachos*.

Another point he was particular about was that his family not read secular books on Shabbos. His rule of thumb: whatever you're allowed to read in the bathroom, you may not read on Shabbos. Since he viewed Shabbos as a Beis HaMikdash (see above, Chapter 7), he held that introducing anything mundane into Shabbos is tantamount to desecrating the sacred.

Melaveh Malkah

The Rav ate *Melaveh Malkah* every week, including food designated specifically for this meal rather than just Shabbos leftovers. On *motza'ei Shabbos* he would drink water just taken from the tap — "new" water that had not been drawn *erev Shabbos*.[5]

He sometimes debated whether to leave over Shabbos food for his *Melaveh Malkah*. He would deliberate: "I want to eat the fish now, at *seudah shelishis*. If so, am I allowed to leave it for my *Melaveh Malkah*? On the other hand, the *Melaveh Malkah* is also in honor of Shabbos..."

The Rav always ate *Melaveh Malkah* before midnight. But in his last years he began eating right after Havdalah, in both summer and winter. "Actually, it's a lot easier this way," he explained. "It eliminates the worry over forgetting to eat this important meal!" He also commented that eating *Melaveh Malkah* is simply a matter of developing the habit. Once one gets used to it, it's easy.

The Rav ate his *Melaveh Malkah* with his family. In honor

5. See *Rema, Orach Chayim* 299:10.

of this meal, he lit candles and sang *zemiros,* such as "*Eliyahu HaNavi.*" Even if he was flying abroad on *motza'ei Shabbos* and therefore had no time for *zemiros,* he brought along a *zemiros* booklet, so he could sing the special *Melaveh Malkah* melodies on the plane.

Afterword

We clearly will never do justice to our subject: the ways and practices of a towering *talmid chacham* and tzaddik, a leader of his generation. About the likes of Rav Shimshon Dovid Pincus, *zt"l,* we could say, "If I knew him, I would be him." It's particularly difficult to describe his greatness because he was so modest. He went to great lengths to hide his piety — as have tzaddikim throughout the ages — and his true greatness lay in the inner recesses of his soul. His close associates and family were occasionally privileged to glimpse the holiness that shone within him, especially on Shabbos.

The Rav's soul was aflame with *emunah,* with *tzidkus,* with purely felt *bitachon,* with exceptional wisdom. And *Shabbos Kodesh* was a means of his magnifying the powers of his soul. The perceptive eye could discern how his soul was aflame within him, while his face glowed with a touch of the *deveikus* and joy that burned fiercely within his heart. On Shabbos he was engrossed in Torah study on all levels, from which he derived immense pleasure.

When the Rav passed away, our generation lost the spice called "Shabbos." None of us tastes its full flavor in all its Heavenly glory as he did. But his example is alive and well and continues to inspire Jews everywhere, as do his rich and varied writings and talks. May his teachings illuminate the path of Torah and lead us to true *yir'as Shamayim*!